Arbitrability

Fundamentals and Major Approaches

Fabien Gélinas
Leyla Bahmany

Wolters Kluwer

Published by:
Kluwer Law International B.V.
PO Box 316
2400 AH Alphen aan den Rijn
The Netherlands
E-mail: lrs-sales@wolterskluwer.com
Website: www.wolterskluwer.com/en/solutions/kluwerlawinternational

Sold and distributed by:
Wolters Kluwer Legal & Regulatory U.S.
920 Links Avenue
Landisville, PA 17538
United States of America
E-mail: customer.service@wolterskluwer.com

ISBN 978-94-035-3077-2

e-Book: ISBN 978-94-035-3087-1
web-PDF: ISBN 978-94-035-3097-0

Contents (summary)

Contents (detailed)

Introduction

1. "Arbitrability is one of the issues where the contractual and jurisdictional natures of international commercial arbitration meet head on. It involves a simple question of what types of issues can and cannot be submitted to arbitration."[1] However, this "simple question" has resulted in scholars, practitioners, and judges writing books, articles, and judgments in an attempt to draw a predictable line between non-arbitrability and arbitrability. In fact, as simple as the arbitrability question might appear to be, for a legal system to clearly draw that line and set a consistent approach to arbitration, it must consider many, often complicated, factors that relate to public policy and economic priorities as well as international relations.

2. The aim of this book is to identify and analyze the fundamentals of and major approaches to "arbitrability" in the current international context, where disputes concerning almost all economic matters are considered arbitrable (even ones arising under public policy rules) in the majority of jurisdictions that have advanced legal systems.

3. In each jurisdiction, non-arbitrability[2] has its own history that has developed through different legislative and judicial phases.[3] Generally, in the first half of the 20th

1. Julian D M Lew, Loukas A Mistelis & Stefan M Kroll, *Comparative International Commercial Arbitration* (Kluwer Law International, 2003) at para. 9(1).
2. This book uses the terms "non-arbitrability" and "inarbitrability" interchangeably. It should be noted that, in this book, the term "non-arbitrability" is used in the sense of "objective non-arbitrability" (that is, discussing the subject matter of a dispute) and not "subjective non-arbitrability" (that is, discussing the parties' capacity to submit their dispute to arbitration). *See* Emmanuel Gaillard & John Savage, eds, *Fouchard Gaillard Goldman on International Commercial Arbitration* (Kluwer Law International, 1999) at para. 533. It should also be noted that the term "arbitrability" as used in this book is not as broad as the American conception of the term, which also encompasses discussion about the validity and scope of parties' consent to the arbitration agreement. *See ibid.*, at para. 532; W Laurence Craig, William W Park & Jan Paulsson, *International Chamber of Commerce Arbitration*, 3rd ed (Oceana Publications & ICC Publishing, 2000) at para. 5(07).
3. For example, for the evolution of arbitrability in France, *see* Emmanuel Gaillard & John Savage, eds, *Fouchard Gaillard Goldman on International Commercial Arbitration* (Kluwer Law International, 1999) at paras. 562–566. For the evolution of arbitrability in the United States, *see* Gary B Born, *International Commercial Arbitration*, 3rd ed (Kluwer Law International, 2021) at

century, law-making authorities or courts (depending on the legal tradition in a particular jurisdiction) marked a wide range of subject matters—from family and criminal matters to antitrust and securities—as incapable of being settled through private dispute resolution methods like arbitration because they engage the public interest. The reason given for this approach was most often that arbitrators could not be trusted to correctly apply or interpret public policy rules.[4]

4. However, as states' distrust of arbitrators gradually subsided over the second half of the 20th century, states began to liberalize their approach to arbitrability. The current trend towards the maximum expansion of arbitrability began in the United States (US), when the US Supreme Court, in its 1985 landmark decision in *Mitsubishi Motors v. Soler Chrysler-Plymouth*,[5] held international antitrust disputes to be arbitrable. The rationale of the *Mitsubishi* decision not only changed US courts' approach in favor of the maximum expansion of arbitrability but its effects were felt beyond US borders as it influenced a large number of other jurisdictions.

5. In the current legal context, the position that economic disputes arising under public policy rules should be inarbitrable has been abandoned, to a great degree. This expansion of arbitrability is due to the growing universal tendency to use arbitration as an alternative to litigation in national courts, as well as a result of a growing confidence that arbitrators can properly apply public policy rules.[6] Furthermore, the possibility of judicial review of awards at the award-enforcement stage is believed to empower national courts to ensure that public policy rules are duly observed.[7]

6. Although questions of whether the current approach has valid bases and is sustainable may legitimately be asked, they are not within the scope of this book. Rather, the aims of this book are to identify and analyze the fundamentals of arbitrability and the major approaches to arbitrability taken by different jurisdictions. To that end, the authors have selected nine major jurisdictions on which to focus, namely: the US, Canada, France, England and Wales, Switzerland, Germany, China (Mainland), Hong Kong,[8] and Singapore. The authors have studied the case law and

---

§6.03[C][4]; Andrew T Guzman, "Arbitrator Liability: Reconciling Arbitration and Mandatory Rules" (2000) 49 Duke L J 1279 at 1288 DOI: 10.2307/1373012.

4. Emmanuel Gaillard & John Savage, eds, *Fouchard Gaillard Goldman on International Commercial Arbitration* (Kluwer Law International, 1999) at paras. 562–563. The term "public policy" as used here broadly captures any rule or standard from which parties cannot depart by agreement.
5. *Mitsubishi Motors Corp v. Soler Chrysler-Plymouth, Inc*, 473 US 614 (1985).
6. *Ibid.*, at paras. 563, 564, 566.
7. *Ibid.*
8. The book discusses Hong Kong and China (Mainland) separately because despite China's resumption of sovereignty over Hong Kong in 1997, the two have different legal systems. China (Mainland) is primarily a civil law jurisdiction and has a socialist system whereas Hong Kong remained a common law jurisdiction after the transfer of sovereignty from the United Kingdom to China and is also entitled to keep its capitalist system for fifty years, according to the principle of "one country, two systems." The Basic Law of Hong Kong Special Administrative Region of the People's Republic of China, Chapter I, Arts. 5, 8, online: https://www.basiclaw.gov.hk/en/basiclaw/index.html (last visited 7 February 2022). For these two jurisdictions, the authors acknowledge the kind assistance of Ms Junpei Ren, a doctoral candidate at the McGill University Faculty of Law.

legislative framework of each of these jurisdictions as well as reviewed relevant commentary.

7. For nearly all the nine jurisdictions, the arbitrability of disputes in the following fields of law is discussed: antitrust/competition, bankruptcy/insolvency, consumer, corporate, family/domestic relations, intellectual property, labour/employment, securities, and torts.[9] The result of the study is set out in the last chapter (Chapter 4) of this book, in the form of nine detailed reports by jurisdictions. The reports are intended to present a comprehensive picture of the status of arbitrability in each jurisdiction, as regulated by law-making authorities, applied by courts, and interpreted by commentators.[10] Given the enormous size of Chapter 4, it is available only in the online version of the book on the website of Kluwer Arbitration.

8. Based on the analysis of different jurisdictions set out in the reports, the authors have identified key areas in which the selected jurisdictions share relevant similarities and evince differences with respect to arbitrability. A discussion of these fundamental similarities and differences is set out in Chapter 2. Chapter 3 provides a more detailed discussion of certain similarities and differences that exist among those jurisdictions by organizing the discussion in terms of the different fields of law that indicate certain major approaches to arbitrability. For example, Chapter 3 includes a comparative analysis of how different jurisdictions address the arbitrability of securities disputes. Chapter 1 is the only chapter of the book that does not draw directly upon the reports by jurisdictions.[11] Chapter 1 outlines and discusses key terms that are often encountered in discussions pertaining to arbitrability.

9. Some reports, depending on the jurisdiction, also cover criminal law, insurance law, or real property law. We recognize that other subject matters, such as organized competitive sport, may engage arbitrability in some jurisdictions.
10. It should be noted that, although a thorough study has been conducted, this book does not claim to be based on an exhaustive study of the nominated jurisdictions.
11. Chapter 1 of this book draws from a chapter in Dr Bahmany's LLM thesis which was written under the supervision of Professor Gélinas at the McGill University Faculty of Law. *See* Leyla Bahmany, *Sustainable Development of International Arbitration: Rethinking Subject Matter Arbitrability* (LLM Thesis, McGill University, 2013).

CHAPTER 1

Key Terms and Concepts

9. The aims of this book are to identify and analyze the fundamentals of and major approaches taken to arbitrability, through a study of nine major jurisdictions. However, before embarking on this task, it is necessary to discuss certain key terms and concepts that are often encountered in the literature on arbitrability. As such, this chapter contains six sections. The first section sets out the definitions of arbitrability, public policy, and mandatory rules; the second section is about distinguishing certain types of public policy rules; the third section discusses the impact of inarbitrability on the arbitration process; the fourth section clarifies the differences between inarbitrability and public policy; the fifth section sets out the differences between arbitrability and commerciality; the sixth section explains the law governing the arbitrability question; and the seventh section is an executive summary of this chapter.

A. DEFINITIONS: ARBITRABILITY, PUBLIC POLICY, AND MANDATORY RULES

1. Arbitrability

10. Three questions may arise at the outset of an arbitration: (i) whether there is a valid arbitration agreement between the parties; if so, (ii) whether the scope of the agreement covers the parties' dispute(s); and if the answer is in the affirmative, (iii) whether any public policy rules bar the arbitration of the subject matter of the dispute (i.e., whether the dispute is subject to the exclusive jurisdiction of local courts). The international understanding of the term "arbitrability" relates only to the third question, whereas the same term in the US encompasses all three questions.[12] This book follows the international usage of the term.

12. Laurence Shore, "The United States' Perspective on Arbitrability" in Loukas A Mistelis & Stavros L Brekoulakis, eds, *Arbitrability: International and Comparative Perspective* (Kluwer Law International, 2009) 69, para. 4(3). For case law, *see, e.g.*, *First Options of Chicago, Inc v. Kaplan*,

11. The UNCITRAL Model Law on International Commercial Arbitration[13] (UNCITRAL Model Law) does not set out any definition of non-arbitrability. In civil law jurisdictions, relevant Codes/Acts often discuss non-arbitrability at a general level.[14] As such, civil law jurisdictions, like common law jurisdictions, mostly rely on case law to clarify details of the concept of inarbitrability.

12. The Convention on the Recognition and Enforcement of Foreign Arbitral Awards[15] (New York Convention) discusses arbitrability without using the term "arbitrability" or expressly defining it. Under the New York Convention, signatory states may refrain from enforcing arbitration agreements and arbitral awards where the matter is inarbitrable. According to Article II, for an arbitration agreement to be enforceable, the agreement should, inter alia, "concern matters capable of settlement by arbitration," which refers to the arbitrability of a subject matter.[16] Article V sets out the grounds for refusing recognition and enforcement of awards. With respect to inarbitrability, Article V states that:

> Recognition and enforcement of an arbitral award may also be refused if the competent authority in the country where recognition and enforcement is sought finds that: (a) The subject matter of the difference is not capable of settlement by arbitration under the law of the country.[17]

13. In the absence of a definition for inarbitrability in international texts and national legislative Codes, this chapter discusses the term as it is understood in legal practice and scholarship. Arbitrability (or its negative, inarbitrability) involves a discussion of whether the subject matter of a dispute is, legally speaking, capable of being settled through arbitration.[18] This is determined based largely on the degree to which a subject

---

514 US 938 (1995) at 943 (stating that the parties' disagreement on whether they agree to arbitrate their dispute concerns the arbitrability issue).

13. UNCITRAL Model Law on International Commercial Arbitration, United Nations Commission on International Trade Law, 112th Mtg, UN Doc A/40/17, Annex I (1985).
14. *See, e.g.*, French Civil Code, Art. 2059 "All persons may enter into arbitration agreements in relation to the rights they can freely waive", and Art. 2060 "One may not enter into arbitration agreements in ... more generally in all matters concerning public policy"; Swiss Private International Law Act (PILA 1987), Art. 177 "All pecuniary claims may be submitted to arbitration"; German Code of Civil Procedure (ZPO 2005), Art. 1030(1) "Any claim under property law may become the subject matter of an arbitration agreement. An arbitration agreement regarding non-pecuniary claims has legal effect insofar as the parties to the dispute are entitled to conclude a settlement regarding the subject matter of the dispute"; Civil Code of Québec, CQLR c C-1991, Art. 2639 "Disputes over the status and capacity of persons, family matters or other matters of public order may not be submitted to arbitration."
15. Convention on the Recognition and Enforcement of Foreign Arbitral Awards, 10 June 1958, 330 UNTS 38.
16. Albert Jan van den Berg, *The New York Arbitration Convention of 1958* (Kluwer Law and Taxation Publishers, 1981) at 359.
17. Convention on the Recognition and Enforcement of Foreign Arbitral Awards, 10 June 1958, 330 UNTS 38, Art. V(2).
18. Emmanuel Gaillard & John Savage, eds, *Fouchard Gaillard Goldman on International Commercial Aritration* (Kluwer Law International, 1999) at para. 533.

matter engages sensitive public policy concerns and mandatory rules.[19] This is because arbitration, as a private adjudication method, has "public consequences" when it comes to the enforcement of awards by courts.[20] Therefore, it is not possible to discuss the concept of non-arbitrability without also studying the concepts of public policy and mandatory rules.

2. Public Policy and Mandatory Rules

14. Public policy rules are broader than mandatory rules and encompass them. At the International Law Association (ILA) Conference in London in 2000, the Committee on International Commercial Arbitration issued a report (ILA Report) that reviewed the development of public policy doctrine in relation to the enforcement of awards since 1950.[21] The ILA Report defines public policy as a notion that describes four categories of rules: (i) mandatory rules (in French: *lois de police*), (ii) fundamental principles of law (e.g., *pacta sunt servanda*),[22] (iii) "public order/good morals" (e.g., the prohibition against smuggling or piracy), and (iv) "national interests/foreign relations."[23]

15. Mandatory rules—category (i) above—are defined as:

> [I]mperative provision[s] of law which must be applied to an international relationship irrespective of the law that governs that relationship. To put it another way: mandatory rules of law are a matter of public policy (*ordre public*), and moreover reflect a public policy so commanding that they must be applied even if the general body of law to which they belong is not competent by application of the relevant rule of conflict of laws.[24]

Likewise, the 2008 European Union (EU) Rome I Regulation defines mandatory rules as:

> [P]rovisions the respect for which is regarded as crucial by a country for safeguarding its public interests, such as its political, social or economic organisation, to such an extent that they are applicable to any situation falling within their scope, irrespective of the law otherwise applicable to the contract under this Regulation.[25]

---

19. *See* Julian D M Lew, Loukas A Mistelis & Stefan M Kroll, *Comparative International Commercial Arbitration* (Kluwer Law International, 2003) at para. 9(2); French Civil Code, Art. 2060.
20. Alan Redfern et al, *Redfern and Hunter on International Arbitration*, 6th ed (Oxford University Press, 2015) at para. 2.126.
21. ILA, Committee on International Commercial Arbitration, *Interim Report on Public Policy as a Bar to Enforcement of International Arbitral Awards* (London Conference, 2000).
22. The ILA Report noted that this group "may or may not be a distinct group from mandatory rules." *Ibid.*, at 20.
23. *Ibid.*, at 15, 17–23.
24. ILA, Committee on International Commercial Arbitration, *Interim Report on Public Policy as a Bar to Enforcement of International Arbitral Awards* (London Conference, 2000) at 15; *see* Pierre Mayer, "Mandatory Rules of Law In International Arbitration" (1986) 2:4 Arb Int'l 274 at 275 DOI: 10.1093/arbitration/2.4.274.
25. Regulation (EC) No 593/2008 of the European Parliament and of the Council of 17 June 2008 on the Law Applicable to Contractual Obligations, Art. 9(1), online: http://eur-lex.europa.eu/legal-content/EN/TXT/PDF/?uri=CELEX:32008R0593&from=EN (last visited 7 February 2022).

Recital 37 to the Regulation distinguishes mandatory rules from those "provisions which cannot be derogated from by agreement," in that mandatory rules "should be construed more restrictively."[26]

16. Mandatory rules usually take the form of legislative provisions,[27] and the rationale behind enacting such rules can be explained as follows. In economic terms, parties to a transaction try to maximize their joint benefit and minimize their costs. As long as such benefit maximization and cost minimization have no negative impact on society, the parties' intent is respected and society has no reason to interfere with the agreement.[28] However, the rule is different if parties intend to impose their costs on society in order to minimize their own costs. In such a case, the state's intervention is justified and takes the form of mandatory rules that are imposed on the parties, regardless of their intent, to protect public interests.[29]

B. DISTINGUISHING CERTAIN TYPES OF PUBLIC POLICY RULES

17. Public policy rules can be categorized into two groups, defined by their respective purposes: rules that cover the procedural aspects of a proceeding to ensure the "basic requirements of procedural justice" are met; and rules that are substantive in nature and concern other important interests of a society.[30] In this book, the term "public policy rules" generally refers to substantive public policy rules.

18. This section clarifies the different types of public policy rules that are relevant to defining the field of non-arbitrability. The first subsection explains the difference between *ordre public de protection* and *ordre public de direction*. The second subsection discusses international public policy, and the third subsection explains the relation between truly international public policy and transnational public policy.

1. *Ordre Public de Protection and Ordre Public de Direction*

19. Public policy rules, particularly in civil law jurisdictions, are generally divided into two groups: rules of *ordre public de direction* and rules of *ordre public de protection*. Both groups are generally considered to encompass economic public policy rules, but the purpose of the former is "to regulate the economy for the general good of the society," whereas the purpose of the latter is to provide protection for an "economically weaker contracting party."[31]

---

26. *Ibid.*
27. Gary B Born, *International Commercial Arbitration*, 3rd ed (Kluwer Law International, 2021) at §6.02[G], n 39.
28. Andrew T Guzman, "Arbitrator Liability: Reconciling Arbitration and Mandatory Rules" (2000) 49 Duke L J 1279 at 1284–85 DOI: 10.2307/1373012.
29. *Ibid.*
30. Emmanuel Gaillard & John Savage, eds, *Fouchard Gaillard Goldman on International Commercial Aritration* (Kluwer Law International, 1999) at paras. 1651–62.
31. Quebec Research Centre of Private and Comparative Law, *Private Law Dictionary and Bilingual Lexicons*, 2nd ed (1991) at 348–49.

20. Therefore, rules of *ordre public de direction* aim to protect the interests of society as a whole (e.g., antitrust laws), while rules of *ordre public de protection* aim to protect those who are believed to be in a weaker bargaining position (e.g., employment laws and consumer protection laws), where the interests that are engaged are narrower.[32] As a result, violation of *ordre public de direction* usually brings about absolute nullity of any offensive agreement, whereas a violation of *ordre public de protection* usually results in relative nullity.[33] The nullity is "relative" when only the person whose right is concerned (i.e., the protected person) may invoke the nullity; but in the case of absolute nullity, anyone (including a judge acting of their own motion) may invoke it.[34]

2. International Public Policy

21. The focus on arbitrability, in the past five decades, has generally been on the facilitation of international arbitration.[35] One of the methods employed by legislatures and courts has been to reduce the scope of public policy rules previously used as a ground for refusing enforcement of international arbitration agreements and awards. In this regard, states have been encouraged to distinguish between domestic and international arbitration. This enables them to draw a distinction between domestic public policy and so-called international public policy. The rationale behind drawing this distinction is that not all of the mandatory provisions of a domestic legal order should bar enforcement of international arbitral awards.

22. For example, the French Code of Civil Procedure—both in its former Book on Arbitration (Article 1502.5)[36] and in its amended Book on Arbitration[37] (Article 1514)—distinguishes international public policy from domestic public policy. It explicitly states that only international public policy can bar recognition and enforcement of an international arbitral award.[38]

23. Although the meaning of "international public policy" appears to be clear on its face, jurists have offered different definitions. Pierre Lalive is of the opinion that international public policy refers to: (i) the fundamental concerns of the domestic law of a given state, (ii) a state's international obligations (e.g., obligations under the treaties to which a state is a signatory), and (iii) the fundamentals of public

32. *See* Tibor Varady, John J Barcelo III & Arthur T von Mehren, *International Commercial Arbitration: A Transnational Perspective*, 4th ed (West, 2009) at 233.
33. Quebec Research Centre of Private and Comparative Law, *Private Law Dictionary and Bilingual Lexicons*, 2nd ed (1991) at 348–49.
34. George A Bermann & Étienne Picard, *Introduction to French Law* (Kluwer Law International, 2008) at 222; and *see* Civil Code of Québec, CQLR c C-1991 (consolidated version as of October 2021), Arts. 1418, 1420.
35. For a brief discussion on the current legal context, *see* above, paras. 2–5.
36. French Code of Civil Procedure, amended by Decree No 81-500 of 12 May 1981.
37. French Code of Civil Procedure, amended by Decree No 2011-48 of 13 January 2011.
38. *Ibid.*, Art. 1514.

international law.[39] However, according to the book *Fouchard Gaillard Goldman on International Commercial Aritration*, international public policy refers to mandatory rules that are so fundamental to the state, that violation would not be tolerable even in international cases.[40] According to Fouchard et al., when a national court reviews an arbitral award, it does so to ascertain that the award does not stand against fundamental considerations of the enforcing state.[41]

24. Bernard Hanotiau and Olivier Caprasse, however, consider that international public policy means the mandatory rules that reflect either fundamental convictions of the enforcing state, or the rules "having an absolute, universal value."[42] Alan Redfern and Martin Hunter set forth another definition: "international public policy would not concern itself with matters of form, or of a purely domestic nature; it would look to the broader public interest of honesty and fair dealing" and, therefore, it is less restrictive.[43]

25. The ILA Report (2000),[44] based on a review of the development of public policy doctrine since 1950,[45] explains that although the term "international public policy" suggests a supra-national principle reflecting an international consensus as to universal standards, it is no more than the "public policy of a state as applied to foreign awards, and its content and application remain subject to [the determination of] each state."[46] Based on the ILA Report, the ILA adopted a Resolution at its Delhi Conference in 2002.[47] The Annex to the Resolution reads:

> The international public policy of any State includes: (i) fundamental principles, pertaining to justice or morality, that the State wishes to protect even when it is not directly concerned; (ii) rules designed to serve the essential political, social or economic interests of the State, these being known as "*lois de police*" or "public policy rules"; and (iii) the duty of the State to respect its obligations towards other States or international organizations.[48]

This book adopts the ILA's definition of the term "international public policy."

---

39. Pierre Lalive, "Transnational (or Truly International) Public Policy and International Arbitration" in Pieter Sanders, ed, *ICCA Congress Series No 3: Comparative Arbitration Practice and Public Policy in Arbitration* (Kluwer Law International, 1987) 257 at paras. 8, 20, 35, 90.
40. Emmanuel Gaillard & John Savage, eds, *Fouchard Gaillard Goldman on International Commercial Aritration* (Kluwer Law International, 1999) at para. 1648.
41. *Ibid.*
42. Bernard Hanotiau & Olivier Caprasse, "Arbitrability, Due Process, and Public Policy Under Article V of the New York Convention: Belgian and French Perspectives" (2008) 25:6 J Int'l Arb 721 at 730 DOI: 10.54648/joia2008058.
43. Alan Redfern et al, *Redfern and Hunter on International Arbitration*, 6th ed (Oxford University Press, 2015) at paras. 10(85), 10(87).
44. Discussed above, para. 14.
45. ILA, Committee on International Commercial Arbitration, *Interim Report on Public Policy as a Bar to Enforcement of International Arbitral Awards* (London Conference, 2000).
46. *Ibid.*, at 2.
47. ILA, *International Law Association Recommendations on the Application of Public Policy as a Ground for Refusing Recognition or Enforcement of International Arbitral Awards* (2002), Res 2/2002.
48. *Ibid.*, at recommendation 1(d).

3. Truly International Public Policy and Transnational Public Policy

26. The terms "international public policy," "truly international public policy," and "transnational public policy" have been used interchangeably by commentators.[49] It has been suggested that, since international arbitral tribunals do not serve in the name of any particular national legal system, they should adopt a "truly international public policy."[50]

27. Pierre Mayer's definition of these terms sheds light on the relevant differences. He explains that:

- "public policy" rules are a set of rules imposed by the legal system of a state on its subjects and, in the case of non-compliance, courts have the duty to restore the situation according to their public policy rules;[51]
- "international public policy" rules are a limited part of a state's public policy rules. They allow courts to bar the application of a foreign law or an international arbitral award;[52]
- "truly international public policy" rules, however, are part of public international law, which even an agreement between two states may not violate, such as an embargo issued by the Security Council of the United Nations against one state;[53] and
- "transnational public policy" rules, on the other hand, are a set of public policy rules for which a broad consensus has emerged in the international community, and do not belong to a particular state. Examples of such rules are the prohibition of racial and religious discrimination, drug trafficking, and trafficking in human organs.[54]

Among the four abovementioned terms, this book is mainly concerned with "international public policy" from the perspective of the jurisdictions under review.

49. *See, e.g.*, Pierre Lalive, "Transnational (or Truly International) Public Policy and International Arbitration" in Pieter Sanders, ed, *ICCA Congress Series No 3: Comparative Arbitration Practice and Public Policy in Arbitration* (Kluwer Law International, 1987) 257 at paras. 8, 20, 35, 90. Even the Interim Report by the ILA's Committee on International Arbitration has used the terms "truly international public policy" and "transnational public policy" as having the same meaning. *See* ILA, Committee on International Commercial Arbitration, *Interim Report on Public Policy as a Bar to Enforcement of International Arbitral Awards* (London Conference, 2000) at 6.
50. Emmanuel Gaillard & John Savage, eds, *Fouchard Gaillard Goldman on International Commercial Aritration* (Kluwer Law International, 1999) at para. 1648.
51. Pierre Mayer, "Effect of International Public Policy in International Arbitration?" in Loukas A Mistelis & Julian D M Lew, eds, *Pervasive Problems in International Arbitration* (Kluwer Law International, 2006) 61 at para. 2(12).
52. *Ibid.*, at paras. 2(2)–(3).
53. *Ibid.*, at paras. 2(3), 2(12).
54. *Ibid.*, at paras. 2(6), 2(8), 2(10). It is understood that those treatises, which suggest that the "truly international public policy" and "transnational public policy" are the same, combine the meanings suggested by Mayer for the two terms.

C. IMPACT OF INARBITRABILITY ON THE ARBITRATION PROCESS

28. The arbitrability question may arise in any of the four following scenarios: (i) when a national court decides on the request of one of the parties for enforcement of an arbitration agreement or for staying an already-commenced arbitration proceeding; (ii) when an arbitral tribunal decides the scope of its jurisdiction; (iii) when a national court reviews the preliminary ruling of a tribunal on its jurisdiction; and (iv) when a national court decides a request for annulment or for recognition/enforcement of an award.[55]

29. Whether the parties' dispute is arbitrable is an important question to be raised at an early stage of proceedings. If the subject matter of a dispute is non-arbitrable, the arbitration agreement is not enforceable with respect to that specific matter.[56] Therefore, the tribunal will lack jurisdiction (in relation to that specific matter) and, consequently, its award (concerning that specific matter) will not be enforceable.[57]

D. DIFFERENCES BETWEEN INARBITRABILITY AND PUBLIC POLICY

30. Article V(2) of the New York Convention sets out the limitations on recognition and enforcement of awards and discusses public policy and inarbitrability in two separate provisions. Article V(2) reads:

> Recognition and enforcement of an arbitral award may also be refused if the competent authority in the country where recognition and enforcement is sought finds that: (a) The subject matter of the difference is not capable of settlement by arbitration under the law of the country [the inarbitrability issue]; or (b) The recognition or enforcement of the award would be contrary to the public policy of that country [the public policy issue].[58]

31. It has been argued that the inarbitrability and public policy grounds for refusing enforcement are identical means to protect the public interests, or alternatively, that inarbitrability is an aspect of public policy.[59] Discussing that issue in detail is not within

55. Tibor Varady, John J Barcelo III & Arthur T von Mehren, *International Commercial Arbitration: A Transnational Perspective*, 4th ed (West, 2009) at 234; David St John Sutton, Judith Gill & Matthew Gearing, *Russell on Arbitration*, 23rd ed (Sweet & Maxwell, 2007) at para. 1(034).
56. Gary B Born, *International Commercial Arbitration*, 3rd ed (Kluwer Law International, 2021) at §6.01.
57. Julian D M Lew, Loukas A Mistelis & Stefan M Kroll, *Comparative International Commercial Arbitration* (Kluwer Law International, 2003) at para. 9(3).
58. Convention on the Recognition and Enforcement of Foreign Arbitral Awards, 10 June 1958, 330 UNTS 38, Art. V(2).
59. *See, e.g.*, Pieter Sanders, "A Twenty Years' Review of the Convention on the Recognition and Enforcement of Foreign Arbitral Awards" (1979) 13:2 Int'l Law 269 at 270; Thomas E Carbonneau, "Mitsubishi: The Folly of Quixotic Internationalism" (1986) 2:2 Arb Int'l 116 at 118, 134. It should be noted that although the discussion focuses on Article V(2) of the New York Convention, inarbitrability and public policy may also render the arbitration agreement ineffective under other provisions of the New York Convention.

the scope of this chapter.[60] However, it suffices to say that those arguments fail to account for a key difference between public policy and inarbitrability.

32. Public policy enables a state to refuse recognition or enforcement of an arbitral award because the *result(s)* reached by the award contradict(s) the public policy of that state. However, the inarbitrability defense "provides that the *arbitral process* itself cannot be used to produce a binding decision in cases related to a particular subject matter (regardless of what its results are)."[61]

33. In other words, although both inarbitrability and public policy are intended to protect public interests, their nature and the way in which they operate are different: inarbitrability challenges the enforceability of an *arbitration agreement* (even when it is raised at the award-enforcement stage) whereas, in this setting, public policy normally challenges only the *award*. Therefore, when a state court relies on inarbitrability, it bars enforcement of the award because that award has been rendered on the basis of an unenforceable arbitration agreement and not because there is a problem with the award itself.

34. The foregoing difference might be the reason why the New York Convention discusses inarbitrability and public policy in two separate provisions, recognizing them as two separate grounds for barring the recognition and enforcement of an award.[62] This argument is supported by the fact that, in drafting the New York Convention, the French delegate's suggestion to merge the two provisions was not implemented.[63]

35. In conclusion, the inarbitrability issue is normally raised by the party who argues that the subject matter of the dispute is non-arbitrable[64] and, if the court accepts the defense, it bars enforcement of the relevant arbitration agreement or the arbitral award, depending on the stage of proceeding. In this setting, the public policy issue, however, can only be raised as such at the award-enforcement stage to bar enforcement of an arbitral award on the grounds that the award contradicts public policy rules of the enforcing state. Thus, both inarbitrability and public policy are to protect public interests, but their nature and the way each operates are different.

E. DIFFERENCES BETWEEN ARBITRABILITY AND COMMERCIALITY

36. Neither the UNCITRAL Model Law nor the New York Convention has defined arbitrability, but both make reference to commerciality. According to the UNCITRAL

60. For further discussion, *see* Emmanuel Gaillard & John Savage, eds, *Fouchard Gaillard Goldman on International Commercial Aritration* (Kluwer Law International, 1999) at para. 1704.
61. Gary B Born, *International Commercial Arbitration*, 3rd ed (Kluwer Law International, 2021) at §6.02[G] (emphasis added).
62. Convention on the Recognition and Enforcement of Foreign Arbitral Awards, 10 June 1958, 330 UNTS 38, Art. V(2)(a), V(2)(b).
63. United Nations Conference on International Commercial Arbitration, 11th Mtg, 27 May 1958, UN Doc E/Conf26/SR 11 at 7, online: https://uncitral.un.org/en/texts/arbitration/conventions/foreign_arbitral_awards/travaux (last visited 7 February 2022).
64. It should be noted that the inarbitrability issue can also be raised by the judge sua sponte.

Model Law, Article 1, the Model Law applies only to commercial matters, of which a number of examples have been set out in a footnote to Article 1.[65] Unlike the UNCITRAL Model Law, the New York Convention does not limit itself to commercial matters. Nevertheless, Article I(3) of the Convention has made it possible for signatory states to make a reservation whereby they could apply the Convention only to commercial matters.

37. The question, therefore, is (1) what does commerciality of a matter mean, in precise terms, and (2) how does it relate to arbitrability?

1. Meaning of "Commercial"

38. As noted above, relevant international instruments do not provide a definition for the term "commercial." The same is true for the official guides and explanatory notes of these instruments. For example, the UNCITRAL Secretariat Guide on the New York Convention does not provide a clear definition for the term "commercial."[66] The Explanatory Note to the 1985 UNCITRAL Model Law has observed that "[a]s regards the term 'commercial', no hard and fast definition could be provided."[67] With respect to the European Convention on International Commercial Arbitration of 1961, it has been noted that "[t]here was general agreement among the drafters that an attempt to provide a uniform definition of the commercial character of the dispute would be exceedingly difficult owing to the variety of meanings and scope given by the various legal systems to this concept."[68]

39. In the course of drafting the 1985 UNCITRAL Model Law, it was suggested that the words "international commercial arbitration" be replaced by "international arbitration in commercial matters, including services and other economic relations," which was not accepted on the grounds that the term "international commercial arbitration" was a commonly used term.[69]

---

65. The footnote reads: "The term 'commercial' should be given a wide interpretation so as to cover matters arising from all relationships of a commercial nature, whether contractual or not. Relationships of a commercial nature include, but are not limited to, the following transactions: any trade transaction for the supply or exchange of goods or services; distribution agreement; commercial representation or agency; factoring; leasing; construction of works; consulting; engineering; licensing; investment; financing; banking; insurance; exploitation agreement or concession; joint venture and other forms of industrial or business cooperation; carriage of goods or passengers by air, sea, rail or road."
66. *UNCITRAL Secretariat Guide on the Convention on the Recognition and Enforcement of Foreign Arbitral Awards* (2016 ed) at paras. 85–87, online: https://uncitral.un.org/sites/uncitral.un.org/files/media-documents/uncitral/en/2016_guide_on_the_convention.pdf (last visited 7 February 2022).
67. *Explanatory Note by the UNCITRAL Secretariat on the Model Law on International Commercial Arbitration* (1985) at para. 11; *see also* the *Explanatory Note* to the 2006 version of the Model Law, at para. 12.
68. Dominique T Hascher "European Convention on International Commercial Arbitration of 1961: Commentary" in Van den Berg, ed, *ICCA Yearbook Commercial Arbitration*, vol XXXVI (Kluwer Law International, 2011) 504 at para. 10.
69. Report of the United Nations Commission on International Trade Law on the work of its Eighteenth Session (*Official Records of the General Assembly, Fortieth Session, Supplement No 17* (A/40/17)) at paras. 24–26.

40. In the 1990s, Fouchard, Gaillard, and Goldman stated that the distinction between commercial and non-commercial matters—as known historically in the domestic laws of civil law jurisdictions—should not extend to international arbitration because the significance of this difference has diminished, even at the domestic level, in those jurisdictions.[70] According to them, in international arbitration, commerciality relates to *economic* matters, and even the footnote to Article 1 of the UNCITRAL Model Law extends to "all economic relations the object of which is the production, transformation or circulation of goods or services associated with those goods, or financial and banking activities."[71]

41. Likewise, Gary Born is of the opinion that commerciality includes "international trade, financial, investment and related economic transactions" and international commercial arbitration, by comparison, is a means to resolve "international business disputes."[72]

2. Commerciality v. Arbitrability

42. After elaborating on the meaning of commerciality, the discussion now turns to the question of how commerciality relates to arbitrability. In other words, if a matter is not considered commercial, does it mean that it is non-arbitrable? This is an important question, because a considerable number of states have made the commercial reservation to the New York Convention,[73] and a considerable number of jurisdictions have adopted the UNCITRAL Model Law.[74]

43. Gary Born correctly points out that arbitrability concerns the *subject matter of a dispute*, whereas commerciality has nothing to do with the subject matter of a dispute: commerciality only concerns the *underlying relationship* between the parties.[75] If the underlying relationship is considered to be commercial, then the commercial requirement is satisfied regardless of whether the dispute arising out of that relationship is commercial or not.[76]

44. As a result, the fact that a relationship is not commercial does not entail that any dispute arising out of that relationship is non-arbitrable; rather, it only means that the *favorable regime* governing international commercial arbitration (be it the New York

70. Emmanuel Gaillard & John Savage, eds, *Fouchard Gaillard Goldman on International Commercial Arbitration* (Kluwer Law International, 1999) at paras. 58, 64, 67.
71. *Ibid.*, at para. 63.
72. Gary B Born, *International Commercial Arbitration*, 3rd ed (Kluwer Law International, 2021) at §§1.02, 2.03[B].
73. Out of the 169 signatory states, 54 states have made the commercial reservation. UNCITRAL Website, status of the New York Convention, online: https://uncitral.un.org/en/texts/arbitration/conventions/foreign_arbitral_awards/status2 (last visited 7 February 2022).
74. UNCITRAL website, status of the UNCITRAL Model Law (both the 1985 and the 2006 versions), online: https://uncitral.un.org/en/texts/arbitration/modellaw/commercial_arbitration/status (last visited 7 February 2022).
75. Gary B Born, *International Commercial Arbitration*, 3rd ed (Kluwer Law International, 2021) at §2.03[B][1][b][ii].
76. *Ibid.*

Convention or the domestic law of the state that is based on the UNCITRAL Model Law) would not apply and, as such, the relevant default domestic law will instead apply. In that case, the dispute may still be arbitrable under the default law of the enforcing state. On the other hand, if the relationship is commercial, the favorable regime for international commercial arbitration applies, but the local court may still find that the subject matter of the parties' dispute is not arbitrable.

F. LAW GOVERNING THE ARBITRABILITY QUESTION

45. This section briefly discusses which law should apply to the arbitrability question. To this date, this issue has remained unsettled within the arbitration community.[77] There are five possible options in relation to identifying the applicable law: (i) the law governing the arbitration agreement; (ii) the law governing the substantive claim, the arbitrability of which has been challenged by one of the parties; (iii) the law of the state where enforcement of the arbitration agreement is sought; (iv) the law of the seat of the arbitration; or (v) the law of the state(s) where enforcement of the award is sought or will be sought.[78]

46. The answer to the question hinges mainly upon whether it is raised before a tribunal or a national court. Thus, the discussion in this section includes two subsections: (1) The Arbitrability Question Before a Tribunal and (2) The Arbitrability Question Before a National Court.

1. The Arbitrability Question Before a Tribunal

47. The arbitration rules of major arbitration institutions—such as the International Chamber of Commerce (ICC), the London Court of International Arbitration (LCIA), and the American Arbitration Association (AAA)—endorse the freedom of parties to choose the substantive law governing their dispute and the procedural law that applies to it.[79] There is, however, no reference in the above rules as to whether parties are free to choose the law governing the arbitrability question.

48. Craig, Park, and Paulsson are of the view that allowing parties the freedom to choose the law governing the arbitrability question "appears to be a necessity for contractual security."[80] They argue that, under Article 6(2) of the European

77. *See, e.g.*, Karl-Heinz Böckstiegel, "Public Policy and Arbitrability" in Pieter Sanders, ed, *ICCA Congress Series No 3: Comparative Arbitration Practice and Public Policy in Arbitration* (Kluwer Law International, 1987) 177 at 184; Gary B Born, *International Commercial Arbitration*, 3rd ed (Kluwer Law International, 2021) at §4.05. For a recent court decision on the matter, *see* the 2023 decision of the Singapore Court of Appeal in *Anupam Mittal v. Westbridge Ventures II Investment Holdings* [2023] SGCA 1.
78. *See Ibid.*
79. ICC Arbitration Rules (2021), Arts. 19, 21; LCIA Arbitration Rules (2020), Arts. 16(4), 22(3); AAA International Dispute Resolution Procedures (2021), Art. 34.
80. W Laurence Craig, William W Park & Jan Paulsson, *International Chamber of Commerce Arbitration*, 3rd ed (Oceana Publications & ICC Publishing, 2000) at 61.

Convention on International Commercial Arbitration (1961), the parties' choice of law has the first priority in determining the arbitrability question.[81] Their argument is arbitration-friendly and respects the parties' will, but fails to take into account an important consideration: it is very unlikely that parties who wish to arbitrate their dispute (at least at the contract formation stage) would choose a law that considers their dispute to be inarbitrable. It is, therefore, up to the tribunal to be pragmatic about the future of the award by considering the role of the seat and the state(s) in which the parties might seek enforcement of the award.

49. Needless to say, an arbitration proceeding has solid ties with the seat jurisdiction, due to the proceedings' reliance on the courts of the seat for potentially needed interim measures, as well as the risk of potential annulment proceedings at the seat. Such factors should make an arbitrator consider the law of the seat with respect to the arbitrability question. Furthermore, the ultimate goal of every winning party is to enforce the award, in the event that the losing party does not voluntarily honor the award. In order not to frustrate the winning party's goal, the tribunal should therefore also consider the law of the state(s) where the award is most likely to be enforced.

50. The point of the preceding analysis is not to argue that the parties' choice of law should be ignored but to emphasize the fact that there are at least two other jurisdictions (the seat and the enforcing state) that should be taken into consideration.

2. The Arbitrability Question Before a National Court

51. When the arbitrability question arises before a national court, the answer, to some extent, depends on the stage of the arbitration process: the pre-award stage or the post-award stage.

52. The answer is clearer when the arbitration is at the post-award stage. According to Article V(2) of the New York Convention, at the award-enforcement stage the governing law is the law of the enforcing state. Similarly, in set-aside or annulment proceedings, the lex arbitri, as exemplified by Article 34(2)b) of the Model Law, generally ties the arbitrability ground to the law of the seat where the proceedings take place. However, where the question arises at the pre-award stage (e.g., when one of the parties seeks enforcement of the arbitration agreement), these instruments do not provide any clear guidance. It has been reported that the majority of national courts actually apply their own national law even at the pre-award stage.[82] This obviously makes for a significant measure of uncertainty in international practice and requires

81. *Ibid.*
82. Gary B Born, *International Commercial Arbitration*, 3rd ed (Kluwer Law International, 2021) at §4.05[B]; Julian D M Lew, Loukas A Mistelis & Stefan M Kroll, *Comparative International Commercial Arbitration* (Kluwer Law International, 2003) at paras. 9(10), 9(13). For further discussion, *see* Stavros L Brekoulakis, "Law Applicable to Arbitrability: Revisiting the Revisited *Lex Fori*" in Loukas A Mistelis & Stavros L Brekoulakis, eds, *Arbitrability International and Comparative Perspective* (Kluwer Law International, 2009) at 99.

familiarity with several national approaches to arbitrability even in a relatively simple international arbitral configuration.

EXECUTIVE SUMMARY 1

53. Chapter I explained the key terms surrounding non-arbitrability and provided clarifications for those terms that tend to be vague or confusing. The arbitrability question is whether public policy rules bar arbitration of a dispute because of its subject matter. The question is significant because inarbitrability of a dispute renders the arbitration agreement unenforceable with respect to that dispute.

54. Arbitrability has a close relationship with mandatory rules and public policy, despite the fact that these are often distinct concepts. Public policy rules can be divided into categories based on different criteria, such as the division between rules of *ordre public de direction* and rules of *ordre public de protection*. The former concerns rules protecting interests of the society at large, whereas the latter protects interests of sectors of society that are in weaker bargaining positions. Public policy rules can also be divided into domestic, international, truly international, and transnational public policy rules.

55. This chapter explained that arbitrability and commerciality are two different concepts. Arbitrability concerns the subject matter of a dispute whereas commerciality only concerns the underlying relationship between the parties. If the underlying relationship is considered commercial, the commercial requirement will be satisfied regardless of whether the dispute arising out of that relationship is commercial or not. As a result, irrespective of whether the relationship between the parties is commercial, the dispute arising out of that relationship could be arbitrable or not.

56. Having clarified certain terms regarding the field of arbitrability, the discussion now turns to the fundamentals of arbitrability law.

CHAPTER 2

Fundamentals of Arbitrability

57. This chapter aims to provide an international perspective on arbitrability by outlining the fundamentals of arbitrability law in different jurisdictions. After studying the different approaches to arbitrability adopted in nine jurisdictions[83] (presented in Chapter 4, which is available only in the online version of this book), the authors compared the approaches taken in those jurisdictions to determine their key similarities and differences, which are outlined in this chapter.

58. This chapter contains six Sections: the first section discusses "Jurisdictional Categories: Common Law Group v. Civil Law Group"; the second section ("Criterion for Arbitrability") categorizes the different criteria that the nine jurisdictions rely on in determining arbitrability into four groups; the third section discusses the "Presumption of Arbitrability"; the fourth section addresses the issue of "Inarbitrability v. Limitation on Remedies"; the fifth section discusses the "Commercial Reservation to the New York Convention"; and the final section presents an executive summary of this chapter in the form of a table.

A. JURISDICTIONAL CATEGORIES: COMMON LAW GROUP V. CIVIL LAW GROUP

59. Of the nine jurisdictions that are the focus of this research, four follow the civil law tradition (namely, France, Germany, Switzerland, and China [Mainland]) and four are common law jurisdictions (including the US, England and Wales, Hong Kong, and Singapore). The ninth jurisdiction, Canada, falls into both categories in that the legal system in one of its major provinces, Québec, is patterned on civil law principles, whereas all other Canadian provinces, including the three that are studied as part of this research (namely, Ontario, Alberta, and British Columbia—collectively "common

83. Including the US, Canada, France, England and Wales, Switzerland, Germany, China (Mainland), Hong Kong, and Singapore.

law provinces") follow the common law tradition.[84] Therefore, this study in fact covers ten jurisdictions: five jurisdictions in the common law group and five jurisdictions in the civil law group.

60. In studying arbitrability, categorizing jurisdictions into civil law and common law groups is helpful, because each jurisdiction shares significant similarities with other jurisdictions of the same civil/common law group. For example, all the five jurisdictions in the civil law group have a legislative criterion for arbitrability,[85] whereas the majority of jurisdictions in the common law group (namely, England and Wales, the common law provinces of Canada, and Hong Kong) do not. Likewise, the majority in the common law group (the common law provinces of Canada, Hong Kong, and Singapore) have based their legislative arbitration texts on either the 1985 UNCITRAL Model Law or its 2006 version,[86] whereas the majority in the civil law group (France, Switzerland, and China) have not.

61. However, the categorization of jurisdictions into civil law and common law groups is not comprehensive, as each jurisdiction also has differences from the others in the same group while also sharing similarities with jurisdictions classed into the other group. For example, France (unlike the majority of civil law jurisdictions studied here, but like the common law group) applies a presumption of arbitrability that requires, for example, an express or implied restriction in the relevant statute for a dispute to be non-arbitrable.[87]

B. CRITERION FOR ARBITRABILITY

62. Seven out of the ten jurisdictions have enacted a specific legislative criterion for arbitrability. The three jurisdictions that do not have a legislative criterion are all common law jurisdictions: England and Wales, the common law provinces of Canada, and Hong Kong. The criteria that those seven jurisdictions have adopted can be generally categorized into four major groups: (1) the economic interest criterion, (2) the public policy criterion, (3) the waivability criterion (based on the waivability of the right in dispute); and (4) the commerce criterion (based on the commercial nature of a dispute). The four categories are discussed below, in turn. It should be noted that some

84. The four provinces that were selected are the most significant in terms of both gross domestic product (GDP) and population. *See* Statistics Canada website, *Table 36-10-0222-01 on Gross Domestic Product, Expenditure-based, Provincial and Territorial*, online: https://www150.statcan.gc.ca/t1/tbl1/en/tv.action?pid=3610022201; *Ibid.*, *Table 17-10-0005-01 on Population by Year, By Province and Territory*, online: https://www150.statcan.gc.ca/t1/tbl1/en/tv.action?pid=1710000501 (last visited 16 October 2021).

85. *See* French Civil Code, Arts. 2059, 2060; German Code of Civil Procedure, Art. 1030; Swiss Private International Law Act, Art. 177(1) and Swiss Civil Procedure Code, Art. 354; Arbitration Law of the People's Republic of China, Art. 2.

86. For Canada, *see* Alberta's International Commercial Arbitration Act, RSA 2000, c I-5; British Columbia's International Commercial Arbitration Act, RSBC 1996, c 233; Ontario's International Commercial Arbitration Act, 2017, SO 2017, c 2, Schedule 5. For Hong Kong and Singapore, *see* Arbitration Ordinance (Cap 609) and International Arbitration Act 1994.

87. Discussed below, same Chapter, Section "Presumption of Arbitrability."

of the jurisdictions have adopted more than one of these criteria in their requirements of arbitrability.

1. Economic-Interest Criterion

63. The economic-interest criterion provides for the arbitrability of any disputes that concern economic interests. Of the seven jurisdictions that have a specific legislative criterion for arbitrability, three (all from the civil law group) have framed their criterion based on economic interests. The three jurisdictions are Switzerland, Germany, and China. Switzerland was the first to adopt such a criterion in 1987, followed by China in 1994, and Germany in 1998.

i. Economic-Interest Criterion in Switzerland

64. The Swiss Private International Law Act (PILA), Article 177(1), defines arbitrable matters as "*toute cause de nature patrimoniale*" (any dispute of a patrimonial nature). There is no statutory definition of the term "patrimonial," but according to the decision of the Federal Supreme Court in *BGE 118 II 353, 23 June 1992*, the term includes any claim that has an economic value for at least one of the parties, whether it is in the form of an asset or a liability, and regardless of whether the right in dispute could be waived or not. In addition to the economic-interest criterion, Swiss law applies the public-policy criterion (which is discussed next).[88]

65. Switzerland, unlike Germany and China, applies a dual regime to international and domestic arbitrations and, as such, its economic-interest criterion for arbitrability is applicable only to international disputes (as defined in Chapter 12 of the PILA), unless the parties to a domestic arbitration choose Chapter 12 of the PILA to apply to their arbitration.[89] Where the PILA does not apply, arbitration is governed by Part III of the Civil Procedure Code. For arbitrations governed by the Civil Procedure Code, Switzerland applies the waivability criterion for arbitrability (which is discussed further in this chapter).[90]

ii. Economic-Interest Criterion in Germany

66. Section 1030(1) of the German Code of Civil Procedure reads: "Any claim under property law [pecuniary claims] may become the subject matter of an arbitration

88. Discussed below, para. 77.
89. Swiss Civil Procedure Code, Art. 353(2). In 2019, the Swiss Federal Supreme Court clarified that in order for an opt-out from the PILA in favor of the Code of Civil Procedure (or vice versa) to be valid, the parties must (i) in a written format and expressly (ii) exclude the application of one law and (iii) include the application of the other law. However, according to the Court, the term "expressly" does not mean that the parties are required to name the law that is being excluded, i.e., as long as they "clearly" indicate their shared intention that they submit their dispute to one law in exclusion of the other, the requirements are met. *Case No 4A_540/2018, 7 May 2019*, reason 1.
90. *See* below, para. 79.

agreement." Commentators have interpreted section 1030(1) to include "claims for the payment of a sum of money," "declaratory claims and actions for the change of a legal relationship," and "prohibitory actions and actions for revocations, if they are raised to protect business interests."[91]

iii. Economic-Interest Criterion in China (Mainland)

67. According to Article 1 of the Arbitration Law of the People's Republic of China, "economic disputes" are in principle arbitrable, and according to Article 2, "contractual disputes" and "disputes over rights and interests in property" may be submitted to arbitration. Further, the Civil Code, Article 233, provides for the arbitrability of disputes over "real rights" which, according to Article 115, includes rights in both movable and immovable properties. Thus, one could argue that disputes over real estate and lands should be arbitrable, but it is not clear whether that argument will hold. This is so because, according to Article 34 of the Civil Procedure Law of the People's Republic of China, real estate disputes are within the exclusive jurisdiction of the People's Courts and may not be submitted to arbitration. The Civil Procedure Law (last amended in 2021) is more recent, compared to the Civil Code (enacted in 2020). Also, the relevant article in the Civil Code (Article 233) has a general scope covering both movable and immovable properties, whereas the relevant article of the Civil Procedure Law (Article 34) is addressed specifically to real estate and lands and, as such, may be viewed as a lex specialis that should be applied with respect to the question of arbitrability of real estate/land disputes.

2. Public Policy Criterion

68. Three jurisdictions (of the seven that have a legislative criterion for arbitrability) have adopted a criterion based on public policy. These jurisdictions are France and Québec (both in the civil law group) and Singapore from the common law group.

69. None of the aforementioned jurisdictions defines public policy in their relevant legislation. However, they are not the only jurisdictions without a statutory definition for public policy. According to the report issued in 2015 by the International Bar Association (IBA)'s Sub-committee on the Recognition and Enforcement of Arbitral Awards, only two jurisdictions out of the 40 that the IBA report covers have a statutory definition for public policy.[92]

91. Rolf Trittmann & Inka Hanefeld, "Commentary on the German Arbitration Law (10th Book of the German Code of Civil Procedure), Chapter II Arbitration Agreement, § 1030" in Karl-Heinz Böckstiegel et al, eds, *Arbitration in Germany: The Model Law in Practice*, 2nd ed (Kluwer Law International, 2015) 94 at para. 9.

92. IBA Subcommittee on Recognition and Enforcement of Arbitral Awards, *Report on the Public Policy Exception in the New York Convention* (October 2015) at 2, online: https://uk.practicallaw.thomsonreuters.com/8-619-5912?transitionType=Default&contextData=(sc.Default)&firstPage=true (last visited 11 March 2023).

i. Public Policy Criterion in France

70. The French public policy criterion for arbitrability has undergone substantial changes over the past decades. Article 2060 of the French Civil Code—which concerns the non-arbitrability of public policy matters—if not abandoned completely, has at least not been applied in international matters for some time.[93] Rather, since the 1950s, "French courts have simply ignored the legislative text [of article 2060] and explicitly ruled out the restrictive association of public policy and arbitrability."[94] French courts "gradually associated [non-arbitrability] with a more international and less restrictive notion."[95]

71. In this regard, it is important to understand the definition that French law has offered for international arbitration. Article 1504 of the Code of Civil Procedure reads: "An arbitration is international if it involves the interests of international commerce." According to the book *Fouchard Gaillard Goldman on International Commercial Arbitration*, Article 1504 has adopted an economic definition of "internationality", in that it includes "[a]ny transaction involving a movement of goods, services or funds across national [borders], or concerning the economies or currencies of at least two countries."[96]

72. Therefore, the matters that are within the scope of Article 2060 of the Civil Code can be categorized into two groups:

- The first group includes matters where the public interest element is so strong that their inarbitrability has survived the liberalization of French arbitration law over the past decades. These include: matters relating to the status and capacity of persons, matters relating to divorce and judicial separation, criminal matters, and disputes relating to the invalidity of a patent in rem.
- The second group consists of a broader range of matters, mostly involving economic interests—such as antitrust, securities, and intellectual property—that concern public policy and, as such, are within the scope of Article 2060, but where the public interest element has not been deemed as strong as in the first group so as to justify their non-arbitrability. Therefore, although matters that fall within this group have a public interest element and remain subject to mandatory rules, French courts have preferred to perform a

93. Emmanuel Gaillard & John Savage, eds, *Fouchard Gaillard Goldman on International Commercial Arbitration* (Kluwer Law International, 1999) at 330–38, paras. 560–68.
94. Karim Youssef, "The Death of Inarbitrability" in Loukas A Mistelis & Stavros L Brekoulakis, eds, *Arbitrability: International and Comparative Perspective* (Kluwer Law International, 2009) 47 at 59; *see* Jean Rouche, Gerald H Pointon & Jean-Louis Delvolvé, eds, *French Arbitration Law and Practice: A Dynamic Civil Law Approach to International Arbitration*, 2nd ed (Kluwer Law International, 2009) at paras. 11, 73.
95. Karim Youssef, "The Death of Inarbitrability" in Loukas A Mistelis & Stavros L Brekoulakis, eds, *Arbitrability: International and Comparative Perspective* (Kluwer Law International, 2009) 47 at 59.
96. Emmanuel Gaillard & John Savage, eds, *Fouchard Gaillard Goldman on International Commercial Arbitration* (Kluwer Law International, 1999) at 55–58, paras. 107–108, 115, 120–121.

supervisory role rather than a primary role in the enforcement of these mandatory rules whenever there is a valid arbitration agreement.

73. It should be noted that the public-policy criterion is not the only criterion governing arbitrability in the Civil Code. French law also applies the waivability criterion, which is discussed later in this chapter.[97]

ii. Public Policy Criterion in Québec

74. Under the first part of Article 2639 of the Québec Civil Code, "matters of public order" are not arbitrable. This includes disputes over the status and capacity of persons and family matters. The second part of the same article, however, stresses that the mere fact that the applicable rules to a dispute are rules of public order does not render the dispute non-arbitrable. In *Desputeaux v. Éditions Chouette (1987) Inc*—which originated in Québec—the Supreme Court of Canada held that Québec courts may not bar arbitration of copyright ownership disputes by associating them with the status and capacity of a person or public order under Article 2639 of the Québec Civil Code or Article 946.5 of the then Code of Civil Procedure (now Article 646 of the new Code).[98]

iii. Public Policy Criterion in Singapore

75. Singapore has two distinct regimes for international and domestic arbitrations: international arbitration is governed by the International Arbitration Act and domestic arbitration is governed by the Arbitration Act. Section 3(1) of the International Arbitration Act gives the 1985 UNCITRAL Model Law the force of law in Singapore. In relation to arbitrability, section 11(1) of the same Act provides that a non-arbitrable dispute is one where it would be contrary to "public policy" to refer it to arbitration, but section 11 does not define "public policy."

76. The legislative history of the Arbitration Act sheds some light on the contours of arbitrability in Singapore. According to the final report issued by the Review of the Arbitration Act Committee,[99] "[i]t is generally accepted that issues, which may have public-interest elements, may not be arbitrable, e.g. citizenship or legitimacy of marriage, grants of statutory licenses, validity of registration of trade marks or patents, copyrights, winding of companies, bankruptcy of debtors, administration of

97. *See* below, Subsection "Waivability Criterion in France."
98. *Desputeaux v. Éditions Chouette (1987) Inc*, 2003 SCC 17 at paras. 40, 42, 49–51, 56–59, 61, 62, [2003] 1 SCR 178.
99. The committee formed by Singapore Attorney General to review the then arbitration legislation, i.e., prior to the enactment of the International Arbitration Act.

estates."[100] However, since 2019, disputes as to the validity of trademarks, patents, and copyrights have become arbitrable through new legislation.[101]

iv. Public Policy Criterion in Switzerland

77. It should be noted that, although the public policy criterion for arbitrability was not the choice of the Swiss legislature,[102] it has found its way into Swiss law through another door. Commentators consider that "the only bar to arbitrability, outside article 177(1) of the PILA [the article containing the economic interest criterion] is the principle of public policy as developed by the Federal Supreme Court in the application of article 190(2)(e) PILA in the context of setting aside proceeding."[103]

3. **Waivability Criterion**

78. Of the seven jurisdictions that have a specific criterion for arbitrability, three have adopted a criterion based on whether the right in dispute is waivable, that is: whether the parties may conclude a settlement with respect to their dispute. The three jurisdictions are Switzerland, Germany, and France. However, each defines and applies the waivability criterion in a different way.

i. Waivability Criterion in Switzerland

79. As explained previously, Switzerland applies the economic-interest criterion in international arbitrations as well as in those domestic arbitrations where the parties have elected for their arbitration to be governed by Chapter 12 of the PILA.[104] For domestic arbitrations that are governed by Part III of the Civil Procedure Code, Switzerland applies the waivability criterion. The rights that one may not waive under Swiss law can be categorized into two groups.

80. The first group includes matters such as employment and consumer disputes where inarbitrability could be linked to *ordre public de protection*.[105] The limitation on

---

100. Review of Arbitration Act Committee, *Review of Arbitration Laws*, LRRD No 3/2001, online: https://www.sal.org.sg/sites/default/files/PDF%20Files/Law%20Reform/1993-08%20-%20Review%20of%20Arbitration%20Laws.pdf (last visited 8 April 2023).
101. The Intellectual Property (Dispute Resolution) Act 2019 amended the Arbitration Act and the International Arbitration Act to provide for the arbitrability of a wide range of intellectual property disputes, including the validity disputes. *See* Part 2A of the International Arbitration Act, and Part 9A of the Arbitration Act.
102. Discussed above, para. 64.
103. Philippe Bärtsch & Dorothee Schramm, *Arbitration Law of Switzerland: Practice and Procedure* (Juris, 2014) at 30; Robert Briner & Paolo Michele Patocchi, "National Report for Switzerland (2008)" in Jan Paulsson & Lise Bosman, eds, *ICCA International Handbook on Commercial Arbitration* (Kluwer Law International, 2008) 1 at 14, 15.
104. *See* above, paras. 64–65.
105. Economic public policy rules are divided, particularly in civil law jurisdictions, into two groups: rules of *ordre public de direction* and rules of *ordre public de protection*. The former is "to regulate the economy for the general good of the society," whereas the latter is to provide

the arbitration of such disputes is not based on a concern for the interests of society as a whole, but rather the right-holder who is presumed to be in a weaker bargaining position.[106] This inarbitrability is neither inherent to the subject matter nor permanent, and could be lifted as soon as the protected person is no longer presumed to be in the weaker position. For example, in employment disputes, the limitation on arbitration only applies during the employment relationship and until one month after its end (Articles 361, 362, 341 of the Swiss Code of Obligations).[107] Likewise, in consumer disputes, only pre-dispute arbitration agreements are invalid under Article 35 of the Civil Procedure Code, with the parties free to conclude an agreement after the dispute arises.

81. The second group includes matters such as family disputes and matters of "voluntary jurisdictions" (i.e., matters involving an entry or a change in a public registry such as a change of name, a declaration of disappearance, or a grant of a patent).[108] Inarbitrability in this context is intended to protect the interests of both the right-holder and the public at large. Therefore, unlike the first group, their inarbitrability is permanent.

ii. Waivability Criterion in Germany

82. Unlike Switzerland, Germany has a single regime for international and domestic arbitrations. The default criterion for arbitrability, under section 1030(1) of the Code of Civil Procedure, is that claims involving economic interests are arbitrable. However, section 1030(1) also provides that, if a claim does not involve any economic interest, it could be submitted to arbitration only if the parties to the dispute are entitled to conclude a settlement regarding the subject matter of the dispute (i.e., the waivability criterion). In German law, only a few matters have been considered to be non-arbitrable under the waivability criterion, including divorce, establishing the legitimacy of a child, custody, protection from family violence, and non-pecuniary matters involving a guardian.[109]

---

protection for an "economically weaker contracting party." Quebec Research Centre of Private and Comparative Law, *Private Law Dictionary and Bilingual Lexicons*, 2nd ed (1991) at 348–49.

106. *See* Tibor Varady, John J Barcelo III & Arthur T von Mehren, *International Commercial Arbitration: A Transnational Perspective*, 4th ed (West, 2009) at 233.

107. Federal Act on the Amendment of the Swiss Civil Code (Part Five: The Code of Obligations).

108. Bernhard Berger & Franz Kellerhals, International and Domestic Arbitration in Switzerland, 3rd ed (Hart, 2015) at para. 259; Matthias Scherer, "New Rules for Litigation and Domestic Arbitration in Switzerland" (2011) 8: 29 Revista Brasileira de Arbitragem 121 at 124.

109. Civil Code, §§ 1564, 1822(12); Act on Proceedings in Family Matters and in Matters of Non-Contentious Jurisdiction (FamFG), §§ 36, 86(1)(2), 156(2), 121, 122; Stephanie Uta Gilfrich, *Schiedsverfahren im Scheidungsrecht: eine rechtvergleichende Untersuchung* (Mohr Siebeck, 2007) at 33, 34, 36, 49, 57–59; Rolf Trittmann & Inka Hanefeld, "Commentary on the German Arbitration Law (10th Book of the German Code of Civil Procedure) § 1030" in Karl-Heinz Böckstiegel et al, eds, *Arbitration in Germany: The Model Law in Practice*, 2nd ed (Kluwer Law International, 2015) 94 at para. 21; Hilmar Raeschke-Kessler, "Arbitrability of Disputes Concerning Resolutions of a Limited Liability Company (GmbH)" (1996) 14:3 ASA Bulletin 355 at 358, para. 3 DOI: 10.54648/asab1996022.

iii. Waivability Criterion in France

83. As previously discussed, Article 2060 of the French Civil Code provides for the non-arbitrability of public policy disputes.[110] However, the public policy criterion is not the only criterion determining arbitrability in the Civil Code. Article 2059 sets out a criterion that provides for the non-arbitrability of rights that one may not freely waive. The nature of such inarbitrability has been linked to *ordre public de protection*,[111] which means that this inarbitrability is usually neither inherent to the subject matter nor permanent and could be lifted as soon as the protected person is no longer considered to be in the weaker position.[112] There are two matters that are within the scope of Article 2059, namely support payment (alimony) disputes[113] and lease disputes.[114]

84. However, it should be noted that typical examples of rules of *ordre public de protection* in French law are consumer and employment rules, where arbitrability of a dispute is decided based on other legislative provisions. Under Article 2061 of the French Civil Code, *pre-dispute* arbitration agreements are *not enforceable* against consumers. That means: when there is a pre-dispute arbitration agreement with a consumer, the clause is not invalid, but may be relied on only by the consumer.[115]

85. Likewise, arbitration provisions in employment agreements are not enforceable against employees. Previously, employment disputes were considered non-arbitrable, due to the exclusive jurisdiction of the Labour Court over employment disputes under Articles L1411-1 and L1411-4 of the Labour Code.[116] However, the Court of Cassation, in a line of cases,[117] held that an arbitration clause may not be enforced against an employee, which means that the clause is not invalid, but may be relied on only by the employee.

---

110. *See* above, paras. 70–73.
111. Éric Loquin, JurisClasseur Procédure Civile, Fasc 1024 (May 2016) at nos. 5, 17, 22, 24; *but see* Jean Rouche, Gerald H Pointon & Jean-Louis Delvolvé, eds, *French Arbitration Law and Practice: A Dynamic Civil Law Approach to International Arbitration*, 2nd ed (Kluwer Law International, 2009) at para. 65 (arguing that the rule in Article 2059 relates to the incapacity of persons).
112. Éric Loquin, JurisClasseur Procédure Civile, Fasc 1024 (May 2016) at no 89.
113. *Ibid.*, at nos. 90–91.
114. *Ibid.*, at nos. 93–105.
115. Thomas Clay, "La réforme des articles du Code civil sur l'arbitrage en France" (2017) 35:1 ASA Bulletin 40 at 47 DOI: 10.54648/asab2017004.
116. Philippe Fouchard, "La laborieuse réforme de la clause compromissoire par la loi du 15 mai 2001" (2001) 3 Rev Arb 397 at para. 29; Beatrice Castellane, "Arbitration in Employment Relationship in France" (2009) 26:2 J Int'l Arb 293 at 294; Estelle Courtois-Champenois, "L'Arbitrage des litiges en droit du travail: à la redécouverte d'une institution française en disgrâce" (2003) 2 Rev Arb 349 at paras. 3, 19; Éric Loquin, JurisClasseur Procédure Civile, Fasc 1024 (May 2016) at nos. 107, 108.
117. *Société Kis France v. Lopez-Alberdi*, Court of Cassation (Social Chamber), 9 October 2001, Decision No 99-43.288, reported in (2002) 2002:2 Rev Arb 347; *Société Taiphoon limited v. Bobinet*, Court of Cassation (Social Chamber), 28 June 2005, Decision No 03-45.042, reported in (2005) 2005:3 Rev Arb 799; *Société Sportive IL Gabbiano v. [not indicated]*, Court of Cassation (Social Chamber), 12 March 2008, Decision No 01-44.654; *Société Deloitte conseil v. M E Serant*, Court of Cassation (Social Chamber), 30 November 2011, Decision nos. 11-12.905 & 11-12.906.

4. Commerce Criterion

86. Of the seven jurisdictions that have a legislative criterion for arbitrability, only the US (which is within the common law group) has a legislative criterion that is based on the commercial nature of the matter in dispute. The US Federal Arbitration Act (FAA), originally enacted in 1925, clearly predates the UNCITRAL Model Law and, therefore, it is important to note that the term "commerce" in this context has a different meaning than term "commerciality" discussed in Chapter 1.[118]

87. The FAA provides for the arbitrability of any "*maritime transaction* or a contract evidencing a transaction involving *commerce*" (emphasis added). Section 1 of the FAA defines both maritime transactions and commerce. For maritime transactions, the definition reads: "charter parties, bills of lading of water carriers, agreements relating to wharfage, supplies furnished vessels or repairs to vessels, collisions, or any other matters in foreign commerce which, if the subject of controversy, would be embraced within admiralty jurisdiction." For commerce, the definition reads:

> [C]ommerce among the several States or with foreign nations, or in any Territory of the United States or in the District of Columbia, or between any such Territory and another, or between any such Territory and any State or foreign nation, or between the District of Columbia and any State or Territory or foreign nation.

88. The term "commerce" has been construed very broadly in this context. The US Supreme Court has repeatedly held that the FAA was enacted pursuant to Congress' Commerce Clause authority,[119] which has given the FAA a preemptive effect over contrary state laws.[120] This means that, in principle, where a state law and the FAA conflict over the arbitrability of a matter, the FAA prevails.[121]

89. The FAA § 1 excludes from the coverage of the FAA any "contracts of employment of seamen, railroad employees, or any other class of workers engaged in foreign or interstate commerce." The Supreme Court, in *Circuit City Stores, Inc v. Adams* (2001), construed the exception as confined to contracts of employment of *transportation* workers only.[122] In *New Prime Inc v. Oliveira* (2019), the same Court held that § 1 not

118. *See* above, Chapter I, Section "Differences Between Arbitrability and Commerciality."

119. The Commerce Clause refers to Art. 1, s. 8, clause 3, of the US Constitution, which gives Congress the power "to regulate commerce with foreign nations, and among the several states, and with the Indian tribes." Online: https://www.archives.gov/founding-docs/constitution-transcript (last visted 15 June 2022).

120. *See, e.g.*, *Prima Paint Corp v. Flood & Conklin Mfg*, 388 US 395 (1967), *Southland Corp v. Keating*, 465 US 1 (1984); *Volt Info Scis, Inc v. Bd of Trs of Leland Stanford Junior Univ*, 489 US 468 (1989).

121. The key cases on this issue are: *Prima Paint Corp v. Flood & Conklin Mfg*, 388 US 395 (1967); *Southland Corp v. Keating*, 465 US 1 (1984); *Volt Info Scis, Inc v. Bd of Trs of Leland Stanford Junior Univ*, 489 US 468 (1989); *Allied-Bruce Terminex v. Dobson*, 513 US 265 (1995); *Preston v. Ferrer*, 552 US 346 (2008); *AT&T Mobility v. Concepcion*, 131 S Ct 1740 (2011).

122. *Circuit City Stores, Inc v. Adams*, 532 US 105 (2001). It should be noted that for a transportation worker to be covered by the exception in § 1, they do not have to actually transport goods interstate or internationally. In *Southwest Airlines v. Saxon*, 2022 WL 1914099 (2022), the Supreme Court held that airline workers who load/unload cargo on/from airplanes that then

only is limited to contracts that establish an employer-employee relationship but also encompasses contracts with independent contractors.[123] In addition, the Courts of Appeals for the Fifth, Ninth, and Eleventh Circuits have held that the exception in § 1 of the FAA is not applicable to *international* employment disputes.[124]

C. PRESUMPTION OF ARBITRABILITY

90. For a dispute to be considered non-arbitrable, all the common law jurisdictions that have been the focus of this research require either an express/implied restriction in the relevant statute or there to be a conflict between arbitration and the statute's underlying purposes. Of the civil law jurisdictions, only France and Québec apply such a presumption. This section elaborates on the presumption of arbitrability in those jurisdictions that apply the presumption.

1. Presumption of Arbitrability in the United States

91. The US Supreme Court has repeatedly held that US statutory rights are considered to be arbitrable unless the opposing party proves that Congress has intended otherwise, and that such intention is deducible from "the statute's text or legislative history or from an inherent conflict between arbitration and the statute's underlying purposes."[125] Furthermore, according to the US Supreme Court, "[a]ny doubts concerning the scope of arbitrable issues should be resolved in favor of arbitration."[126]

2. Presumption of Arbitrability in Canada

92. The Supreme Court of Canada, in *Desputeaux v. Éditions Chouette* (2003), a case from Québec, ruled that the legislative intention behind statutory provisions providing for a court's jurisdiction over a subject matter is not to exclude arbitration of the matter, but rather to identify which court within the judicial system has jurisdiction over that

travel in interstate commerce are considered transportation workers because they are "directly involved in transporting goods across state or international borders" and hence meet the criterion in § 1 (i.e., being "engaged in foreign or interstate commerce"). Moreover, in order for transportation workers to qualify under § 1, the element of timing is also important. In *Hamrick v. Partsfleet, LLC*, 1 F4th 1337 (11th Cir 2021), the Court of Appeals for the Eleventh Circuit held that the worker must be involved in transporting goods across state lines and, as such, it is not sufficient that the goods were only previously transported interstate.

123. *New Prime Inc v. Oliveira*, 139 S Ct 532 (2019).
124. *Francisco v. Stolt Achievement MT*, 293 F3d 270 (5th Cir 2002) at 273–274; *Rogers v. Royal Caribbean Cruise Line*, 547 F3d 1148 (9th Cir 2008) at 1149, 1154, 1159; *Bautista v. Star Cruises*, 396 F3d 1289 (11th Cir 2005) at 1295–1297.
125. *Mitsubishi Motors Corp v. Soler Chrysler-Plymouth, Inc*, 473 US 614 (1985); *Shearson/American Express, Inc v. McMahon*, 482 US 220 (1987) at 226–227.
126. *Moses H Cone Memorial Hospital v. Mercury Construction*, 460 US 1 (1983); *Mitsubishi Motors Corp v. Soler Chrysler-Plymouth, In*, 473 US 614 (1985).

matter and, therefore, "it cannot be assumed to exclude arbitral jurisdiction unless it expressly so states."[127]

93. The *Desputeaux* decision, however, does not mean that, for a matter to be non-arbitrable under Canadian law, an express prohibition of arbitration in the relevant statute is necessary. The *Desputeaux* decision should be read together with another Canadian Supreme Court case: *Seidel v. Telus Communications Inc* (2011), a case from a common law province, which indicates that non-arbitrability could be implied in the relevant statute or be interpreted from other relevant sources.[128]

3. Presumption of Arbitrability in England and Wales

94. The Court of Appeal in *Fulham Football Club v. Richards* (2011) noted that, for a dispute to be considered non-arbitrable, there should be "either an implied restriction in the statute or some equivalent rule of public policy based on the considerations" of whether the matters in dispute "engage third party rights or represent an attempt to delegate to the arbitrators what is a matter of public interest which cannot be determined within the limitations of a private contractual process."[129]

95. Mustill and Boyd were also of the view that:

> English law has never arrived at a general theory for distinguishing those disputes which may be settled by arbitration from those which may not. The general principle is ... that any dispute or claim concerning legal rights which can be the subject of an enforceable award is capable of being settled by arbitration.[130]

4. Presumption of Arbitrability in Hong Kong

96. In Hong Kong, a Model Law jurisdiction, there is no direct authority on the presumption of arbitrability. However, notable commentators such as Michael Moser and Robert Morgan are of the opinion that, in Hong Kong law, "any dispute affecting civil interests of the parties may be the subject of a reference to arbitration."[131] Furthermore, "in the absence of direct Hong Kong authority, it is generally believed that the usual restrictions on arbitrability which apply under English law also apply in Hong Kong."[132] Given that English law applies the presumption of arbitrability,[133] it is arguable that the presumption is also applicable in Hong Kong law.

---

127. *Desputeaux v. Éditions Chouette (1987) Inc*, 2003 SCC 17 at paras. 22, 40, 42, [2003] 1 SCR 178.
128. *Seidel v. Telus Communications Inc*, 2011 SCC 15 at paras. 7, 10, 31–34, 37, 43–45, [2011] 1 SCR 531.
129. *Fulham Football Club (1987) Ltd v. Richards* [2011] EWCA Civ 855 at paras. 43, 40.
130. Michael J Mustill & Stewart C Boyd, *Commercial Arbitration*, 2nd ed (Butterworths, 1989) at 149–150.
131. Michael J Moser & Robert Morgan, "National Report for Hong Kong (2021 through 2022)" in Lise Bosman, ed, *ICCA International Handbook on Commercial Arbitration* (Kluwer Law International, 2022) at 30.
132. John Choong & Michael J Moser, *Asia Arbitration Handbook* (Oxford University Press, 2011) at para. 4.100.
133. *See* above, paras. 94–95.

5. Presumption of Arbitrability in Singapore

97. The case most relevant to the presumption of arbitrability in Singapore is *Larsen Oil & Gas Pte Ltd v. Petroprod Ltd* (2011), in which the Court of Appeal pointed out that:

> There is ordinarily a presumption of arbitrability where the words of an arbitration clause are wide enough to embrace a dispute, unless it is shown that parliament intended to preclude the use of arbitration for the particular type of dispute in question (as evidenced by the statute's text or legislative history), or that there is an inherent conflict between arbitration and the public policy considerations involved in that particular type of dispute.[134]

6. Presumption of Arbitrability in France

98. Although there are specific legislative criteria for arbitrability in France,[135] French courts have played a key role in shaping the rules of arbitrability. Thus, over the past decades, "French courts have simply ignored the legislative text and explicitly ruled out the restrictive association of public policy and arbitrability" because, from their perspective, "[t]he arbitrability of a dispute [should] not [be] excluded by the mere fact that rules pertaining to public policy are applicable to the dispute."[136]

99. As has been observed by leading French commentators, the French approach to arbitrability "consists of allowing the arbitrators to hear disputes relating to matters of public policy, whether or not the main contract containing the arbitration agreement actually contravenes public policy" and then courts are "able to review the public policy issue if an action is subsequently brought to enforce or set aside the resulting award."[137]

D. INARBITRABILITY V. LIMITATION ON REMEDIES

100. Other than the US, the other common law jurisdictions often consider limitations on arbitration in terms of the remedies a tribunal may order, rather than in terms of the arbitrability of the subject matter of a dispute. This approach may lead to the bifurcation of the claims, with the merits to be arbitrated first and then relief to be sought from courts. This section elaborates on the approach of jurisdictions that take this position in relation to the limitations on arbitration.

---

134. *Larsen Oil & Gas Pte Ltd v. Petroprod Ltd* [2011] 3 SLR 414 (CA) at para. 44.
135. *See* above, the discussion on "Public Policy Criterion in France" and "Waivability Criterion in France."
136. Karim Youssef, "The Death of Inarbitrability" in Loukas A Mistelis & Stavros L Brekoulakis, eds, *Arbitrability: International and Comparative Perspective* (Kluwer Law International, 2009) 47 at 59. *See* Jean Rouche, Gerald H Pointon & Jean-Louis Delvolvé, eds, *French Arbitration Law and Practice: A Dynamic Civil Law Approach to International Arbitration*, 2nd ed (Kluwer Law International, 2009) at paras. 11, 73.
137. Emmanuel Gaillard & John Savage, eds, *Fouchard Gaillard Goldman on International Commercial Arbitration* (Kluwer Law International, 1999) at 332.

1. Limitation on Remedies in England and Wales

101. The English view is that "any dispute or claim concerning legal rights which can be the subject of an enforceable award is capable of being settled by arbitration," but the remedies a tribunal may order would be "limited by considerations of public policy and by the fact that [arbitrators are] appointed by the parties and not by the State."[138]

102. The Court of Appeal in *Fulham Football Club v. Richards* (2011) explained that English law distinguishes between the dispute itself and the relevant relief: the fact that a specific relief may not be granted by an arbitral tribunal does not automatically render the dispute inarbitrable.[139] As a result, the Court held, the arbitral tribunal will have to decide the facts and merits of the dispute and then the parties may initiate court proceedings to seek the appropriate relief.[140]

103. For example, in the same case (namely *Fulham*), the Court held that a dispute as to whether there has been any unfair prejudice under the Companies Act 2006 is arbitrable, but there are certain *restrictions as to the type of relief* a tribunal may award; for instance, an arbitral tribunal may not make a winding up order, which rests exclusively with courts.[141] The Court also noted that, in a winding up petition on just and equitable grounds under the Insolvency Act 1986, tribunals may decide the underlying dispute so as to determine whether presenting a winding up petition to courts would be justified.[142]

2. Limitation on Remedies in Hong Kong

104. In *Quiksilver Greater China Ltd v. Quiksilver Glorious Sun JV Ltd* (2014), the Hong Kong Court of First Instance agreed with the English Court of Appeal in the *Fulham Football Club* case[143] and held that a tribunal may not make a winding up order, but it may determine whether the presentation of a winding up petition to courts on just and equitable grounds is justified.[144] Accordingly, the Hong Kong Court of First Instance held that courts should stay the winding up proceeding, pending the outcome of the arbitration.[145]

3. Limitation on Remedies in Canada (Province of British Columbia)

105. In the Canadian province of British Columbia (BC), the case law indicates that oppression claims are arbitrable in the sense that tribunals may make findings of

138. Michael J Mustill & Stewart C Boyd, *Commercial Arbitration*, 2nd ed (Butterworths, 1989) at 149-50.
139. *Fulham Football Club (1987) Ltd v. Richards* [2011] EWCA Civ 855 at paras. 76-78, [2012] 2 WLR 1008 (CA).
140. *Ibid.*
141. *Ibid.*, at paras. 51, 57-58, 61, 76-78, 83-84.
142. *Ibid.*
143. Discussed above, para. 102.
144. *Quiksilver Greater China Ltd v. Quiksilver Glorious Sun JV Ltd*, [2014] HKCFI 1304.
145. *Ibid.*

oppression, but they may not grant a relief that is considered to be within the exclusive jurisdiction of courts, such as the winding-up of a company.[146]

106. The BC approach regarding oppression claims clearly leads to the bifurcation of proceedings, where the merits are arbitrated first, and the relief is sought from courts. This approach has not been well-received by pro-arbitration lawyers and has been described as making "the arbitration process a paper tiger in the resolution of shareholder disputes,"[147] as well as being "unnecessary and inconsistent with the principle that a multiplicity of proceedings should be avoided at all costs."[148]

4. Limitation on Remedies in Singapore

107. The Singapore Court of Appeal in *Tomolugen Holdings Ltd v. Silica Investors Ltd* (2016), held that arbitral tribunals' jurisdictional limitation in granting certain reliefs that are available only to courts, including an order to wind up a company, "does not in and of itself make the subject matter of the dispute non-arbitrable."[149] The Court reasoned that the parties may, upon receiving the award, apply to courts for any relief which is beyond the tribunal's power to grant, without being able to re-litigate the findings of the tribunal.[150]

E. COMMERCIAL RESERVATION TO THE NEW YORK CONVENTION

108. The definition of commerciality and its difference from arbitrability is discussed in Chapter 1 of this book.[151] The New York Convention does not limit itself to commercial matters. Nevertheless, Article I(3) of the New York Convention has made it possible for signatory states to make a reservation whereby they would apply the Convention only to commercial matters.

109. In the course of drafting the New York Convention in 1955, the ad hoc committee established by the United Nations Social and Economic Council noted that not all countries distinguish commercial matters from non-commercial ones, and thus decided not to limit the scope of the Convention to commercial matters, including instead a commercial reservation option for signatory states.[152] In the final rounds of

146. *ABOP LLC v. Qtrade Canada Inc*, 2007 BCCA 290, 72 BCLR (4th) 34.
147. Rebecca Huang, "Shareholders Disputes: Arbitrator's Power to Grant Statutory Oppression Remedy" (2010) 36 Advocates' Q 457 at 427.
148. Byron Shaw, "The Arbitrability of Oppression Claims" (2011) 69:1 Advocate (Vancouver) 21 at 26.
149. *Tomolugen Holdings Ltd and another v. Silica Investors Ltd* [2016] 1 SLR 373 (CA) at paras. 98–99.
150. *Ibid.*, at para. 100.
151. *See* above, Chapter I, Section "Differences Between Arbitrability and Commerciality."
152. *Travaux Préparatoires*, Report of the Committee on the Enforcement of International Arbitral Awards, E/2704, E/AC42/4/Rev1 (28 March 1955) at para. 26.

drafting, the commercial reservation was deleted,[153] only to be reintroduced at the suggestion of the Dutch delegate.[154]

110. Although the commercial reservation to the New York Convention owes its existence to the insistence of certain civil law countries during the drafting phase, the majority of civil law jurisdictions studied here (namely France, Germany, Switzerland, and Québec) have not made the reservation. Only China has made the reservation. However, it should be noted that France initially made the reservation, but withdrew it in 1989.[155] Interestingly, the majority of common law jurisdictions studied here (the US, the common law provinces of Canada, and Hong Kong) have made the commercial reservation; but England and Singapore have not.

111. Overall, of the ten jurisdictions that were studied, the majority (six out of ten) have not made the commercial reservation to the New York Convention.[156]

153. *Text of the Convention as Provisionally Approved by the Drafting Committee on 6 June 1958*, E/CONF26/L61.
154. *Travaux Préparatoires*, United Nations Conference on International Commercial Arbitration, Summary Record of the Twenty-third Meeting, E/CONF26/SR.23 (9 June 1958) at 7–12; *Consideration of the Draft Convention: New Text of Articles 1 (3), 5 (1)(a), (b) and (e) Adopted by the Conference at its 23rd Meeting*, E/CONF26/L63 (9 June 1958).
155. Decree No 90-170 of 16 February 1990, online: https://www.legifrance.gouv.fr/jo_pdf.do?id =JORFTEXT000000714806 (last visited 23 October 2022). For more information, *see* Philippe Fouchard, "La Levée par la France de sa Réserve de Commercialité pour l'application de la Convention de New York" (1990) 1990:3 Rev Arb 571.
156. UNCITRAL website, tab "Texts and Status," hyperlink "International Commercial Arbitration," hyperlink "Convention on the Recognition and Enforcement of Foreign Arbitral Awards," hyperlink "Status," note (h), online: https://uncitral.un.org/en/texts/arbitration/conventions /foreign_arbitral_awards/status2 (last visited 23 October 2022).

Table 2.1 Fundamentals of Arbitrability

Statements	**Jurisdictions**									
This jurisdiction—	**Common Law Jurisdictions**					**Civil Law Jurisdictions**				
	Canada (AB, ON, BC)	**England & Wales**	**Hong Kong**	**Singapore**	**United States**	**Canada (Québec)**	**China (Mainland)**	**France**	**Germany**	**Switzerland**
1. applies a dual regime to international and domestic arbitrations	√			√			[157]	√[158]	[159]	√
2. has based its (international) arbitration law on the UNCITRAL Model Law (1985 or 2006)	√	[160]	√	√		√	[161]		√	

157. The Arbitration Law of the People's Republic of China is applicable to both international and domestic arbitrations, but Chinese arbitration law still applies a distinct set of rules to "foreign-related" arbitrations. However, in terms of the arbitrability criterion, there is generally no difference—from a legislative perspective—between domestic and foreign-related arbitrations.
158. In case law. For example, the French Court of Cassation has repeatedly held that Article 2061 of the French Civil Code does not apply to international arbitration, yet Article 2061 (whether before or after the 2016 amendment) does not make such a qualification.
159. However, it should be noted that the part in Book 10 of the Code of Civil Procedure that concerns the recognition and enforcement of awards distinguishes between awards rendered in Germany (domestic awards) and those rendered in other countries (foreign awards).
160. The drafters of the Arbitration Act 1996 did not adopt the UNCITRAL Model Law but were influenced by it.
161. The Chinese Arbitration Law is not based on the UNCITRAL Model Law but the latter was taken into account when drafting the Arbitration Law.

Statements	Jurisdictions									
This jurisdiction—	Common Law Jurisdictions					Civil Law Jurisdictions				
	Canada (AB, ON, BC)	England & Wales	Hong Kong	Singapore	United States	Canada (Québec)	China (Mainland)	France	Germany	Switzerland
3. has a legislative criterion for arbitrability				√	√	√	√	√	√	√
3.1. the criterion is based on economic interests							√		√	√[162]
3.2. the criterion is based on public policy		[163]		√		√		√[164]		[165]

162. For international disputes as defined by Article 176(1) of the Swiss PILA, or for domestic disputes that the parties have agreed should be governed by Chapter 12 of the PILA.
163. One of the sections of the Arbitration Act 1996 that may seem to be relevant to arbitrability from a "public policy" perspective is s. 1(b) which states that "the parties should be free to agree how their disputes are resolved, subject only to such safeguards as are necessary in the public interest." However, the Court of Appeal, in *Fulham Football Club (1987) Ltd v. Richards* [2011] EWCA Civ 855, pointed out that the term "public interest" in section 1(b) is not likely to refer to "arbitrability."
164. It should be noted that French courts, beginning in the 1950s and onwards, have not applied the public policy criterion of the Civil Code, particularly in international matters.
165. Public policy has not been the choice of the Swiss legislature in framing the arbitrability criterion, but it has found its way in the criterion through another door. Commentators believe that, in addition to the economic-interest criterion in Article 177(1) of the PILA, the public policy criterion is also a criterion for arbitrability in Swiss law, since the Federal Supreme Court has applied it through Article 190(2)(e) of the PILA in setting aside proceedings.

Statements	Jurisdictions									
This jurisdiction—	Common Law Jurisdictions					Civil Law Jurisdictions				
	Canada (AB, ON, BC)	England & Wales	Hong Kong	Singapore	United States	Canada (Québec)	China (Mainland)	France	Germany	Switzerland
3.3. the criterion rules out the arbitrability of the rights one may not freely waive								√[166]	√[167]	√[168]
3.4. the criterion is based on the commercial nature of the subject matter					√					
4. does not allow the arbitration of status matters, e.g., divorce[169]	√	√	√	√	√	√*	√*	√*	√	√

166. In French law, the waivability criterion has been linked to *ordre public de protection*. This type of inarbitrability is usually neither inherent to the subject matter nor permanent, and can be lifted as soon as the protected person is no longer in the weaker position. This is usually expressed in terms of *inopposabilité*, meaning that the rights arising from the arbitration clause (an arbitration agreement concerning future disputes) may be invoked by the protected party but cannot be set up against that party.
167. This criterion applies to matters that are not pecuniary; in other words, claims that do not involve any economic interest could still be arbitrable if the parties to the dispute are entitled to conclude a settlement regarding the subject matter of the dispute.
168. For disputes that are not governed by Chapter 12 of the Swiss PILA.
169. Only the jurisdictions with a star next to them have a legislative provision that expressly prohibits the arbitration of status matters or family matters in general. In the other jurisdictions, the inarbitrability of status matters is understood from the wording of the relevant legislation and case law, as well as from commentary.

Statements	Jurisdictions									
This jurisdiction—	Common Law Jurisdictions					Civil Law Jurisdictions				
	Canada (AB, ON, BC)	England & Wales	Hong Kong	Singapore	United States	Canada (Québec)	China (Mainland)	France	Germany	Switzerland
5. applies a presumption of arbitrability	√	√	√[170]	√	√	√		√[171]		
6. considers limitations on arbitration to be more in the remedies a tribunal may award than the subject matter of dispute	√	√	√	√						
7. has made the commercial reservation to the NY Convention	√		√		√		√	[172]		

170. It is so understood from the commentary.
171. It is so understood from the commentary.
172. France initially made the commercial reservation but withdrew it in 1989.

CHAPTER 3

Major Approaches to Arbitrability in Different Fields of Law

112. After studying the status of arbitrability in nine jurisdictions[173] (presented in Chapter 4 of this book—available only in the online version), the authors compared those jurisdictions to one another, based on the approaches they have adopted in different fields of law. The aim was to identify the major approaches taken to arbitrability in different fields of law. The resulting analysis is presented in this chapter, which is organized as follows: the first section discusses major approaches to arbitrability in antitrust/competition law; the second section covers bankruptcy/insolvency law, the third section addresses consumer law; the fourth section focuses on corporate law; the fifth section concerns family/domestic relations law; the six section addresses intellectual property law; the seventh section focuses on labour/employment law; and the eighth section covers securities law. Finally, there is an executive summary of this chapter in the form of two tables.

A. ANTITRUST/COMPETITION LAW

113. Of the nine jurisdictions studied for this text, seven allow for the arbitration of antitrust disputes, while two jurisdictions (China and Singapore) generally do not. Further, of the seven jurisdictions where antitrust disputes are arbitrable, most impose

173. The nine jurisdictions are the US, Canada, France, England and Wales, Switzerland, Germany, China (Mainland), Hong Kong, and Singapore. It should be noted that when discussing some fields of law in this book, the number of jurisdictions increases from nine to ten. However, this is not because a new jurisdiction is added, but rather because of the division in Canada between the province of Québec and the other major provinces (Alberta, British Columbia, and Ontario—collectively the "common law provinces"). Canada has a federal system that leaves some matters to be regulated at the provincial level. For those matters, Canadian provinces have to be studied in two separate groups, because Québec follows the civil law tradition while the common law provinces follow the common law tradition. As such, in some fields, instead of discussing Canada as a single jurisdiction, the authors discuss Québec and the common law provinces separately.

some sort of restriction: either by limiting the relief a tribunal may grant, or by allowing courts to review the merits of arbitral awards in antitrust matters.

114. As explained below, the US and Switzerland have taken the most liberal approaches to the arbitration of antitrust disputes, while China and Singapore have adopted the most conservative approaches. The other jurisdictions stand somewhere between these two extremes. Thus, this section contains three subsections: (1) Liberal Approaches; (2) Conservative Approaches; and (3) Mixed Approaches.

1. Liberal Approaches

115. Of the jurisdictions assessed here, the US and Switzerland take the most liberal approaches to the arbitrability of antitrust disputes. These approaches are discussed in turn.

The United States

116. Courts in the US have held that both international and domestic antitrust disputes are arbitrable, without imposing any specific restrictions on arbitrability. In the words of the US Supreme Court, this is because "[h]aving permitted the arbitration to go forward, the national courts of the US will have the opportunity at the award-enforcement stage to ensure that the legitimate interest in the enforcement of the antitrust laws has been addressed."[174] This justification has become known as the "Second-Look Doctrine" which has been the focus of substantial expert commentary.[175]

117. The Supreme Court, in the landmark decision of *Mitsubishi Motors Corp v. Soler Chrysler-Plymouth, Inc* (1985), removed *international* antitrust disputes from the category of inarbitrable matters.[176] The bulk of the Supreme Court's analysis in that case was of a general nature and was therefore applicable to nearly all public policy matters. The *Mitsubishi* decision marked a new phase in the history of inarbitrability, as it limited the previous rule that the majority of public policy disputes were inarbitrable, in favor of the maximum expansion of arbitration.[177]

118. After the *Mitsubishi* decision, it did not take long for *domestic* antitrust disputes to become arbitrable in the US. For example, the Court of Appeals for the Ninth Circuit

174. *Mitsubishi Motors Corp v. Soler Chrysler-Plymouth, Inc*, 473 US 614 (1985) at 638.
175. *See, e.g.*, William W Park, "Private Adjudicators and the Public Interest: The Expanding Scope of International Arbitration" (1986) 12 Brook J Int'l 629 at 641; Thomas E Carbonneau, "Mitsubishi: The Folly of Quixotic Internationalism" (1986) 2 Arb Int'l 116 DOI: 10.1093/arbitration/2.2.116; Pierre Mayer, "Mandatory Rules of Law in International Arbitration" (1986) 2:4 Arb Int'l 274 at 279 DOI: 10.1093/arbitration/2.4.274; Luca G Radicati di Brozolo, "Antitrust: A Paradigm of the Relations Between Arbitration and Mandatory Rule—A Fresh Look at the 'Second Look'" (2004) 1 Int'l Arb L Rev 23.
176. *Mitsubishi Motors Corp v. Soler Chrysler-Plymouth, Inc*, 473 US 614 (1985) at 628–38.
177. *See*, Donald Francis Donovan & Alexander K A Greenawalt, "Mitsubishi After Twenty Years: Mandatory Rules Before Courts and International Arbitrators" in Loukas A Mistelis & Julian D M Lew, eds, *Pervasive Problems In International Arbitration* (Kluwer Law International, 2006) 11 at paras. 1-5, 1-6.

in *Nghiem v. NEC Elec, Inc* (1994)—for which the Supreme Court denied a petition for certiorari—held domestic antitrust disputes to be arbitrable.[178] Likewise, the Court of Appeals for the First Circuit in *Seacoast Motors of Salisbury, Inc v. Daimler Chrysler Motors Corp* (2001) ruled for the arbitrability of domestic antitrust disputes in similar terms to *Nghiem*.[179]

119. An exception to this general move in favor of arbitrability was the decision of the Court of Appeals for the Eleventh Circuit in *Kotam Electronics, Inc v. JBL Consumer Products, Inc* (1995), where the Court held that domestic antitrust disputes should remain non-arbitrable.[180] However, shortly after this decision, the Court vacated its decision in an en banc session.[181]

120. In 2019, the Antitrust Division of the US Department of Justice (DOJ) used arbitration—for the first time in its history—to resolve a critical issue in a merger challenge.[182] The DOJ had sought to block the proposed merger between Novelis Inc and Aleris Corporation (two major aluminum producers in North America).[183] The two sides eventually reached an agreement to refer the dispositive issue of "product market definition" to arbitration, in which the DOJ prevailed.[184] In fact, the DOJ has been authorized since 1990—under the Administrative Dispute Resolution Act of 1990 (amended 1996)[185]—to use alternative dispute resolution techniques (including arbitration), but it never acted on that authority until the *Novelis-Aleris* case. Based on the success in that case, the DOJ updated its guidelines on the use of arbitration.[186]

Switzerland

121. The Swiss approach is even more liberal than the US approach, in that Swiss courts not only support the arbitration of antitrust disputes but also consider antitrust rules to fall outside the scope of public policy rules.

122. The Federal Supreme Court, in cases such as *BGE 118 II 193, 28 April 1992, BGE 128 III 234, 1 February 2002,* and *BGE 132 III 389, 8 March 2006,* has supported the

178. *Nghiem v. NEC Elec, Inc*, 25 F3d 1437 (9th Cir 1994) at 1441–42, certiorari denied, 513 US 1044 (1994).
179. *Seacoast Motors of Salisbury, Inc v. Daimler Chrysler Motors Corp*, 271 F3d 6 (1st Cir 2001) at 10, 11.
180. *Kotam Electronics, Inc v. JBL Consumer Products, Inc*, 59 F3d 1155 (11th Cir 1995).
181. 69 F3d 1097 (11th Cir 1995) (en banc).
182. DOJ website, Press Release (4 September 2019), "Justice Department Sues to Block Novelis' Acquisition of Aleris" online: https://www.justice.gov/opa/pr/justice-department-sues-block-noveliss-acquisition-aleris-1 (last visited 15 June 2022).
183. *Ibid.*
184. DOJ website, Press Release (9 March 2020), "Justice Department Wins Historic Arbitration of a Merger Dispute" online: https://www.justice.gov/opa/pr/justice-department-wins-historic-arbitration-merger-dispute (last visited 15 June 2022).
185. Administrative Dispute Resolution Act of 1990 (amended 1996), 5 USC §§ 571-584, online: https://uscode.house.gov/view.xhtml?path=/prelim@title5/part1/chapter5/subchapter4&edition=prelim (last visited 13 December 2021).
186. Memorandum by Assistant Attorney General, "Updated Guidance Regarding the Use of Arbitration and Case Selection Criteria" (12 November 2020).

arbitrability of antitrust disputes. Three main principles may be distilled from these decisions:

> [First], [a]s a general rule, an arbitral tribunal, having its seat in Switzerland, has jurisdiction to examine the validity of an agreement pursuant to foreign competition law.
>
> [Second], [i]f neither party has raised the issue of foreign competition law, an arbitral tribunal, having its seat in Switzerland, is under no obligation to examine that question ex officio and its award is not contrary to public policy if no such examination is made.
>
> [Third], if one of the parties invokes the nullity of the agreement by virtue of applicable foreign competition law, an arbitral tribunal, having its seat in Switzerland, must examine the validity of the agreement in light of such competition law, even if the law chosen by the parties to govern their contract is Swiss law. That being said, as competition law provisions are not considered to be part of public policy within the meaning of Article 190(2)(e) PILA, there is little room [for] review at the stage of a challenge to the award, since [an error in the] application of the law by the arbitral tribunal is not, per se, a ground for setting aside the award.[187]

123. In *BGE 132 III 389, 8 March 2006*, the Federal Supreme Court held that European and national competition laws are not part of public policy rules and, therefore, a violation of such rules would not constitute a ground under Article 190(2)(e) of the PILA for setting aside an award. The Federal Supreme Court's reasoning was that, although many countries share the same concerns about cartels and trusts, different countries have adopted different approaches to protect their economy and market.[188]

124. In the same case, the Federal Supreme Court also held that there would be no contradiction between its decision (that competition laws are not part of public policy rules) and that in which the European Court of Justice[189] held that European Community (EC) competition law is part of the public policy rules of Member States, as well as an example of public policy rules under the New York Convention.[190] The Swiss Federal Supreme Court held that there was no conflict between these positions because the mandatory nature of EC competition law is linked to the existence of internal procedural rules that require Member States' courts to grant applications for annulment on the basis of a failure to observe national rules of public policy.[191] The Federal Supreme Court ruled that no such internal procedural rules are in place in Switzerland, as the country is not an EU Member State.

---

187. Philippe Bärtsch & Dorothee Schramm, *Arbitration Law of Switzerland: Practice and Procedure* (Juris, 2014) at 31.
188. *BGE 132 III 389, 8 March 2006.*
189. *Eco Swiss China Time Ltd v. Benetton International NV*, ECJ Case No C-126/97, Judgment of the Court (1 June 1999) at paras. 35–39.
190. *BGE 132 III 389, 8 March 2006.*
191. *Ibid.*

125. It should be noted that there is no provision on the arbitration of competition disputes either in the relevant Swiss legislative Acts[192] or in relevant ordinances. The same is true with respect to the Agreement Between the European Union and the Swiss Confederation Concerning Cooperation on the Application of Their Competition Laws.

2. Conservative Approaches

126. China and Singapore have adopted approaches that, compared to the other jurisdictions studied, are situated at the most conservative end of the spectrum.

China

127. Neither the Chinese Anti-Monopoly Law nor the Provisions of the Supreme People's Court on Several Issues Concerning the Application of Law in the Trial of Civil Dispute Cases Arising from Monopolistic Conduct prohibit the arbitration of antitrust disputes. However, Article 3(2) of the Arbitration Law expressly prohibits the arbitration of disputes that are within the jurisdiction of administrative authorities. Therefore, antitrust disputes are generally regarded as inarbitrable in China because they normally involve administrative decisions.[193] In fact, the Anti-Monopoly Law has mandated the creation of an administrative body to sanction any violation of Anti-Monopoly Law provisions.[194]

128. In *Nanjing Yuxu Technology Co v. Samsung (China)* (2016), the Higher People's Court of Jiangsu held the antitrust dispute between the parties to be inarbitrable on the grounds that:

- the Anti-Monopoly Law provides for an administrative mechanism for the enforcement of its regime and, under the relevant guidelines of the Supreme People's Court, private remedies in antitrust matters are only available through civil litigation;
- unlike jurisdictions where antitrust matters are arbitrable, in China, antitrust law is relatively new and the judicial practice in the field has yet to develop; and
- antitrust matters generally involve public interest and third-party rights.[195]

129. Based on the *Nanjing* decision, one could conclude that antitrust disputes may be submitted to arbitration if the following two conditions are both met: the dispute does not require any administrative decision to be taken and there are no third-party rights or public interests involved. However, in 2019, the Supreme People's Court made a

192. Including the Federal Act on Cartels and Other Restrictions to Competition (known as the Cartel Act) and the Federal Act Against Competition (known as the Competition Act).
193. Lu Song, "National Report for China (2020 through 2022)" in Lise Bosman, ed, *ICCA International Handbook on Commercial Arbitration* (Kluwer Law International, 2022) at Chapter II.3.a.
194. Anti-Monopoly Law of the People's Republic of China, Arts. 12, 13, 46–67.
195. *Nanjing Yuxu Technology Co, Ltd v. Samsung (China) Investment Co, Ltd*, Higher People's Court of Jiangsu, [2015] 苏知民辖终字第 00072 号, 29 December 2016.

ruling that seemingly imposed a general ban on the arbitration of antitrust disputes. In *Shell (China) v. Hohhot Huili Materials*, the Court ruled that antitrust disputes are not arbitrable under Chinese law, first because arbitration is not among the dispute resolution mechanisms explicitly set out in the Anti-Monopoly Law for antitrust disputes, and second because such disputes are not contractual in nature and involve public policy elements and thus they do not fall within the scope of arbitrable matters in Article 2 of the Arbitration Law.[196] In 2021, the Court held the same position again in *Baicheng Xinniu Dairy Co v. Yili Group Company*.[197]

Singapore

130. The Singapore Competition Act 2004 does not include any provision on arbitration. However, commentators consider that "antitrust regulatory issues" are non-arbitrable.[198] While commentators have not elaborated on the meaning of "antitrust regulatory issues," it is understood that the term conveys restrictions similar to the ones in Chinese law, i.e., that antitrust disputes requiring administrative decisions or involving public interest may not be submitted to arbitration.

3. Mixed Approaches

131. The approaches adopted by France, England, Germany, Canada, and Hong Kong to the arbitrability of antitrust disputes are not as liberal as the US and Swiss approaches, because they impose certain restrictions. However, unlike China and Singapore, these restrictions concern the remedy that a tribunal may award, rather than subject-matter arbitrability.

France

132. The Paris Court of Appeal, in *Société Labinal v. Sociétés Mors et Westland Aerospace* (1993)[199] and *Société Aplix v. Société Velcro* (1993),[200] held that arbitral tribunals may sanction a violation of competition rules and decide disputes arising under EC competition law, but that tribunals may decide *only the civil aspect* of these disputes and may *not* grant exemptions or award financial penalties in the case of a violation.

---

196. *Shell (China) Limited v. Hohhot Huili Materials Co, Ltd*, Supreme People's Court of the People's Republic of China, (2019) Zui Gao Fa Zhi Min Xia Zhong No 47, 21 August 2019.
197. *Baicheng Xinniu Dairy Co, Ltd v. Yili Group Company*, Supreme People's Court of the People's Republic of China, (2021) Zui Gao Fa Min Zhi Zhong No 924, 9 February 2022.
198. Michael Hwang, Lawrence Boo & Eugene Thong, "National Report for Singapore (2018–2022)" in Lise Bosman, eds, *ICCA International Handbook on Commercial Arbitration* (Kluwer Law International, 2022) at sec 3.a (citing *Halsbury's Laws of Singapore*, vol 1(2) (LexisNexis, 2020 Reissue) at para. 20.002); David Joseph & David Foxton, *Singapore International Arbitration: Law & Practice* (LexisNexis, 2014) at para. 5.3.
199. *Société Labinal v. Sociétés Mors et Westland Aerospace*, Paris Court of Appeal, 19 May 1993, reported in (1993) 1993:4 Rev Arb 645 at 650.
200. *Société Aplix v. Société Velcro*, Paris Court of Appeal, 14 October 1993, reported in (1994) 1994:1 Rev Arb 164 at 167–168.

133. In relation to French competition law rules, the Paris Court of Appeal, in *Jacquetin v. Société Intercaves SA* (2008), rejected an application for annulment of an arbitral award in which the arbitrator had ruled on questions of competitive practices and validated an exclusive supply clause in a contract.[201] The Court held that the arbitrator had the competence to decide the arbitrability of disputes arising from public policy rules of the Commercial Code and to apply those rules and sanction any violation thereof.[202] Also, the Court of Cassation, in *Société Scamark v. Société Conserveries des Cinq Oceans* (2015), held that Articles L442-6 and D442-3 of the Commercial Code on practices restricting competition do not exclude recourse to arbitration for settling claims for compensation in disputes between economic players.[203]

134. In accordance with Recital 48 of Directive 2014/104/EU (on actions for damages in competition disputes), dispute resolution mechanisms such as arbitration are "desirable" and should be encouraged. In this regard, Recital 51 stresses that "[t]o encourage consensual settlements, an infringer that pays damages through consensual dispute resolution should not be placed in a worse position vis-à-vis its co-infringers than it would otherwise be without the consensual settlement."[204] France transposed the Directive into its national law in 2017 through an ordinance and a decree, neither of which contains provisions on consensual dispute resolution mechanisms.[205]

England and Wales

135. Both English legislation and case law allow for the arbitration of antitrust disputes. English courts have held that antitrust disputes—whether they arise under English law or EU law—may be submitted to arbitration. For example, in *Electronic Arts CV v. CTO SpA* (2003), the Commercial Court allowed the arbitration of competition disputes governed by English law, regardless of the risk of non-enforcement of the award in the jurisdiction likely to be the place of enforcement.[206] Likewise, in *ET Plus SA v. Welter* (2005), the same Court held that antitrust disputes arising under Articles 81 and 82 of the Treaty Establishing the European Community (now Articles 101 and 102 of the Treaty on the Functioning of the European Union) are arbitrable.[207]

201. *Jacquetin v. Société Intercaves SA*, Paris Court of Appeal, 20 March 2008, Case No 06/06860.
202. *Ibid.*
203. *Société Scamark v. Société Conserveries des Cinq Oceans*, Court of Cassation (1st Civil Chamber), 21 October 2015, Decision No 14-25.080.
204. Directive 2014/104/EU of the European Parliament and of the Council of 26 November 2014 on Certain Rules Governing Actions for Damages Under National Law for Infringements of the Competition Law Provisions of the Member States and of the European Union, online: http://eur-lex.europa.eu/legal-content/EN/TXT/PDF/?uri = OJ:L:2014:349:FULL&from = EN (last visited 30 January 2020).
205. *See* Ordinance No 2017-303 of 9 March 2017 Relating to Actions for Damages due to Anti-Competitive Practices (online: https://www.legifrance.gouv.fr/jorf/id/JORFTEXT000034160223/) and Decree No 2017-305 of 9 March 2017 Relating to Actions for Damages due to Anti-Competitive Practices (online: https://www.legifrance.gouv.fr/loda/id/JORFTEXT000034160256/2021-01-30/) (last visited 30 January 2020).
206. *Electronic Arts CV v. CTO SpA* [2003] EWHC 1020 (Comm) at paras. 86–90.
207. *ET Plus SA v. Welter* [2005] EWHC 2115 at para. 51.

136. From a legislative perspective, before Brexit, the United Kingdom (UK) transposed the EU directive relating to actions for damages in competition disputes[208] into domestic law in 2017, by way of a regulation titled Claims in Respect of Loss or Damage Arising from Competition Infringements (Competition Act 1998 and Other Enactments (Amendment)) Regulations 2017. The Regulation amended the Competition Act 1998 by introducing a new schedule (Schedule 8A) into the Act. Schedule 8A recognizes consensual dispute resolution as a means of settling antitrust disputes and defines this process inclusively as "arbitration, mediation or any other process enabling parties to a dispute to resolve it out of court."

137. However, commentators have noted that arbitrators may not "engage in merger control, conduct a cartel investigation, hear allegations of criminal liability for breach of Article 101 of the Treaty on the Functioning of the European Union (formerly Article 81 of the Treaty Establishing the European Community), impose a fine or penalty for anti-competitive behaviour, or order the restructuring or break-up of a group of companies."[209]

138. Since the UK left the EU, EU competition law is no longer applicable in the UK as EU law. Yet, it remains relevant because any conduct by a UK firm that is implemented in the EU territory or produces effect therein is subject to EU competition law.[210] Further, at the time of leaving the block, the UK converted all EU laws (including its competition law) that were applicable to the UK at the time into UK domestic law.[211] It should also be noted that Chapters I and II of the Competition Act 1998 are, in fact, the equivalents of Articles 101 and 102 of the Treaty on the Functioning of the European Union. Therefore, the UK's departure from the EU has not, to date, affected the arbitrability of competition disputes in English law.

139. In both abovementioned cases—*ET Plus SA v. Welter* and *Electronic Arts CV v. CTO SpA*—the Commercial Court did not deal with a purely domestic antitrust dispute. Nevertheless, disputes arising under English domestic competition law are clearly arbitrable, under the 2017 Regulation that amended the Competition Act 1998. But

208. Directive 2014/104/EU of the European Parliament and of the Council of 26 November 2014 on Certain Rules Governing Actions for Damages Under National Law for Infringements of the Competition Law Provisions of the Member States and of the European Union, online: http://eur-lex.europa.eu/legal-content/EN/TXT/PDF/?uri=OJ:L:2014:349:FULL&from=EN (last visited 12 August 2022). In accordance with recital 48 of the Directive, dispute resolution mechanisms such as arbitration are "desirable" and should be encouraged. Recital 51 stresses that "[t]o encourage consensual settlements, an infringer that pays damages through consensual dispute resolution should not be placed in a worse position vis-à-vis its co-infringers than it would otherwise be without the consensual settlement."

209. Julian D M Lew & Oliver Marsden, "Arbitrability" in Julian D M Lew et al, eds, *Arbitration in England, with Chapters on Scotland and Ireland* (Kluwer Law International, 2013) at paras. 19.40–19.41.

210. *See* European Commission Directorate-General for Competition, *Notice to Stakeholders: Withdrawal of the United Kingdom and EU Rules in the Field of Competition* (2 December 2020) at 1–3, online: https://competition-policy.ec.europa.eu/system/files/2022-12/UK_withdrawal_stakeholders_notice_on_consequences_on_competition_law.pdf (last visited 25 June 2022).

211. European Union (Withdrawal) Act 2018 (amended 2020), ss. 2, 3, online: https://www.legislation.gov.uk/ukpga/2018/16/contents (last visited 12 August 2022).

even prior to the introduction of the 2017 Regulation, commentators considered that purely domestic antitrust matters were arbitrable under English law.[212]

Hong Kong

140. There is no explicit legislative text or case law in relation to the arbitrability of antitrust disputes in Hong Kong. For instance, the Competition Ordinance (Cap 619) includes no provision that prohibits arbitration of antitrust disputes, or that vests exclusive jurisdiction in local courts or the Competition Tribunal. Further, under the Arbitration Ordinance (Cap 609), sections 89(3)(a), 95(3)(a), and 86(2)(a), non-arbitrability is one of the grounds on which it is possible to set aside or to refuse the enforcement of an award, but the Ordinance offers no definition for arbitrability. Commentators are of the view that, in Hong Kong:

> [A]ny dispute affecting civil interests of the parties may be the subject of a reference to arbitration. Thus, arbitration may resolve any dispute involving not only claims for breach of contract but also claims in tort, breach of trust and breach of statutory duty, and claims relating to real or personal property, provided that the arbitration agreement so permits.[213]

141. Given that the Arbitration Ordinance does not limit itself to commercial matters,[214] and given the influence of English law in Hong Kong[215] coupled with the fact that English law allows for the arbitration of antitrust disputes,[216] such disputes are likely to be arbitrable in Hong Kong, with similar restrictions applied in English law.

Canada

142. The federal Competition Act includes no provision on the arbitrability of competition disputes. However, the case law on this point is clear, as federal courts have held that *private claims* for damages under the Competition Act are arbitrable. In *Murphy v. Amway Canada Corp* (2013), the Federal Court of Appeal upheld the Federal

212. *See, e.g.*, Julian D M Lew, "The Basis for Applying Competition Law from an English Law Perspective" in Gordon Blanke and Phillip Landolt, eds, *EU and US Antitrust Arbitration: A Handbook for Practitioners*, (Kluwer Law International, 2011) 519 at para. 14-016; Richard H Kreindler, Paul Gilbert et al, "Impact of Brexit on UK Competition Litigation and Arbitration" (2016) 33:7 J Int'l Arb 521 at 533–534.
213. Michael J Moser & Robert Morgan, "National Report for Hong Kong (2021 through 2022)" in Lise Bosman, ed, *ICCA International Handbook on Commercial Arbitration* (Kluwer Law International, 2022) at 30.
214. The Arbitration Ordinance (Cap 609) is based on the UNCITRAL Model Law (1985, amended in 2006) but, unlike the Model Law, it does not limit its application to "commercial" arbitration. *See* Arbitration Ordinance (Cap 609), s. 2(1), definition of "UNCITRAL Model Law"; UNCITRAL Model Law (1985, amended in 2006), Art. 1.
215. Although Hong Kong is an advanced jurisdiction in terms of arbitration practice, arbitrability under Hong Kong law has not been extensively discussed in academic literature. As such, according to John Choong and Michael J Moser, "in the absence of direct Hong Kong authority, it is generally believed that the usual restrictions on arbitrability which apply under English law also apply in Hong Kong." John Choong & Michael J Moser, *Asia Arbitration Handbook* (Oxford University Press, 2011) at para. 4.100.
216. *See* above, paras. 135–139.

Court's decision that claims for damages under section 36 of the Competition Act are essentially private claims and hence arbitrable.[217]

143. The reasoning of the Federal Court of Appeal in *Murphy* requires specific attention, as the case is the first decision where a Canadian federal court specifically addressed the issue of arbitrability of competition disputes. The Federal Court of Appeal set out two main reasons for its decision. The first was that the Supreme Court of Canada has implemented a principle that appropriate "legislative language in a statute is required before the courts will refuse to give effect to the terms of an arbitration agreement," and that "the Competition Act does not contain language which would indicate that Parliament intended that arbitration clauses be restricted or prohibited."[218]

144. The second reason relates to the difference between public interest remedies and private causes of action, as distinguished by the Supreme Court of Canada in *Seidel v. Telus Communications Inc* (2011).[219] In *Seidel*, the Supreme Court held that only public interest remedies are non-arbitrable.[220] Relying on that distinction, the *Murphy* Federal Court of Appeal held that claims brought under section 36 of the federal Competition Act are private claims and, as such, are arbitrable.[221] Furthermore, the Court rejected the argument that public policy considerations would render private claims for damages under the Competition Act non-arbitrable because the Supreme Court of Canada had already rejected such arguments in *Dell Computer Corp v. Union des Consommateurs* (2007)[222] in relation to consumer disputes.[223]

145. More recently, the BC Supreme Court in *Williams v. Amazon* (2020) applied *Murphy* and held that claims for damages under section 36 of the Competition Act are arbitrable.[224] The Court went on to hold that the ruling as to the arbitrability of private competition claims remains in place even if there is a "realistic prospect" that once those claims are submitted to arbitration, a foreign arbitrator would not apply the Canadian Competition Act given the choice of law clause in the parties' agreement (in the case at bar, US law), so long as an alternative remedy would be available in that foreign jurisdiction.[225]

Germany

146. Considering both legislation and case law, it is clear that antitrust disputes are arbitrable in Germany. Formerly, section 91 of the Act Against Restraints of Competition set out prerequisites for the validity of arbitration agreements in

217. *Murphy v. Amway Canada Corp*, 2013 FCA 38 at paras. 1–5, 40, 46, 63–66, [2014] 3 FCR 478.
218. *Ibid.*, at para. 60.
219. *Ibid.*, at paras. 16, 17.
220. *Seidel v. Telus Communications Inc*, 2011 SCC 15, [2011] 1 SCR 531.
221. *Murphy v. Amway Canada Corp*, 2013 FCA 38 at paras. 42, 43, 46, 60, 63–66.
222. *Dell Computer Corp v. Union des Consommateurs*, 2007 SCC 34, 284 DLR (4th) 577.
223. *Ibid.*, at para. 64.
224. *Williams v. Amazon.com, Inc*, 2020 BCSC 300 at paras. 1–2, 4, 11–12, 59–61, 4 BLR (6th) 271.
225. *Ibid.*, at paras. 69–71, 80, 82, 86.

competition disputes.[226] However, that provision was repealed (as part of the 1998 reform of German arbitration law), which commentators have interpreted to mean that competition disputes are arbitrable now.[227] In fact, in the explanatory section of the Bill of the Arbitration Law Reform Act (applicable to the 1998 reform in the Code of Civil Procedure), the drafters explicitly stated that the restriction on arbitration in section 91 of the Act Against Restraints of Competition was no longer necessary.[228] Further, in *LG Dortmund, 13.09.2017—8 O 30/16 (Kart)*, the Dortmund District Court confirmed the position that antitrust disputes are arbitrable in Germany given the repeal of section 91.

147. The Court also held that tortious liability for damages arising under antitrust law rules are covered by an arbitration clause regardless of whether the clause has a broad or narrow scope.[229] However, according to the Court, if the scope of the arbitration clause is narrow (i.e., when it only covers contractual disputes), the claim sounding in tort must be connected to the contract and be based on the facts in relation to the contract.[230] There are other German court decisions supporting the arbitrability of competition disputes. For example, the Düsseldorf Court of Appeals in *OLG Düsseldorf, 21.7.2004- VI Sch (Kart) 11/02* and the Dresden Court of Appeals in *OLG Dresden, 20.04.2005—11 Sch 01/05* enforced arbitral awards in relation to competition disputes.

148. Based on the above, German law allows for the arbitration of competition disputes. As a rule, German courts may not engage in merits review of awards at the enforcement stage;[231] however, it is likely that awards on competition disputes will face a full merits review. In *OLG Celle, 14.10.2016—13 Sch 1/15 (Kart)*, the Higher Regional Court of Celle (HRCC) held that, when the court is asked to enforce a foreign arbitral award involving issues of EU competition rules (which are also regarded as German public policy rules), the court must review the award in full on questions of

226. Former s. 91 read: "Arbitration agreements regarding future legal disputes arising from agreements or resolutions as designated in sections 1 to 5b ... or from claims within the meaning of section 35 are null and void, unless they give to each participant the right to demand that each specific dispute be decided by an ordinary court instead of an arbitration tribunal." As reported in Ludwig Von Zumbusch, "Arbitrability of Antitrust Claims Under U.S., German, and EEC Law: the International Transaction Criterion and Public Policy" (1987) 22 Tex Int'l L J 291 at 305; Wolfgang Kühn, "Arbitrability of Antitrust Disputes in the Federal Republic of Germany" (1987) 3:2 Arb Int'l 226 at n 4.
227. Patrick M Baron & Stefan Liniger, "A Second Look at Arbitrability: Approaches to Arbitration in the United States, Switzerland and Germany" (2003) 19:1 Arb Int'l 27 at 37, 38; Rolf Trittmann & Inka Hanefeld, "Commentary on the German Arbitration Law (10th Book of the German Code of Civil Procedure), Chapter II Arbitration Agreement, § 1030" in Karl-Heinz Böckstiegel et al., eds, *Arbitration in Germany: The Model Law in Practice*, 2nd ed (Kluwer Law International, 2015) 94 at para. 19; Stefan Michael Kröll, "National Report for Germany (2007)" in Jan Paulsson & Lise Bosman, eds, *ICCA International Handbook on Commercial Arbitration* (Kluwer Law International, 2020) at 17 [the 2020 Note by the editors confirms that the 2007 Report "continues broadly to reflect current arbitral practice in Germany"].
228. *See* Bill of the Arbitration Law Reform Act (12 July 1996), BT-Drs 13/5274 at 70, online (in original language): http://dipbt.bundestag.de/doc/btd/13/052/1305274.pdf (last visited 14 February 2021).
229. *LG Dortmund, 13.09.2017—8 O 30/16 (Kart).*
230. *Ibid.*
231. *See, e.g.*, the decision of the Federal Court of Justice in *BGH, 15.07.1999—III ZB 21.98* (holding that courts may not review the merits of awards).

both fact and law, and should refuse to enforce the award where there is *any* violation of EU antitrust rules, not just manifest violations. The exception, according to the HRCC, is cases where the award is equally justifiable. The HRCC noted that, in *OLG Jena, 08.08.2007—4 Sch 3/06*, the Higher Regional Court of Thuringia was hesitant to review an award for compliance with EU competition law and held that German courts should not generally review the merits of arbitral awards. However, the HRCC finally decided that, where the case concerns competition disputes, courts should conduct a full review of the award.[232] That decision was appealed to the Federal Court of Justice, but the appeal was rejected on procedural grounds,[233] following which the parties reached an out-of-court settlement.[234]

149. As noted earlier, under recital 48 of the Directive 2014/104/EU (on actions for damages in competition disputes), out-of-court dispute resolution mechanisms such as arbitration are considered "desirable" and should be encouraged.[235] Further, recital 51 stresses that "[t]o encourage consensual settlements, an infringer that pays damages through consensual dispute resolution should not be placed in a worse position vis-à-vis its co-infringers than it would otherwise be without the consensual settlement."[236] Germany transposed the Directive into its national law through the Ninth Amendment to the Act Against Restraints of Competition (2017).[237] The amendment introduced, among other things, Article 33f into the Act Against Restraints of Competition,[238] which sanctions the conclusion of settlement agreements in competition disputes.

B. BANKRUPTCY/INSOLVENCY LAW

150. Determining the major approaches to the arbitrability of bankruptcy/insolvency disputes is more challenging, compared to the analysis of other fields of law. First, there is a difference between bankruptcy/insolvency law and other laws: bankruptcy/insolvency law is more procedural in nature (rather like arbitration itself), whereas other fields of law (such as antitrust law and consumer law) are more

232. *OLG Celle, 14.10.2016—13 Sch 1/15 (Kart).*
233. *BGH, 28.06, 2017, I ZB 100/16.*
234. *BGH, 14.01.2019, KZR 62/16.*
235. Directive 2014/104/EU of the European Parliament and of the Council of 26 November 2014 on Certain Rules Governing Actions for Damages Under National Law for Infringements of the Competition Law Provisions of the Member States and of the European Union, online: http://eur-lex.europa.eu/legal-content/EN/TXT/PDF/?uri=OJ:L:2014:349:FULL&from=EN (last visited 15 February 2021).
236. *Ibid.*
237. Online: https://eur-lex.europa.eu/legal-content/en/NIM/?uri=CELEX:32014L0104 (last visited 15 February 2021).
238. Ninth Law Amending the Act Against Restraints of Competition, Federal Law Gazette 2017 Part I No 33 (8 June 2017), in original language, online: https://www.bgbl.de/xaver/bgbl/start.xav?startbk=Bundesanzeiger_BGBl&jumpTo=bgbl117s1416.pdf#__bgbl__%2F%2F*%5B%40attr_id%3D%27bgbl117s1416.pdf%27%5D__1613412968000 (last visited 15 February 2021).

substantive in nature. Second, the meaning of the terms "bankruptcy" and "insolvency" is not consistent across all the jurisdictions that were studied.

151. For example, English law and Hong Kong law share the same approach of using the term "bankruptcy" only in relation to individuals, but the two jurisdictions then differ in the meaning they attach to "insolvency." English law uses "insolvency" for both individuals and companies, whereas in Hong Kong, "insolvency" is used only in relation to companies.[239] By comparison, Canada takes a completely different approach to that of England and Hong Kong, in that "bankruptcy" and "insolvency" do not refer to different kinds of persons (natural versus legal), but rather refer to different stages of a proceeding. In Canada, "insolvency" is used to describe a debtor, whether legal or natural, who is unable to pay their debts when due, while the term "bankruptcy" is used to refer to an insolvent person who has filed for bankruptcy.[240] Such differences make it complicated to study and categorize similarities in various jurisdictional approaches to arbitrability.

152. To overcome these difficulties, we apply two criteria to categorize the jurisdictions. First, we assess the type of bankruptcy/insolvency-related dispute, i.e., whether the dispute is a core bankruptcy/insolvency dispute or not; and second, we identify the location of the bankruptcy/insolvency proceeding, i.e., whether the bankruptcy/insolvency proceeding is opened in the same jurisdiction as the seat of the arbitration or in a foreign jurisdiction. Therefore, the discussion in this section contains two Subsections: (1) Core Bankruptcy/Insolvency Disputes v. Non-core Disputes; and (2) Local Bankruptcy/Insolvency Proceedings v. Foreign Proceedings.

1. Core Bankruptcy/Insolvency Disputes v. Non-Core Disputes

153. In seven out of the nine jurisdictions that were studied, if one party objects to the arbitrability of a bankruptcy/insolvency dispute, the forum before which the objection is raised (be it court or tribunal) will have to first decide whether or not the dispute is a "core" bankruptcy/insolvency dispute. The only two jurisdictions where there is no specific discussion in the literature as to whether the dispute is a core bankruptcy/insolvency dispute are Canada and Hong Kong.

---

239. For English law, *see* the Insolvency Act 1986 (the First Group of Parts [Parts A1—VII] concerns companies and is titled "Company Insolvency, Companies Winding up" whereas the Second Group of Parts [Parts 7A—XI] concerns individuals and is titled "Insolvency of Individuals, Bankruptcy"). For Hong Kong, *see* Charles D Booth, "Current Trends in Consumer Insolvency in Hong Kong" in Johanna Niemi-Kiesiläinen, Iain Ramsay & William Whitford, eds, *Consumer Bankruptcy in Global Perspective* (Hart Publishing, 2003) at 187, n 1.

240. Regarding the difference between the terms "insolvency" and "bankruptcy" in Canadian law, it has been said that "[a] debtor is an insolvent person who is unable to pay their debts when they are due" but "[a] bankrupt is an insolvent person who has filed for bankruptcy." Therefore, insolvency (as the status of not being able to pay one's debts) is a condition for bankruptcy, but not all insolvents are bankrupt. *See* the definition of "Debtor" provided by the Office of the Superintendent of Bankruptcy Canada website, tab "Bankruptcy and Insolvency at a Glance," online: https://www.ic.gc.ca/eic/site/bsf-osb.nsf/eng/h_br01545.html (last visited 16 October 2021).

i. Jurisdictions Where "Coreness" Is a Criterion

154. This Subsection discusses the seven jurisdictions where "coreness" is a criterion for the arbitrability of bankruptcy/insolvency disputes, namely, the US, England, France, Germany, Switzerland, China (Mainland), and Singapore. Although each of those seven jurisdictions defines "coreness" differently, the definitions all share the same spirit: core disputes are generally considered inarbitrable while non-core disputes are arbitrable.

155. Of the seven jurisdictions that have coreness as a criterion, five jurisdictions (the US, England, France, China [Mainland], and Singapore) offer similar definitions of this term. The essence of these definitions—acknowledging that they may use different terminologies and provide different exceptions to their application—is that core disputes:

- arise *after* the bankruptcy/insolvency is opened; *and*
- arise as a result of the operation of the bankruptcy/insolvency regime.[241]

As such, for those five jurisdictions, non-core disputes concern the parties' pre-bankruptcy/insolvency relationship.

156. The remaining two jurisdictions are Germany and Switzerland. Their definitions of "coreness" are narrower in scope, compared to the other five jurisdictions in the group. This means that, in Germany and Switzerland, more bankruptcy/insolvency disputes are considered non-core, which would in turn mean that more bankruptcy/insolvency disputes are arbitrable.

157. Each of the seven jurisdictions are discussed in more detail below and are organized in decreasing order by the relevance they assign to "coreness."

241. For the US, *see Wood v. Wood*, 825 F2d 90 (5th Cir 1987) at 97; *Hays and Co v. Merrill Lynch, Pierce, Fenner & Smith, Inc* 885 F2d 1149 (3d Cir 1989) at 1155–1161; *In re National Gypsum Co*, 118 F3d 1056 (5th Cir 1997) at 1066–1067; *PSINet, Inc v. Cisco Systems Capital Corp*, 271 BR 1 (Bankr SD NY 2001) at 29; *In re Tyson*, 433 BR 68 (SD NY 2010) at n 11; *In re Hagerstown Fiber Ltd. P'ship*, 277 BR 181 (Bankr SD NY 2002) at 203, 204; and § 157(b)(2) of the Judiciary and Judicial Procedure Code. For England, *see Fulham Football Club (1987) Ltd v. Richards* [2011] EWCA Civ 855 at paras. 73–75, [2012] 2 WLR 1008 (CA). However, since Brexit, English courts have relaxed the sharp distinction between disputes arising from a company's pre-insolvency and post-insolvency rights. *See, e.g., Nori Holding Ltd & Ors v. Public Joint-Stock Company, Bank Otkritie Financial Corporation* [2018] EWHC 1343 (Comm) at paras. 1, 6–13, 16–18, 43–47, 50–54, 57, 60–66. For France, *see* Jean Rouche, Gerald H Pointon & Jean-Louis Delvolvé, eds, *French Arbitration Law and Practice: A Dynamic Civil Law Approach to International Arbitration*, 2nd ed (Kluwer Law International, 2009) at para. 75; Laurence Kiffer, "National Report for France (2020)" in Jan Paulsson & Lise Bosman, eds, *ICCA International Handbook on Commercial Arbitration* (Kluwer Law International, 2020) at Chapter II.2.a.ii. For Hong Kong, *see* Neil Kaplan & Robert Morgan, "National Report for Hong Kong (2013)" in Jan Paulsson & Lise Bosman, eds, *ICCA International Handbook on Commercial Arbitration* (Kluwer Law International, 2013) at 25 [the 2015 Note by the editors confirms that the 2013 National Report "generally continues to reflect current arbitral practice" in Hong Kong]. For Singapore, *see Larsen Oil & Gas Pte Ltd v. Petroprod Ltd* [2011] 3 SLR 414 (CA) at paras. 36, 45–47, 51.

The United States

158. It is understood from the US case law analyzing the interplay between arbitration and bankruptcy that, in order to determine whether a bankruptcy-related claim is arbitrable or not, the first step for bankruptcy courts is to determine whether the claim is "core" or "noncore."[242] However, US courts have not applied a unanimous test of "coreness." For instance, the Court of Appeals for the Fifth Circuit, in *Wood v. Wood* (1987), set out the following test:

> [I]f the proceeding involves a right created by the federal bankruptcy law, it is a core proceeding. If the proceeding is one that would arise only in bankruptcy, it is also a core proceeding. If the proceeding does not invoke a substantive right created by the federal bankruptcy law and is one that could exist outside of bankruptcy it is not a core proceeding; it may be related to the bankruptcy because of its potential effect, but it is an otherwise related or non-core proceeding.[243]

However, the Second Circuit expressly rejected the abovementioned test in *PSINet, Inc v. Cisco Systems Capital Corp* (2001)[244] and *In re Tyson* (2010).[245]

159. The Bankruptcy Court for the District of Maryland in *In re McPherson* (2005) considered the following claims to be "core": claims arising directly under the Bankruptcy Code which the "Debtor could not have asserted … against [the other party] prior to the petition date"; "an objection to discharge or the dischargeability of a claim in a bankruptcy case under section 523"; "an objection to claim under section 502, a preference claim under section 547, a turnover action under section 543, or a subordination claim under section 510."[246] The Court then found these claims to be "non-core": the prepetition contract claims that are grounded in state law as well as the claims arising under the Fair Debt Collection Practices Act.[247]

160. To determine whether a matter is core or not in US law, one should also consult the Judiciary and Judicial Procedure Code, § 157(b)(2), which sets out a non-exhaustive list of matters that are regarded as indicating a "core proceeding," for example: "matters concerning the administration of the estate," "allowance or disallowance of claims against the estate or exemptions from property of the estate," "orders in respect to obtaining credit," and "proceedings to determine, avoid, or recover preferences."[248]

---

242. *See Hays and Co v. Merrill Lynch, Pierce, Fenner & Smith, Inc*, 885 F2d 1149 (3d Cir 1989); *In re National Gypsum Co*, 118 F3d 1056 (5th Cir 1997); *Wood v. Wood*, 825 F2d 90 (5th Cir 1987); *PSINet, Inc v. Cisco Systems Capital Corp*, 271 BR 1, 29 (Bankr SD NY 2001); *In re Tyson*, 433 BR 68 (SD NY 2010); *In re National Gypsum Co*, 118 F3d 1056 (5th Cir 1997). *See also In Re Ben Cooper, Inc*, 896 F2d 1394 (2d Cir 1990) at 1400 (holding that "the timing of a dispute may render it uniquely a bankruptcy case").
243. *Wood v. Wood*, 825 F2d 90 (5th Cir 1987) at 97.
244. *PSINet, Inc v. Cisco Systems Capital Corp*, 271 BR 1 (Bankr SD NY 2001) at 29.
245. *In re Tyson*, 433 BR 68 (SD NY 2010) at n 11.
246. *In re McPherson*, 630 BR 160 (Bankr D MD 2005) at 172–173.
247. *Ibid.*, at 175–176.
248. US Code, Title 28 (Judiciary and Judicial Procedure), 28 USC § 157(b)(2), online: http://uscode.house.gov/view.xhtml?req = granuleid:USC-prelim-title28-section157&num = 0&edition = prelim (last visited 15 June 2022).

161. If the claim is considered *noncore*, the dispute is likely to be arbitrable, as per the decisions of the Court of Appeals for the Third and Fifth Circuits in *Hays and Co v. Merrill Lynch, Pierce, Fenner & Smith, Inc* (1989)[249] and *In re National Gypsum Co* (1997).[250] However, if the matter is considered *core*, that does not automatically render the claim non-arbitrable. According to the Court of Appeals for the Fifth Circuit in *In re National Gypsum Co* (1997), when it is established that the claim is core, the second step is to examine whether arbitration would undermine the underlying purposes of the Bankruptcy Code.[251]

162. In order to conduct this examination, the New York Bankruptcy Court in *In re Hagerstown Fiber Ltd Partnership* (2002) stated that courts should examine whether the matter is "procedurally core" or "substantively core."[252] According to the Court, one example of a procedurally core dispute is a prepetition contract dispute which is dubbed "core" because of how the dispute arises or gets resolved, whereas a substantively core matter is not based on the parties' prepetition relationship and involves rights that are created under the Bankruptcy Code.[253] The Court asserted that arbitration of "procedurally core" disputes is less likely to conflict with any underlying policies of the Bankruptcy Code, whereas arbitration of substantively core disputes is more likely to conflict, which would in turn render the claim non-arbitrable.[254]

163. In terms of arbitration proceedings that are already pending when the bankruptcy proceeding commences, the arbitration proceeding generally becomes subject to an automatic stay under § 362 of the Bankruptcy Code. However, § 362 provides for certain exceptions, as well as allowing the possibility of lifting the stay under certain conditions. In *In re McPherson* (2005), the Bankruptcy Court for the District of Maryland dealt with the automatic stay that was imposed on the parties' pending arbitration when one of them became subject to Chapter 11.[255] The Court lifted the stay with respect to the claims that it considered "non-core" and kept the stay with respect to the "core" claims, which bifurcated the claims.[256] The Court then stayed the bankruptcy proceeding pending the result of the arbitration of the non-core claims and noted that the parties could only seek enforcement of their arbitral award before the Bankruptcy Court.[257]

France

164. Commentators consider that, in French law, disputes arising from the bankruptcy procedure (i.e., core claims) may not be submitted to arbitration.[258] However, disputes

---

249. *Hays and Co v. Merrill Lynch, Pierce, Fenner & Smith, Inc*, 885 F2d 1149 (3d Cir 1989) at 1155–1161.
250. *In re National Gypsum Co*, 118 F3d 1056 (5th Cir 1997) at 1066–1067.
251. *Ibid.*
252. *In re Hagerstown Fiber Ltd P'ship*, 277 BR 181 (Bankr SD NY 2002) at 203, 204.
253. *Ibid.*
254. *Ibid.*
255. *In re McPherson*, 630 BR 160 (Bankr D MD 2005) at 165.
256. *Ibid.*, at 171–179.
257. *Ibid.*
258. *See, e.g.*, Jean Rouche, Gerald H Pointon & Jean-Louis Delvolvé, eds, *French Arbitration Law and Practice: A Dynamic Civil Law Approach to International Arbitration*, 2nd ed (Kluwer Law

relating to pre-bankruptcy relations between a debtor and creditors (i.e., non-core claims) are generally arbitrable, but there are limitations, as discussed below.

165. If, when the bankruptcy proceeding is opened, there is an arbitration agreement but no pending arbitration yet, the applicable rule can be extracted from three decisions of the Court of Cassation handed down in 2004: *Société Gaussin et autres v. Société Alstom Power Turbomachines* (2004),[259] *Société Prodim v. Société Logidis* (2004),[260] and *Société Industry et autres v. Société Alstom Power Turbomachines* (2004).[261] The rule arising from these cases is that, if a creditor wishes to initiate arbitration proceeding against the debtor, the bankruptcy judge should first check the legality of the creditor's claim declaration and should then refer the matter to arbitration so that the tribunal may decide its jurisdiction, including the arbitrability of the dispute.[262] Prior to these three decisions of the Court of Cassation, the Paris Court of Appeal in *Dont et Cts de Cominck v. Zanzi ès qual et autre* (1999), had held that if there was no pending arbitration once the insolvency proceeding was opened, creditors could not initiate a new arbitration.[263]

166. If, when a bankruptcy proceeding is commenced, there is already a pending arbitration, the bankruptcy proceeding does not render the dispute inarbitrable, but it does affect the pending arbitration proceeding. The degree of the impact depends on factors such as the procedural position of the bankrupt person in the arbitration proceeding (i.e., whether they are the claimant or the respondent).[264]

167. When the person subject to the bankruptcy proceeding is the respondent in the pending arbitration proceeding, the commencement of the bankruptcy proceeding would stay the arbitration proceeding, according to Article L622-21 of the Commercial Code. According to Article L622-22, the stay of the arbitration proceeding will continue only until the claimant creditor files the declaration of their claim. However, after resuming the arbitration proceeding, the arbitral tribunal may only validate the claims and quantify their amount, *without* having the jurisdiction to order the debtor to pay (Article L622-22 of the Commercial Code). The Court of Cassation in *Lion et Compagnie v. International Company for Commercial Exchanges (INCOME—Egypt)* (2009), and the

---

International, 2009) at para. 75; Laurence Kiffer, "National Report for France (2020)" in Jan Paulsson & Lise Bosman, eds, *ICCA International Handbook on Commercial Arbitration* (Kluwer Law International, 2020) at Chapter II.2.a.ii.

259. *Société Gaussin et autres v. Société Alstom Power Turbomachines*, Court of Cassation (Commercial Chamber), 2 June 2004, reported in (2004) 2004:3 Rev Arb 593.

260. *Société Prodim v. Société Logidis*, Court of Cassation (Commercial Chamber), 14 January 2004, reported in (2004) 2004:3 Arb Rev 591.

261. *Société Industry et autres v. Société Alstom Power Turbomachines*, Court of Cassation (Commercial Chamber), 2 June 2004, reported in (2004) 2004:3 Rev Arb 595.

262. *See* Laurence Kiffer, "National Report for France (2020)" in Jan Paulsson & Lise Bosman, eds, *ICCA International Handbook on Commercial Arbitration* (Kluwer Law International, 2020) at Chapter II.2.a.ii.

263. *Dont et Cts de Cominck v. Zanzi ès qual et autre*, Paris Court of Appeal, 30 March 1999, Case No 97/25592.

264. Laurence Kiffer, "National Report for France (2020)" in Jan Paulsson & Lise Bosman, eds, *ICCA International Handbook on Commercial Arbitration* (Kluwer Law International, 2020) at Chapter II.2.a.ii.

Paris Court of Appeal in *Dont et Cts de Cominck v. Zanzi ès qual et autre* (2009), both made the same finding.[265]

168. When the person subject to a bankruptcy proceeding is the claimant of the pending arbitration proceeding, Article L622-21 of the Commercial Code does not require the proceeding to be stayed because the article only concerns proceedings initiated by creditors against the person who is subject to the bankruptcy proceeding.

169. However, once the court order as to liquidation or receivership is issued, *any* arbitration proceeding will be stayed, regardless of whether the bankrupt is the respondent or the claimant (Article 1471 together with Article 369 of the Civil Code).

Singapore[266]

170. The legislative history of the Arbitration Act 2001 shows that the drafters considered "bankruptcy of debtors" and the "winding up of companies" to be non-arbitrable matters.[267] As concerns corporate insolvency disputes, the Court of Appeal in its 1999 decision in *Four Pillars Enterprises Co v. Beiersdorf Aktiengesellschaft* noted that an arbitral tribunal may not grant a winding up order.[268] However, it was more than a decade later, in *Larsen Oil & Gas Pte Ltd v. Petroprod Ltd* (2011), that the same Court discussed the matter in detail and ruled on the types of dispute that may be submitted to arbitration when one of the parties to an arbitration agreement becomes subject to insolvency proceedings. The Court distinguished two general categories of disputes:

- First, disputes "that arose only upon the onset of insolvency due to the operation of the insolvency regime" (i.e., core disputes), which are non-arbitrable per se.
- Second, disputes "involving an insolvent company that stemmed from its pre-insolvency rights and obligations" (i.e., non-core disputes), which are:
    - non-arbitrable, if they affect the rights of other creditors; but
    - arbitrable, "where the [arbitration] agreement is only to resolve the prior private inter se disputes between the company and another party … without creat[ing] new rights in the creditors or destroy[ing] old ones."[269]

---

265. *Lion et Compagnie v. International Company for Commercial Exchanges (INCOME—Egypt)*, Court of Cassation (1st Civil Chamber), 6 May 2009, reported in Albert Jan van den Berg, ed, *ICCA Yearbook Commercial Arbitration*, vol 35 (Kluwer Law International, 2010) 353 at paras. 9–12; *Dont et Cts de Cominck v. Zanzi ès qual et autre*, Paris Court of Appeal, 30 March 1999, Case No 97/25592.
266. In Singapore law, the term "bankruptcy" is used only in relation to individuals (*see* the definition of "bankrupt" in s. 2 of the Insolvency, Restructuring and Dissolution Act 2018) whereas the term "insolvency" is used in relation to both companies and individuals (*see* ss. 3, 47).
267. Review of Arbitration Act Committee, *Review of Arbitration Laws*, LRRD No 3/2001, online: https://www.sal.org.sg/sites/default/files/PDF%20Files/Law%20Reform/1993-08%20-%20 Review%20of%20Arbitration%20Laws.pdf (last visited 9 April 2023).
268. *Four Pillars Enterprises Co Ltd v. Beiersdorf Aktiengesellschaft* [1999] 1 SLR(R) 382 (CA) at paras. 9–17, 23.
269. *Larsen Oil & Gas Pte Ltd v. Petroprod Ltd* [2011] 3 SLR 414 (CA) at paras. 36, 45–47, 51.

171. A decade later, in *AnAn Group Pte Ltd v. VTB Bank* (2021), the Court of Appeal brought a clarification to its ruling in *Larsen Oil*.[270] The question before the Court was who should pay the liquidators' remuneration in an aborted winding up proceeding: the debtor company who was no longer subject to the liquidation proceedings or the creditor who, instead of pursuing arbitration for its claim against the debtor company as per their arbitration agreement, sought to wind up that company? The Court of Appeal held that the issue, despite arising from the winding up proceedings, is arbitrable and can be referred to arbitration as part of the debtor's claim for damages in relation to the creditor's breach of the arbitration agreement.[271] According to the Court:

> The observations in *Larsen Oil* certainly do not mean that any dispute with a connection to insolvency law, no matter how tangential, would be deemed non-arbitrable. In so far as a head of relief is not one that the court is only empowered to make under "statutory provisions of the insolvency regime," such relief would prima facie fall outside of the prohibitive rule in *Larsen Oil*. Here, it is important to bear in mind that the court is not being asked to exercise any of its powers in relation to insolvency such as an order for judicial management, winding up or the appointment of a liquidator, etc. Such powers are vested in the courts by virtue of insolvency legislation and in that sense, such applications are non-arbitrable because arbitrators do not have the powers to grant such orders. But the present case does not involve any of these.[272]

172. Another relevant case is *Tomolugen Holdings Ltd v. Silica Investors Ltd* (2015), in which the Court of Appeal observed that a dispute as to the liquidation of an insolvent company is "non-arbitrable because such a liquidation is a process in which the greater public beyond the parties to the dispute have an interest. A creditor's winding up petition seeks 'an order to put a company into an insolvent liquidation that will affect the interests of all creditors as well as of all members.'"[273]

173. Also, in *Duncan, Cameron Lindsay v. Diablo Fortune Inc* (2017), the High Court applied both *Larsen Oil* and *Tomolugen* to rule that the following question may not be submitted to arbitration: whether a ship owner's unregistered lien is, under section 131 of the Companies Act, a void charge against the liquidators of the chartering company.[274]

174. It should be noted that the Insolvency, Restructuring and Dissolution Act 2018 (IRDA) identifies four circumstances where no arbitration may be commenced *against* a company:

270. *AnAn Group (Singapore) Pte Ltd v. VTB Bank (Public Joint Stock Company)* [2021] SGCA 112.
271. *Ibid.*, at paras. 1–9, 33, 42–59.
272. *Ibid.*, at para. 48.
273. *Tomolugen Holdings Ltd and another v. Silica Investors Ltd* [2016] 1 SLR 373 (CA) at paras. 78, 83.
274. *Duncan, Cameron Lindsay v. Diablo Fortune Inc* [2017] SGHC 172 at paras. 15–21, appeal dismissed, [2018] SGCA 26.

- Under section 133, once the winding up order is made, or a provisional liquidator is appointed, no proceeding (including arbitration) against the company may be commenced except by leave of the court.
- The same rule applies, under sections 95(1)(c) and 96(4)(c), when the company applies for a judicial management order and, if such an order is made, during the time that the order is in force.
- The same rule applies again, under section 72K(1)(c), when a company is in a simplified debt restructuring, during a specified period.
- The same rule applies, under section 64(8)(c), when the company applies for an arrangement order, during the automatic moratorium period.

175. Although the rule established by the Court of Appeal in *Larsen Oil* (that distinguishes between core disputes and non-core disputes) concerns corporate insolvency, it seems to be applicable (by analogy) to bankruptcy of individuals as well. As such, in non-core disputes, the commencement of a bankruptcy proceeding does not invalidate the arbitration agreement per se.[275] However, under section 420 of the IRDA, if a party to an arbitration agreement becomes bankrupt, the Official Assignee has the discretion to decide whether to adopt the underlying contract (the contract containing the arbitration agreement). If the Official Assignee does not adopt the contract, the matter can then be referred to a court to decide whether to enforce the arbitration agreement (section 420(3)). However, the bankrupt themselves remain incompetent to *commence* any proceeding, including arbitration, until they are discharged of the bankruptcy (section 401(1) and (4)).

176. The discussion above concerns circumstances where the insolvency/bankruptcy proceeding has commenced and there is an arbitration agreement, but as yet no pending arbitration. However, there is another scenario: when the bankruptcy/insolvency proceeding is opened, there is already a pending arbitration proceeding.

177. With respect to corporate insolvencies, upon receiving a winding up application from the company or a creditor, courts have the discretion to stay any proceeding (including arbitration) *against* the insolvent company at any time after the making of a winding up application but before a winding up order is made (section 258 of the IRDA). However, once a winding up order is made or a provisional liquidator is appointed, any proceeding against the company, including arbitration, must be stayed except by leave of the court (section 133). A similar automatic-stay rule applies in the following circumstances:

- the company applies for a judicial management order and, if such an order is made, during the time the order is in force (sections 95(1)(c) and 96(4)(c));
- the company applies for an arrangement order, during the automatic moratorium period (section 64(8)(c)); and

275. Andrew Chan Chee Yin et al, "Cross-border Bankruptcy and its Implications on Arbitration" (2014) 26 SAcLJ 999 at para. 6.

- the company is in a simplified debt restructuring, during a specified period (section 72K(1)(c)).

178. Similarly, for bankruptcy of individuals, the bankrupt becomes incompetent, under section 401(1) and (4) of the IRDA, to continue any proceeding, including a pending arbitration, until they are discharged. Further, section 325 confers on the court the discretion to order the stay of any legal proceeding against the debtor or their property.

England and Wales

179. From the case law perspective, initially, the Court of Appeal in *Fulham Football Club v. Richards* (2011) agreed in *dictum* with the Singapore Court of Appeal's approach in the *Larsen Oil* case,[276] distinguishing between disputes involving an insolvent company that stem from its pre-insolvency rights and obligations (i.e., non-core claims) and those disputes that arise only following the onset of insolvency due to the operation of the insolvency regime (i.e., core claims).[277] The English Court of Appeal noted that disputes arising under provisions of the Insolvency Act 1986 which apply to liquidation, as well as those provisions that apply to liquidators' power to intervene in and set aside transactions with third parties in the context of the insolvency regime, may not be submitted to arbitration.[278]

180. However, in the Brexit era, English courts adopted a more pro-arbitration approach by relaxing the sharp distinction between disputes arising from a company's pre-insolvency and post-insolvency rights. For example, in *Nori Holding v. Bank Otkritie Financial* (2018), the Commercial subdivision of the High Court regarded the Singapore Court of Appeal's approach in *Larsen Oil* as "outmoded" for being based on the old English law view that considered arbitration "a procedure depriving a party of its inalienable rights".[279] Accordingly, the Court held that avoidance claims are arbitrable because, in English law, such claims—despite having the label of insolvency claims—are factual in nature: they involve the question of whether the transactions that were carried out immediately prior to a party's insolvency constitute a fraud on that party to replace its valuable assets with worthless assets, in which case the insolvent party has the right to avoid those transactions.[280]

181. In *Riverrock Securities v. International Bank of St Petersburg* (2020), the same Court (the Commercial Court) made a similar ruling and elaborated further on its view: in English law, the fact that a claim and the relevant relief concern insolvency law does

276. Discussed above, in the current Chapter, para. 170.
277. *Fulham Football Club (1987) Ltd v. Richards* [2011] EWCA Civ 855 at paras. 73–75, [2012] 2 WLR 1008 (CA).
278. *Ibid.*
279. *Nori Holding Ltd & Ors v. Public Joint-Stock Company, Bank Otkritie Financial Corporation* [2018] EWHC 1343 (Comm) at paras. 65–66.
280. *Ibid.*, at paras. 43–47, 50–54, 57, 60–64.

not automatically render the claim non-arbitrable.[281] The Court even rejected the following argument: because avoidance claims are brought by a liquidator (who is not a party to the arbitration agreement), those claims belong to the liquidator and are not covered by the arbitration agreement.[282] Instead, the Court ruled that the avoidance claims belong to the insolvent party and that the liquidator's role is only to bring those claims on behalf of the insolvent party and, as such, the avoidance claims are covered by the arbitration agreement and are arbitrable.[283]

182. It should be noted that both *Nori* and *Riverrock* involved foreign insolvency proceedings, which makes the situation different from a scenario involving English insolvency/bankruptcy proceedings. However, both cases demonstrate that English law is moving toward a more favorable approach to the arbitration of insolvency-related claims. This means that, England and Wales are likely to move from their current category (those jurisdictions that differentiate between core and non-core disputes) to the other category (those jurisdictions that do not recognize such difference).

183. From a legislative perspective, the insolvency of companies is governed by the first group of Parts (Part AI to Part VII) of the Insolvency Act 1986, while the insolvency and bankruptcy of individuals is governed by the second group of Parts (Part 7A to Part XI) of the Act.[284] The group of Parts that governs the insolvency of companies has no provision that expressly addresses the arbitrability of insolvency disputes. However, two provisions should be noted:

- Under section 130(2), when a winding up order has been made or a provisional liquidator has been appointed, *any* proceeding (including arbitration) against the insolvent person will be *automatically stayed* and *no proceedings may be commenced* without the permission of the court.
- Under Schedule B1, paragraph 43(6), which applies to a company in administration, *no legal proceeding may be continued* or *commenced* without the administrator's consent or the permission of the court.

184. Unlike the first group of Parts of the Insolvency Act 1986, the second group of Parts (which governs insolvency and bankruptcy of individuals) includes a section on arbitration: section 394A. It applies to the scenario where the bankruptcy proceeding has commenced and there is an arbitration agreement, but as yet no pending arbitration. If the trustee adopts the underlying contract, the arbitration clause in that contract will also be enforceable by or against the trustee (section 394A(2)). If the trustee chooses not to adopt the underlying contract, the court may under certain

281. *Riverrock Securities Ltd v. International Bank of St Petersburg (Joint Stock Company)* [2020] EWHC 2483 (Comm) at para. 76.
282. *Ibid.*, at paras. 49–50.
283. *Ibid.*, at paras. 56, 66.
284. The Act has a third group of Parts (Part XII to Part XIX), which applies to insolvency of both companies and individuals. Online: https://www.legislation.gov.uk/ukpga/1986/45/contents (last visited 31 October 2022).

conditions refer the parties to arbitration on the basis of the arbitration agreement (section 394A(3)). Nevertheless, once a bankruptcy order is made, creditors may not commence any arbitration proceeding against the bankrupt in relation to a debt provable in the bankruptcy, except with the leave of the court (section 285(3)).

185. Another scenario concerns the circumstances where the bankruptcy proceeding is commenced while there is already a pending arbitration. The mere opening of the bankruptcy proceeding does not cause an automatic stay of other proceedings including arbitration proceedings. However, under section 285(1), the court has the discretion to stay other proceedings (including arbitration) at any time.

186. Moreover, under Schedule 1 of the Insolvency Act 1986, the administrator or administrative receiver has the power to refer any question affecting the company to arbitration. Further, in accordance with Schedule 5, the trustee has the power to refer to arbitration: "any debts, claims or liabilities subsisting or supposed to subsist between the bankrupt and any person who may have incurred any liability to the bankrupt."

China

187. Article 3 of the Law on Enterprise Bankruptcy provides that bankruptcy disputes are subject to the exclusive jurisdiction of Chinese courts. Therefore, core claims (i.e., claims arising as a result of the operation of the bankruptcy regime) are inarbitrable. The next question is whether non-core-claims (i.e., claims concerning the parties' pre-bankruptcy relationship) may be submitted to arbitration. Two scenarios should be considered.

188. In the first scenario, there is already a pending arbitration proceeding when the bankruptcy/insolvency proceeding is opened. According to Article 20 of the Law on Enterprise Bankruptcy, any pending arbitration proceedings must be automatically suspended but may then be resumed when an administrator takes over the debtor's property. In addition, under Article 25(7), one of the duties of an administrator is to participate in "actions, arbitrations or any other legal procedures on behalf of the debtor."

189. However, Chinese courts do not seem to apply the above rule strictly with respect to "foreign" awards. For example, in *Johann MK Blumenthal GmbH v. Jiangsu Rongsheng Heavy Industry Co et al* (2015), the claimant secured, based on the New York Convention, the recognition and enforcement of a London award which was issued while one of the respondents had entered into bankruptcy proceedings in China.[285] The bankrupt respondent argued that the award should not be recognized and enforced in China because the bankruptcy administrator was not aware of the arbitration proceeding and that the claimant should only be allowed to declare its claims within the bankruptcy framework like any other creditor.[286] However, the

285. *Johann MK Blumenthal GmbH & Co KG v. Jiangsu Rongsheng Heavy Industry Co, Ltd et al*, Shanghai Maritime Court, (2015) Hu Hai Fa Min Ren Zi No 3, 22 March 2016.
286. *Ibid.*

Shanghai Maritime Court rejected the objections and reasoned that the bankruptcy administrator was deemed to be aware of the arbitration proceeding given the presence of the respondents' agent in the proceeding and that the other objection was "not within the scope of review on the application for the recognition and enforcement of a *foreign* maritime arbitral award."[287]

190. The second scenario involves a situation in which the bankruptcy/insolvency proceeding commences and there is an arbitration agreement between the debtor and a creditor, but no pending arbitration yet. It is not clear from the Chinese literature whether it is possible to initiate a new arbitration for non-core bankruptcy disputes. However, when Articles 3, 20, and 25(7) of the Law on Enterprise Bankruptcy (discussed above) are read together, one could argue that, in Chinese law, non-core disputes are arbitrable but may be submitted to arbitration only after the administrator takes over the debtor's property.

Germany

191. In Germany, for a dispute to be considered "core" (and thus inarbitrable), not only does it have to be a post-insolvency dispute that arises from the operation of the insolvency regime (like the approach adopted in the five jurisdictions discussed above), but the dispute must also arise *as a result of the administrator's application of specific rights granted to them by the German Insolvency Act.*[288] For example, sections 103 and 129 et seq of the Insolvency Act grant rights that concern the insolvency administrator's power to object to and avoid certain contracts into which the debtor has entered prior to insolvency. The Federal Court of Justice has held that disputes arising under sections 103 and 129 et seq are inarbitrable.[289]

192. Given that the scope of core disputes is more limited in German law (compared to the other jurisdictions discussed above), the scope of arbitrable insolvency-related matters is also broader. In addition, the German definition of core disputes has its own, internal exception. That is, disputes that arise due to the administrator's application of their rights under section 166(2) of the Insolvency Act, and that concern the administrator's rights to collect the claims which the debtor has previously assigned as security to a third party, have been held to be arbitrable by the Federal Court of Justice in *BGH, 25.04.2013—IX ZR 49/12*. Such an exception further adds to the scope of arbitrable insolvency-related matters in Germany.

193. None-core disputes are considered to be arbitrable. The Federal Court of Justice, in *BGH, 20.11.2003—III ZB 24.03*, held that the insolvency proceeding does not affect the validity of an arbitration agreement and that the insolvency administrator replaces the debtor and remains bound to the arbitration agreement.[290] Moreover, in *BGH,*

---

287. *Ibid.* (emphasis added).
288. *See* the decisions of the Federal Court of Justice in *BGH, 20.11.2003—III ZB 24.03* and *BGH, 30.06.2011—II ZB 59/10.*
289. *See BGH, 20.11.2003—III ZB 24.03* and *BGH, 30.06.2011—II ZB 59/10.*
290. This position is supported by the fact that German state courts do not enjoy an "all-embracing exclusive jurisdiction over any insolvency or insolvency-related disputes." Stefan Kröll,

09.08.2016—I ZB 1/15I, the same Court held that the parties' insolvency does not affect the validity of the arbitration clause even when the underlying agreement has a provision whereby that agreement becomes ineffective once one of the parties becomes insolvent.

194. However, there is one exception to the arbitrability of non-core disputes in German law: when the assets of an insolvent party are not sufficient to conduct the arbitration. The Federal Court of Justice in *BGH 14.09.2000—III ZR 33/00* held that, when the insolvent party does not have sufficient funds to participate in the arbitration proceeding, and the other party cannot shoulder the insolvent's portion of the costs, the arbitration agreement becomes *incapable of being performed*. Commentators have noted this same exception.[291]

Switzerland

195. Switzerland has adopted the most liberal approach, in that the scope of core matters is very limited. It includes "the initiation of insolvency proceedings; appointment of trustees; verification and acceptance of the creditor's claims and the administration of the reorganization or liquidation of a company pursuant to the [Federal Act on Debt Enforcement and Bankruptcy]."[292] And of course, arbitral tribunals may not declare a person bankrupt.[293]

196. Non-core disputes are arbitrable. The Federal Supreme Court in *BGE 136 III 107, 8 December 2009* noted that, generally, bankruptcy will not affect the validity of an arbitration agreement that was entered into prior to the commencement of the bankruptcy proceeding. According to commentators, in this situation, the parties may proceed to constitute the arbitral tribunal, but arbitrators will have to take into consideration the insolvency/bankruptcy of the relevant party and apply relevant public policy rules.[294]

"Insolvency and Arbitration—Effects of Party Insolvency on Arbitral Proceedings in Germany" in Karl-Heinz Böckstiegel et al, eds, *Arbitration in Germany: The Model Law in Practice*, 2nd ed (Kluwer Law International, 2015) 981 at paras. 27–29, 33–37; Christoph Liebscher, "Insolvency and Arbitrability" in Loukas A Mistelis & Stavros L Brekoulakis, eds, *Arbitrability: International and Comparative Perspectives* (Kluwer Law International, 2009) 165 at paras. 9.39, 9.41; Rolf Trittmann & Inka Hanefeld, "Commentary on the German Arbitration Law (10th Book of the German Code of Civil Procedure) § 1030" in Karl-Heinz Böckstiegel et al, eds, *Arbitration in Germany: The Model Law in Practice*, 2nd ed (Kluwer Law International, 2015) 94 at para. 25.

291. Rolf Trittmann & Inka Hanefeld, "Commentary on the German Arbitration Law (10th Book of the German Code of Civil Procedure) § 1030" in Karl-Heinz Böckstiegel et al, eds, *Arbitration in Germany: The Model Law in Practice*, 2nd ed (Kluwer Law International, 2015) 94 at para. 25.

292. Robert B Kovacs, "A Transnational Approach to the Arbitrability of Insolvency Proceedings in International Arbitration" (2012) 21 J Bankr L & Prac 5 Art 3 at para. 7.2.2.1.

293. *Case No 4A_12/2017, 19 September* 2017. *See also* Paolo Michele Patocchi, "National Report for Switzerland (2018–2020)" in Jan Paulsson & Lise Bosman, eds, *ICCA International Handbook on Commercial Arbitration* (Kluwer Law International, 2020) 1 at 31; Martin Wiebecke & Anwaltsbüro Wiebecke, "Switzerland" in James H Carter, ed, *The International Arbitration Review*, 11th ed (Law Business Research Ltd, 2020) at 3.

294. Christoph Liebscher, "Insolvency and Arbitrability" in Loukas A Mistelis & Stavros L Brekoulakis, eds, *Arbitrability: International and Comparative Perspectives* (Kluwer Law International, 2009) 165 at paras. 9-44, 9-45.

197. Nevertheless, there are exceptions to this general rule. In *BGE 136 III 107, 8 December 2009*, a creditor (who was also a shareholder of the company in bankruptcy) was assigned a liability claim in the bankruptcy proceeding and later filed the liability claim in court against the board members. The Federal Supreme Court—although noting the rule that bankruptcy does not generally affect the validity of the arbitration agreement entered into prior to the bankruptcy—held that the board members of the company in the bankruptcy proceeding could not rely on the arbitration clause in the articles of association because the liability claim is for the creditor and not the company, and the arbitration agreement set out in the articles of association is not binding on creditors.

198. Further, it is true that arbitral tribunals may decide the existence of an alleged debt, but if the debt is subject to a "collection order" under Swiss law,[295] only state courts may set aside the debtor's objection (definitively or provisionally).[296] According to the Federal Supreme Court, those objections are not arbitrable under Article 177 of the PILA because debt collection proceedings are in nature an enforcement procedure and do not concern the merits of the claim.[297] However, it should be noted that the scope of the exception is limited and does not extend to an application to validate a freezing order (in the context of the debtor's objection to a collection order), and thus arbitrators may rule on such applications.[298]

199. If there is already a pending arbitration when the bankruptcy proceeding is commenced, under Article 207(1) of the Federal Act on Debt Enforcement and Bankruptcy, the pending arbitration proceeding must be stayed. However, the same article provides that, in ordinary liquidations, arbitration may be resumed after 10 days following the second meeting of creditors, but in summary liquidations, arbitration may be resumed after 20 days following the filing of the schedule of claims.

295. In Switzerland, "the creditor of a sum of money can already start debt collection proceedings before it has obtained an enforceable judgment or award. Upon the creditor's application, the enforcement office issues and serves the (alleged) debtor with a summons to pay, to which the debtor can object within 10 days without stating its reasons. If there is no objection, the summons to pay becomes enforceable. If the debtor objects, the proceedings hinge on whether the creditor has already obtained a judgment or an award. If the creditor has obtained a judgment or an award, it can apply to the court to definitively set aside the objection and then proceed to enforcement measures. If the creditor has not yet obtained a judgment or an award but is in possession of certain documents, it can apply to the court to provisionally set aside the objection. This provisional setting aside of the objection ... does not entitle the creditor to proceed to enforcement measures, but it entitles the creditor to certain provisional measures, for example a provisional freezing order against the debtor's assets." Georg von Segesser & Dorothée Schramm, "X. SA v. Y. BV, Federal Supreme Court, 5A_225/2010, 2 November 2010" *A contribution by the ITA Board of Reporters* (Kluwer Law International).

296. *BGE 136 III 583, 2 November 2010.*

297. *Ibid.*

298. *Case No 4A_12/2017, 19 September 2017.*

ii. Jurisdictions Where "Coreness" Is Not a Criterion

200. Canada and Hong Kong are the only jurisdictions (of the nine jurisdictions studied) where the arbitrability of bankruptcy/insolvency does not revolve around the "coreness" criterion. Also, England and Wales, as discussed in the previous Subsection, are likely to move to this category as well. The discussion in the following paragraphs show that, in Hong Kong, the criterion is whether there is a particular court or tribunal nominated to settle the bankruptcy/insolvency-related dispute. Where this is the case, the matter is rendered inarbitrable. Canada has adopted the most conservative approach in practice, in that it either imposes legislative limitations on the arbitration of bankruptcy/insolvency-related disputes, or where legislation does not impose such a limitation, it grants courts the discretion to refuse to enforce arbitration agreements when one of the parties is involved in bankruptcy/insolvency proceedings. This is a discretion which courts have generally exercised against arbitration.

Canada[299]

201. The major legislative Acts are the Bankruptcy and Insolvency Act (BIA), the Companies' Creditors Arrangements Act (CCAA), and the Winding-Up and Restructuring Act (WURA).

202. Once the insolvency/bankruptcy proceeding is opened, under the BIA, *no* "proceedings" may *commence* against the debtor (sections 69, 69.1, 69.2, 69.3, 69.31). Sections 11.02, 11.03 of the CCAA give courts the *discretion* to issue an order staying any "proceedings" that "might be taken" against the debtor company and its directors. Section 17 of the WURA gives courts the same discretion.

203. The courts of the common law provinces have broadly interpreted the term "proceeding" in the BIA, the CCAA, and the WURA to include arbitration proceedings and therefore have refused to enforce arbitration agreements, out of a concern that arbitration could jeopardize the efficiency of CCAA or WURA proceedings. For instance, in *Luscar Ltd v. Smoky River Coal Ltd* (1999), the Alberta Court of Appeal held that arbitration is not always an expeditious proceeding, since it can be subject to judicial review which could "lengthen and complicate" the CCAA proceedings.[300] Likewise, the British Columbia Supreme Court, in *Hayes Forest Services Ltd (Re)* (2009), ruled that, if a company is under the protection of the CCAA, the court may "override" the arbitration agreement to allow court determination of the dispute.[301] The rationale for this position is to improve efficiency, as arbitration is subject to judicial review, which could make the entire process less expeditious and more expensive.[302] In Ontario, the Superior Court of Justice in *Canada (Attorney General) v.*

299. Bankruptcy and insolvency are matters within the exclusive legislative authority of the Parliament of Canada. Constitution Acts, 1867 to 1982, s. 91(21), online: http://laws-lois.justice.gc.ca/eng/const/ (last visited 4 May 2022).
300. *Luscar Ltd v. Smoky River Coal Ltd*, 1999 ABCA 179 at paras. 1–6, 9, 10, 31–33, 73–76, 237 AR 326.
301. *Hayes Forest Services Ltd (Re)*, 2009 BCSC 1169 at paras. 1, 2, 23–25, 30, [2009] BCJ No 1725.
302. *Ibid.*

Reliance Insurance Co (2007), held that enforcing an arbitration clause against a company that is the subject of a winding up order would go against the "merits of the public policy that favors single control or a single proceeding."[303]

204. Brian Casey is of the opinion that an arbitration agreement may become "inoperative" when one of the parties becomes insolvent and under court protection.[304] As discussed below, courts in Alberta, Ontario, and most recently, the Supreme Court of Canada support the view that an arbitration agreement *may* become *inoperative or incapable of being performed* once the company is the subject of a CCAA proceeding or a winding up order.

205. In Alberta, in *Smoky River Coal Ltd (Re)* (1999), the King's Bench first refused to enforce the arbitration agreement against the company (Smoky) that was reorganizing under the CCAA and was the subject of a judicial order staying all proceedings against it.[305] The Court's reasoning was that the arbitration agreement was "incapable of being performed due to a lack of capacity" of the company which "stems from the fact that the operations of Smoky are being supervised by this Court under the CCAA."[306] The decision was appealed, and the Alberta Court of Appeal upheld the King's Bench's decision without examining the correctness of the characterization of the arbitration agreement, i.e. that the arbitration agreement becomes "incapable of being performed" as a result of the CCAA proceeding.[307] The Court of Appeal held that, even if the lower court had erred in this respect, the result would still be the same because the CCAA is a federal law which prevails in case of any conflict with the provincial Arbitration Act.[308]

206. Likewise, in Ontario, in the matter of *Canada (Attorney General) v. Reliance Insurance Co* (2007), the Superior Court of Justice refused to enforce an arbitration agreement against an insurance company that was subject to a winding up order providing for the stay of any proceedings against the company.[309] One of the reasons the Court gave for its decision was that the winding up order and the mandatory stay of "any proceedings" under section 21 of the WURA rendered the arbitration agreement "inoperative."[310]

207. However, the most important case on this topic originated in British Columbia. In *Peace River Hydro Partners v. Petrowest Corp* (2022), the Supreme Court of Canada held that a court proceeding launched by a company's receiver might continue despite an

303. *Canada (Attorney General) v. Reliance Insurance Co* (2007), 87 OR (3d) 42 (Ont Sup Ct) at paras. 2–10, 20, 21, 27–32.
304. Brian Casey, *Arbitration Law of Canada: Practice and Procedure*, 3rd ed (Juris, 2017) at chap 7.18.2.
305. *Smoky River Coal Ltd (Re)*, 1999 ABQB 202 at paras. 1–4, 8, 9, 17–19, 37, [1999] AJ No 272.
306. *Ibid.*
307. *Luscar Ltd v. Smoky River Coal Ltd*, 1999 ABCA 179 at paras. 1–6, 9, 10, 31–33, 73–76, 237 AR 326.
308. *Ibid.*
309. *Canada (Attorney General) v. Reliance Insurance Co* (2007), 87 OR (3d) 42 (Ont Sup Ct) at paras. 2–10, 20, 21, 27–32.
310. *Ibid.*

otherwise valid arbitration clause in the company's contracts because the arbitration clause became "inoperative" under section 15(2) of the BC Arbitration Act.[311] The Court first clarified that a receiver may not *unilaterally* disclaim an arbitration agreement and render it "void, inoperative or incapable of being performed," as only courts can make such a finding.[312] According to the Court, if the receiver establishes "on a balance of probabilities" that "enforcing [the arbitration agreement] would compromise the orderly and efficient resolution of the receivership," the arbitration agreement becomes "inoperative."[313] The Court also held that the statutory jurisdiction for courts to make such a ruling arises from sections 183(1) and 243(1)(c) of the BIA and hence there is no need to resort to courts' inherent jurisdiction to stay a proceeding.[314]

208. It should be noted that the operability of an agreement will be completely different from the above scenario if the person who has entered into the arbitration agreement is a trustee. In *Experts en traitement de l'information (ETI) Montréal Inc (Syndic de)* (2005), the Québec Court of Appeal held that arbitration agreements concluded by trustees are enforceable against them.[315]

209. If there is a pending arbitration proceeding when a bankruptcy/insolvency proceeding is opened, *no* "proceedings" against the debtor may *continue*, in accordance with sections 69, 69.1, 69.2, 69.3 and 69.31 of the BIA. The CCAA also gives courts the *discretion* to issue an order staying any "proceedings" against the debtor company and its directors (sections 11.02 and 11.03). Section 17 of the WURA gives the same discretion to the courts. Courts in the common law provinces have interpreted the term "proceeding" in section 11.02 of the CCAA and section 69.3 of the BIA broadly to cover arbitration proceedings and enforcement of arbitral awards.[316]

210. However, just as courts have the discretion to stay other proceedings in favor of the bankruptcy proceedings, they have the discretion (under sections 43(10) and 43(11) of the BIA) to stay the bankruptcy proceeding in favor of other proceedings. In *Syndic de Station Touristique Massif du Sud v. 9367-3085 Québec Inc* (2018), the Québec Superior Court held that one of the circumstances allowing courts to exercise such discretion is when the debtor could show that there is a real dispute as to the existence of the alleged debt.[317] To do so, according to the Court, one could show that

311. *Peace River Hydro Partners v. Petrowest Corp*, 2022 SCC 41 at paras. 1–7.
312. *Ibid.*, at paras. 6, 123, 124.
313. *Ibid.*, at paras. 34, 35, 89.
314. *Ibid.*, at para. 152.
315. *Experts en traitement de l'information (ETI) Montréal Inc (Syndic de)*, 2005 QCCA 1257, [2006] RJQ 146.
316. *See, e.g.*, *Luscar Ltd v. Smoky River Coal Ltd*, 1999 ABCA 179 at paras. 22, 31–33, 237 AR 326; *Quintette Coal Ltd v. Nippon Steel Corp* (1990), 51 BCLR (2d) 105 (Bc CA) at 2, 8–10, 24 ACWS (3d) 172; *Hayes Forest Services Ltd (Re)*, 2009 BCSC 1169 at paras. 1, 2, 23–25, 30, [2009] BCJ No 1725; *Universal Settlements International Inc v. Duscio*, 2012 ONCA 215 at paras. 40, 41, 349 DLR (4th) 181.
317. *Syndic de Station Touristique Massif du Sud (1993) Inc v. 9367-3085 Québec Inc*, 2018 QCCS 3605 at paras. 1–2, 8–14, 17–19, 24.

there is a pending arbitration between the creditor and the debtor concerning the alleged debt.

211. Finally, it should be noted that, even if a creditor secures a favorable award against a debtor, that would not necessarily allow the debtor to enforce it. This is so because courts in the common law provinces have also generally favored the approach of guaranteeing the equality of creditors. For example, in *Universal Settlements International Inc v. Duscio* (2010) and *Thibodeau v. Thibodeau* (2011), the Ontario Court of Appeal held that, even if a creditor secures a favorable arbitration award, it may not enforce it and would only become an unsecured creditor.[318] Likewise, the BC Court of Appeal, in *Quintette Coal Ltd v. Nippon Steel Corp* (1990), refused to enforce an arbitral award against a debtor company.[319]

Hong Kong[320]

212. Disputes that are settled through particular courts or tribunals, including bankruptcy, company liquidation and winding up disputes, may not be submitted to arbitration.[321] In *In the Matter of Mech-Power Hong Kong-China Ltd* (1996), the Court of First Instance held that a petition to wind up a company is not a matter that could be submitted to arbitration pursuant to an arbitration agreement because "[t]he prayer for winding up is not something which is or could be the subject of an arbitration. The jurisdiction to wind up resides solely in the Court on the hearing of a petition to wind up."[322] The Court also reasoned that a petition to wind up is not a dispute which falls within the scope of the arbitration agreement because it does not arise out of, or in connection with the container contract, but is rather a dispute as to the operation of the company.[323] As such, according to the Court, even if such a dispute could fall within the scope of the arbitration agreement, it would render the agreement "inoperable."[324]

213. As such, arbitral tribunals do not have the authority to decide on a winding up petition, but the story is different when it comes to ruling on the underlying debt in a winding up petition. In *Lasmos Ltd v. Southwest Pacific Bauxite (HK) Ltd* (2018), the Court of First Instance held that a creditor's winding up petition regarding a company's

318. *Universal Settlements International Inc v. Duscio*, 2012 ONCA 215 at paras. 40, 41, 349 DLR (4th) 181; *Thibodeau v. Thibodeau*, 2011 ONCA 110 at paras. 1–10, 25, 43, 55, 331 DLR (4th) 606.
319. *Quintette Coal Ltd v. Nippon Steel Corp* (1990), 51 BCLR (2d) 105 (Bc CA) at 2, 8–10, 24 ACWS (3d) 172.
320. The term "bankruptcy" in Hong Kong law is applied in relation to individuals and is governed by the Bankruptcy Ordinance (Cap 6), while the term "insolvency" is used in relation to companies and is governed by the Companies (Winding Up and Miscellaneous Provisions) Ordinance (Cap 32). Charles D Booth, "Current Trends in Consumer Insolvency in Hong Kong" in Johanna Niemi-Kiesiläinen, Iain Ramsay & William Whitford, eds, *Consumer Bankruptcy in Global Perspective* (Hart Publishing, 2003) 187 at n 1.
321. Michael J Moser & Robert Morgan, "National Report for Hong Kong (2021 through 2022)" in Lise Bosman, ed, *ICCA International Handbook on Commercial Arbitration* (Kluwer Law International, 2022) at 30, 31.
322. *In the Matter of Mech-Power Hong Kong-China Ltd*, [1996] HKCFI 307, HCCW 281/1995 (4 June 1996) at paras. 1–12.
323. *Ibid.*
324. *Ibid.*

insolvency should be dismissed in favor of arbitration if three conditions are present: (i) the debt that the creditor relied on in the winding up petition originates from an agreement with the debtor company, which contains a broad arbitration clause; (ii) the company disputes the debt; and (iii) the company has taken the required steps as per the arbitration clause to commence the process and has filed an Affirmation under rule 32 of the Companies (Winding Up) Rules (Cap 32H).[325] The Court reasoned that a creditor who has made a contractual bargain to arbitrate its disputes should be held to it.[326] Further, according to the Court, the creditors can still have immediate access to the insolvency regime if they can "demonstrate a prima facie case for a winding up and a risk of misappropriation of assets or some other matter, which would normally justify the court appointing provisional liquidators, a petition could be issued and *stayed* [instead of dismissing it] ... pending determination of the arbitration."[327] In adopting this approach (i.e., dismissing/staying the winding up proceedings due to the existence of an arbitration clause), the Court departed from earlier Hong Kong case law[328] which would require the debtor company to establish, like in any other case, that there was a bona fide dispute on substantial grounds.

214. In determining how a bankruptcy proceeding may impact a *pending* arbitration proceeding and the arbitrability of the dispute, section 14(1) of the Bankruptcy Ordinance (with respect to individuals) does not require a mandatory stay of proceedings against the debtor but leaves the matter to the court's discretion. In addition, under section 61(f), a trustee may, with the permission of the creditors' committee, refer any dispute to arbitration.

215. The same rules apply to company insolvency proceedings. Under section 181 of the Companies (Winding Up and Miscellaneous Provisions) Ordinance, it is within the court's discretion to decide whether to stay any proceeding, including arbitration, against a company in a winding up proceeding. However, once the winding up order is made, the stay of any proceeding becomes mandatory except by leave of the court (section 186).

216. In *In the Matter of B + B Construction Company Ltd (In Liquidation)* (2001), the Court of First Instance granted leave under section 186 of the Companies Ordinance (Cap 32) for the applicant to proceed with an arbitration that had commenced prior to the respondent's insolvency and was already at a mature stage.[329] In another matter brought by a different applicant against the same respondent, the judge set out the legal

325. *Lasmos Ltd v. Southwest Pacific Bauxite (HK) Ltd*, [2018] HKCU 702 (22 January 2018, 2 March 2018) at paras. 1, 4, 5, 31, [2018] HKCFI 426.
326. *Ibid.*, at para. 28.
327. *Ibid.*, at paras. 29, 30 (emphasis added).
328. *See Hollmet AG v. Meridian Success Metal Supplies Ltd*, [1997] 4 HKC 343 at 347; *Re Sky Datamann (HK) Ltd*, HCCW 487/2001 (29 January 2002) at paras. 10–12, 31; *Hoo Cheong Building Construction Co Ltd v. Jade Union Investment Ltd*, HCCW 400/2003 (5 March 2004) at para. 21; *Re Southern Materials Holding (HK) Co Ltd*, HCCW 281/2007 (13 February 2008) at para. 7; *Quiksilver Greater China Ltd v. Quiksilver Glorious Sun JV Ltd and Another*, [2014] HKCFI 1304, HCCW 364/2013 (25 July 2014) at para. 18.
329. *In the Matter of B + B Construction Company Ltd (In Liquidation)*, [2001] HKCFI 779, HCCW 114/2001 (12 June 2001) at paras. 1, 4, 5, 9, 14, 15, 19–23, 28, 30.

principles applicable to the exercise of the court's discretion in granting leave under section 186:

- (1) the test is "what is right and fair according to the circumstances of each case and this involves a balancing exercise";
- (2) "[i]f the issue can be conveniently decided in the course of the winding up, leave will be refused in the absence of special circumstances, as there is a positive benefit in having the issue decided by the liquidator";
- (3) "[p]roceedings will be allowed to be commenced or continued where an action is the most convenient method of trying a question, and specifically so when the questions would involve substantial issues of facts that are in dispute and also matters of law of complexity"; and
- (4) "[l]eave is more likely to be granted where the company in liquidation is insured in respect of the claim made against it as the judgment will be funded to the limit of the cover by the insurance company and the costs of the action will be borne by the insurance company."[330]

2. Local Bankruptcy/Insolvency Proceedings v. Foreign Proceedings

217. When deciding on the arbitrability of a bankruptcy/insolvency-related dispute, a key factor that courts and arbitral tribunals consider is whether the proceeding is local or foreign. The location of the bankruptcy/insolvency proceeding is an important factor because it determines the law applicable to the proceeding. Based on the location of a bankruptcy/insolvency proceeding, three scenarios should be considered, each of which will be discussed in a separate Segment: (i) Local Bankruptcy/Insolvency Proceedings; (ii) Foreign Bankruptcy/Insolvency Proceedings; and (iii) Foreign Bankruptcy/Insolvency Proceedings within the European Union.

218. Here, it is important to note the relation between this Section (on the location of a proceeding) and the previous Section (on the coreness versus non-coreness of a dispute): the previous Section falls within the scope of the discussion on local proceedings. The legislative texts and case law discussed in the previous Section (in relation to each jurisdiction) shared the underlying assumption that the bankruptcy/insolvency proceeding is a local proceeding subject to the law of that jurisdiction.

i. Local Bankruptcy/Insolvency Proceedings

219. This scenario is when the bankruptcy/insolvency proceeding is opened in the same jurisdiction as the seat of arbitration and therefore is subject to the law of the seat. The scenario consists of two sub-scenarios: (a) the bankruptcy/insolvency proceeding has commenced, and there is an arbitration agreement between the debtor and a

330. *In the Matter of B + B Construction Company Ltd (In Liquidation)*, [2003] HKCFI 33, HCCW 114/2001 (4 April 2003) at paras. 1, 4–8.

creditor, but no pending arbitration yet; and (b) there is already a pending arbitration proceeding when the bankruptcy/insolvency proceeding is opened.

Sub-Scenario (a): No Pending Arbitration

220. The question is whether, in the jurisdictions studied for this text, creditors are able to commence arbitration against a debtor despite a pending local bankruptcy/insolvency proceeding and, if yes, under what conditions they may do so. The authors have identified four approaches that the selected jurisdictions take in this regard.

221. The first approach is the most conservative: imposing a general ban on the commencement of any proceedings (including arbitration) against the debtor, with certain exceptions, as set out in the applicable law. This approach is adopted in the US[331] and Canada (although only with respect to proceedings that are subject to the BIA,[332] and not the proceedings that are subject to the CCAA or the WURA).

222. The second approach is the most liberal: allowing creditors to commence arbitration as per the agreement they had with the debtor, regardless of the pending bankruptcy/insolvency proceeding. This approach has been adopted in Switzerland[333] and Germany.[334] Nevertheless, in German law, there is one exception to the general rule of allowing the arbitration to commence: when the debtor's assets are not sufficient to cover the debtor's share of the arbitration cost, which renders the arbitration agreement inoperative.[335] From a legislative perspective, Canada (with respect to proceedings that are subject to the CCAA and the WURA) should be categorized as falling within the liberal group. However, Canadian practice is more conservative than the scope of its legislative provisions suggests. This is because the CCAA and the WURA have given courts discretion to not allow any proceedings (including arbitration) to commence against a debtor company that is subject to the CCAA or WURA,[336] and Canadian courts have used that discretion to refuse to enforce arbitration agreements.[337]

331. *See* § 362 of the Bankruptcy Code (11 USC § 362).

332. Bankruptcy and Insolvency Act, ss. 69, 69.1, 69.2, 69.3, 69.31.

333. *See* the Federal Supreme Court's decision in *BGE 136 III 107, 8 December 2009*; Christoph Liebscher, "Insolvency and Arbitrability" in Loukas A Mistelis & Stavros L Brekoulakis, eds, *Arbitrability: International and Comparative Perspectives* (Kluwer Law International, 2009) 165 at paras. 9-44, 9-45.

334. Although s. 240 of the Code of Civil Procedure provides for the stay of proceedings against the insolvent, the Hamm Higher Regional Court in *OLG Hamm, 02.11.1983* noted that the rule does not apply to arbitral proceedings. Commentators have expressed the same view. Christoph Liebscher, "Insolvency and Arbitrability" in Loukas A Mistelis & Stavros L Brekoulakis, eds, *Arbitrability: International and Comparative Perspectives* (Kluwer Law International, 2009) 165 at para. 9.40. *See also* Jan Kraayvanger & Mark C Hilgard, "The Effect of German Insolvency Proceedings on International Arbitration" in Mayer Brown LLP, *International Arbitration Perspectives on Insolvency* (2010) 9.

335. Decision of the Federal Court of Justice in *BGH 14.09.2000—III ZR 33/00.*

336. CCAA, ss. 11.02, 11.03; WURA, s. 17.

337. *See, e.g.*, *Luscar Ltd v. Smoky River Coal Ltd*, 1999 ABCA 179 at paras. 1–6, 9, 10, 31–33, 73–76, 237 AR 326; *Hayes Forest Services Ltd (Re)*, 2009 BCSC 1169 at paras. 1, 2, 23–25, 30, [2009] BCJ

223. The third and fourth approaches stand between the two approaches explained above; i.e., creditors are allowed to initiate arbitration but only if certain conditions are met. The difference between the third and fourth approaches is in the nature of the conditions that each approach imposes. In the third approach, the conditions are negative (i.e., certain circumstances must be absent for creditors to be allowed to commence arbitration), whereas in the fourth approach, the conditions are affirmative (i.e., certain conditions must be found to exist before creditors are allowed to submit a dispute to arbitration).

224. The third approach is adopted (with respect to companies, not individuals) in the three jurisdictions of England and Wales, Hong Kong, and Singapore. In English law, a creditor is allowed to initiate arbitration against a debtor company if that company has not gone into administration, or a winding-up order has not been made, or a provisional liquidator has not been appointed.[338] Likewise, in Hong Kong, to submit a dispute to arbitration, no winding-up order should be in place against the debtor company.[339] Similarly, in Singapore, arbitration may not commence if a winding-up order is in place, or if the company has applied for a judicial management order or an arrangement order, or if the company is in a simplified debt restructuring.[340]

225. The fourth approach is applied in France, England and Wales (with respect to individuals), and Singapore (with respect to individuals). In French law, a creditor may commence arbitration against the debtor, but only after a bankruptcy judge checks the legality of the creditor's claim declaration.[341] In English law, creditors may commence arbitration against an individual debtor, if the trustee adopts the underlying contract.[342] Likewise, in Singapore, arbitration may commence if the official assignee adopts the underlying contract; otherwise, the matter can be referred to a court to decide whether to enforce the arbitration agreement.[343]

226. China seems to have adopted the fourth approach. Chinese law is not clear on the question of whether it allows creditors to commence arbitration where the dispute is non-core. However, it is understood from Article 20 of the Law on Enterprise Bankruptcy[344] that it is possible for creditors to commence arbitration, but only after an

No 1725; *Canada (Attorney General) v. Reliance Insurance Co* (2007), 87 OR (3d) 42 (Ont Sup Ct) at paras. 2-10, 20, 21, 27-32.

338. Insolvency Act 1986, s. 130(2) and Schedule B1 para. 43(6).
339. Companies (Winding Up and Miscellaneous Provisions) Ordinance (Cap 32), s. 186.
340. Insolvency, Restructuring and Dissolution Act 2018, ss. 133, 95(1)(c), 96(4)(c), 72K(1)(c), 64(8)(c).
341. The rule is extracted from three decisions of the Court of Cassation handed down in 2004: *Société Gaussin et autres v. Société Alstom Power Turbomachines*, Court of Cassation (Commercial Chamber), 2 June 2004, reported in (2004) 2004:3 Rev Arb 593; *Société Prodim v. Société Logidis*, Court of Cassation (Commercial Chamber), 14 January2004, reported in (2004) 2004:3 Arb Rev 59; *Société Industry et autres v. Société Alstom Power Turbomachines*, Court of Cassation (Commercial Chamber), 2 June 2004, reported in (2004) 2004:3 Rev Arb 595.
342. Insolvency Act 1986, s. 349A.
343. Insolvency, Restructuring and Dissolution Act 2018, s. 420.
344. Article 20 reads: "After the people's court accepts an application for bankruptcy, any civil action or arbitration related to the debtor, which has been started yet not ended, shall be

administrator takes over the debtor's assets. In this case, there is a fine distinction between the condition that Chinese law applies and the ones that the other jurisdictions in the fourth group (namely France, England and Wales, and Singapore) apply. One could see that in the conditions that France, England and Wales, and Singapore apply, an element of discretion is vested in judges (in France) or trustees and official assignees (in England and Wales and Singapore) to approve the legality of a claim or adopt the underlying contract, respectively. However, the condition in Chinese law (that an administrator takes over the debtor's assets) relates to the time it takes for this condition to be fulfilled, rather than the discretion of judges/trustees/assignees.

Sub-Scenario (b): With a Pending Arbitration

227. When a local bankruptcy/insolvency proceeding is opened, and there is already a pending arbitration proceeding, the relevant question is whether jurisdictions allow the arbitration to continue despite the bankruptcy/insolvency proceeding and, if yes, under what conditions. The authors have identified four approaches.

228. The first approach is the most liberal: allowing the arbitration to continue without imposing a stay on the arbitration. This approach is adopted in Germany,[345] Canada (with respect to companies that are subject to the CCAA and WURA),[346] and with respect to individuals in England and Wales,[347] Hong Kong,[348] and Singapore.[349] Nevertheless, the relevant laws in the said jurisdictions, except Germany, give courts the *discretion* to stay any pending proceedings (including arbitration) against the debtor.[350]

229. The second approach is the most conservative: imposing a general, automatic stay on a pending arbitration once one of the parties to that arbitration becomes subject to the bankruptcy/insolvency proceeding, with certain exceptions (as set out in the

suspended. The civil action or arbitration can be resumed after a bankruptcy custodian takes over the debtor's assets."

345. Although s. 240 of the Code of Civil Procedure provides for the stay of proceedings against an insolvent, the Hamm Higher Regional Court in *OLG Hamm, 02.11.1983* noted that the rule does not apply to arbitral proceedings. Commentators have expressed the same view. *See* Christoph Liebscher, "Insolvency and Arbitrability" in Loukas A Mistelis & Stavros L Brekoulakis, eds, *Arbitrability: International and Comparative Perspectives* (Kluwer Law International, 2009) 165 at para. 9.40. *See also* Jan Kraayvanger & Mark C Hilgard, "The Effect of German Insolvency Proceedings on International Arbitration" in Mayer Brown LLP, *International Arbitration Perspectives on Insolvency* (2010) 9.
346. The CCAA, ss. 11.02, 11.03; the WURA, s. 17.
347. Insolvency Act 1986, s. 285(1).
348. Bankruptcy Ordinance (Cap 6), s. 14(1).
349. Insolvency, Restructuring and Dissolution Act 2018, s. 325.
350. Regarding the German approach, it should be noted that although it allows the arbitral proceeding to continue, its public policy rules require three conditions to be met: (i) the claimant creditor must file its claim with the insolvency administrator once the insolvency proceeding is opened; (ii) the insolvent party must be replaced with the insolvency administrator; and (iii) the arbitral tribunal may only establish the validity of the claim and its amount and may not order the insolvency administrator to pay or release any assets. *See BGH, 29.01.2009—III ZB 88/07*; German Insolvency Act, ss. 28, 174.

applicable law). This approach is applied in the US[351] and Canada (with respect to debtors that are subject to the BIA).[352]

230. The third and fourth approaches fall somewhere between the above two approaches. In the third approach, an automatic stay is imposed on pending arbitrations *only if certain circumstances are present*. This approach is adopted in relation to debtor companies in England and Wales, Hong Kong, and Singapore. In English law, a pending arbitration is automatically stayed once a company goes into administration, when a winding up order is made, or when a provisional liquidator is appointed.[353] Likewise, in Hong Kong, any arbitration is automatically stayed when a winding up order is made.[354] In Singapore, arbitration is stayed when a winding up order is made, when the company has applied for a judicial management order or an arrangement order, or when the company is in a simplified debt restructuring.[355]

231. In the fourth approach, an automatic stay is imposed on all pending arbitrations, but it is *temporary* and will be lifted after a short time. This approach is applied in France, Switzerland, and China. In French law, an automatic stay is imposed only until the claimant creditor files a declaration of their claim.[356] Likewise, Swiss law imposes an automatic stay on pending arbitrations, but the stay is lifted after 10 days following the second meeting of creditors (in ordinary liquidations) and 20 days following the filing of the schedule of claims (in summary liquidations).[357] In China, the automatic stay on a pending arbitration is lifted after an administrator takes over the debtor's assets.[358]

ii. Foreign Bankruptcy/Insolvency Proceedings

232. This scenario is seen when the bankruptcy/insolvency proceeding is opened in a jurisdiction other than the seat of the pending arbitration. Excepting Hong Kong, the other four common law jurisdictions (the US, Canada, England and Wales, and Singapore) have adopted the UNCITRAL Model Law on Cross-Border Insolvency

351. Bankruptcy Code § 362 (11 USC § 362).
352. BIA, ss. 69, 69.1, 69.2, 69.3, 69.31.
353. Insolvency Act 1986, s. 130(2), Schedule B1 para. 43(6).
354. Companies (Winding Up and Miscellaneous Provisions) Ordinance (Cap 32), s. 186.
355. Insolvency, Restructuring and Dissolution Act 2018, ss. 133, 95(1)(c) together with 96(4)(c), 64(8)(c), 72K(1)(c).
356. However, it should be noted that after resuming the arbitration, the arbitral tribunal may only validate the claims and quantify their amount, without having the jurisdiction to order the debtor to pay. Commercial Code, Arts. L622-21, L622-22; *see Lion et Compagnie v. International Company for Commercial Exchanges (INCOME—Egypt)*, Court of Cassation (1st Civil Chamber), 6 May 2009, reported in Albert Jan van den Berg, ed, *ICCA Yearbook Commercial Arbitration*, vol 35 (Kluwer Law International, 2010) 353, paras. 9-12; *Dont et Cts de Cominck v. Zanzi ès qual et autre*, Paris Court of Appeal, 30 March 1999, Case No 97/25592.
357. Federal Act on Debt Enforcement and Bankruptcy (Debt Enforcement and Bankruptcy Act, DEBA), Art. 207(1).
358. Law on Enterprise Bankruptcy, Art. 20.

(Insolvency Model Law).[359] However, none of the civil law jurisdictions (France, Germany, Switzerland, and China) has adopted the Insolvency Model Law.

233. Two points should be noted about the common law jurisdictions that adopted the Insolvency Model Law. First, although Canada, England and Wales, and Singapore applied modifications to the Insolvency Model Law when adopting it, they have followed its rule in relation to the effects of recognition of a foreign bankruptcy/insolvency proceeding (Article 20 of the Insolvency Model Law).[360] Article 20 relevantly provides that, upon recognition of a foreign bankruptcy/insolvency proceeding, any other pending proceedings (including arbitration) must be stayed and no new proceeding may commence against a debtor. This is significant because Canada, England and Wales, and Singapore do not provide such a level of protection for all debtors when the bankruptcy/insolvency proceeding is local.[361] By comparison, the US modified the effect section of the Insolvency Model Law upon its adoption, providing that effects are to be governed by the same law that applies to local US bankruptcy proceedings, which is § 362 of the Bankruptcy Code.[362] Nevertheless, the end result is substantially the same in the US because, under § 362, no other proceedings (including arbitration) may commence or continue against the debtor.

234. The second point to note about the common law jurisdictions that adopted the Insolvency Model Law is that Canada,[363] England and Wales[364] and the US[365] all adopted the Insolvency Model Law for both companies and individuals, whereas the relevant law in Singapore applies only to companies.[366]

235. In terms of the civil law jurisdictions—and in Hong Kong—there is no common approach taken to foreign bankruptcy/insolvency proceedings. In this category, the authors note that:

- Germany takes the most liberal approach, as it accords automatic recognition to foreign bankruptcy/insolvency proceedings.[367]
- In France, to have a foreign proceeding recognized, one must obtain an exequatur under Article 509 of the Code of Civil Procedure.[368]

359. Canada in 2005, the US in 2005, United Kingdom in 2006, and Singapore in 2017. UNCITRAL website, tab "Texts and Status," sub-tab "Insolvency," hyperlink "UNCITRAL Model Law on Cross-Border Insolvency," hyperlink "Status," online: https://uncitral.un.org/en/texts/insolvency/modellaw/cross-border_insolvency/status (last visited 15 June 2022).
360. For Canada, *see* CCAA, s. 48(1); BIA, s. 271(1). For England, *see* Cross-Border Insolvency Regulations 2006, Schedule 1, Art. 20. For Singapore, *see* Insolvency, Restructuring and Dissolution Act 2018, Third Schedule, Art. 20.
361. *See* the previous Section on local proceedings.
362. Bankruptcy Code § 1520 (11 USC § 1520).
363. BIA, part XIII; CCAA, part IV.
364. Cross-Border Insolvency Regulations 2006, Schedule 1, Art. 20(2).
365. US Code, Title 11 (on bankruptcy), Chapter 15.
366. Insolvency, Restructuring and Dissolution Act 2018, Third Schedule, Arts. 1, 2(k).
367. Insolvency Act, s. 343(1).
368. The decision of the Court of Cassation in 2000 (Decision No 98-19.913) provides that, for French courts to issue an exequatur, the foreign bankruptcy order does not need to meet all requirements of a bankruptcy order under French law. However, pursuant to the decision of

- Swiss law provides for the recognition of foreign proceedings on the conditions that it is enforceable in the country where it was rendered, and there is no ground for refusal under Article 27 of the PILA.[369]
- In China and Hong Kong, there is (as yet) no statutory regime regulating foreign proceedings.[370] However, in China, if there is a foreign, final bankruptcy judgment, it is possible to apply to Chinese courts to have it recognized under Article 5 of the Law on Enterprise Bankruptcy. According to Article 5, Chinese courts will act based on relevant international treaties or according to the principle of reciprocity.

iii. Foreign Bankruptcy/Insolvency Proceedings Within the European Union

236. With respect to France and Germany (as EU Member States), the approaches described in the previous subsection apply *only* to scenarios where the foreign bankruptcy/insolvency proceeding is opened in a non-EU Member State or in Denmark.

237. The reason is that, if the seat of arbitration is an EU Member State, while a foreign bankruptcy/insolvency proceedings is opened in another EU Member State (except Denmark), Regulation (EU) 2015/848 on Insolvency Proceeding applies.[371] Under the Regulation, any insolvency proceeding opened in an EU Member State will be automatically recognized in other Member States (Article 19), and the effects of insolvency proceedings on pending arbitral proceedings are governed by the law of the Member State in which *the arbitral tribunal has its seat* (Article 18).

238. Prior to Brexit, the same Regulation applied to the UK as an EU Member State, but Brexit brought important changes in this regard. When leaving the block, the UK converted all EU laws applicable to the UK at the time (including the above Regulation)

the Paris Court of Appeal in *République de Côte-d'Ivoire et autre v. Société Norbert Beyrard* (1993), the commencement of foreign bankruptcy proceedings must not offend international public policy rules, such as the principle of good faith. *République de Côte-d'Ivoire et autre v. Société Norbert Beyrard*, Paris Court of Appeal, 12 January 1993, reported in (1994) 1994:4 Rev Arb 685.

369. Private International Law Act, Art. 166(1).

370. For China, *see* Dentons LLP (Xiuchao Yin & Zhiguo Yang), "Restructuring and insolvency in China: Overview" published online at Practical Law a Thomson Reuters Legal Solution (January 2022) at question No 13: https://uk.practicallaw.thomsonreuters.com/7-502-0018?transitionType=Default&contextData=(sc.Default)&firstPage=true. For Hong Kong, *see* Clifford Chance LLP, "Client Briefing: Cross-border insolvency in Hong Kong" (November 2016), online: https://www.cliffordchance.com/briefings/2016/11/cross-border_insolvencyinhongkongpushin0.html (last visited 8 March 2023).

371. Regulation (EU) 2015/848 of the European Parliament and of the Council of 20 May 2015 on Insolvency Proceeding. It should be noted that this Regulation applies only to insolvency proceedings opened after 26 June 2017. For proceedings commenced prior to that date, the former regulation, namely the Council Regulation (EC) No 1346/2000, is applicable. The 2000 Regulation has similar provisions governing insolvency proceedings in its Arts. 15 and 16. However, the application of Art. 15 of the 2000 regulation, unlike Art. 18 of the 2015 regulation, is limited to "lawsuit" and does not expressly mention "arbitral proceedings."

into its domestic law.[372] However, the relevant provisions of the Regulation (Articles 18, 19, and 20) were omitted through a series of amendments that the parliament introduced in 2019 and 2020.[373] As such, insolvency proceedings that are now opened in EU Member States are treated like any other foreign insolvency proceeding in the UK. Therefore, they fall within the scope of application of the Cross-border Insolvency Regulations 2006.

C. CONSUMER LAW

239. Nearly all jurisdictions studied for this book allow the arbitration of consumer disputes. However, the majority of them also impose restrictions on the validity or enforceability of *pre-dispute* arbitration agreements. The authors have identified two major approaches taken by the studied jurisdictions that will be discussed in two Subsections: (1) the liberal approach of allowing the arbitration of consumer disputes without imposing any specific restrictions; (2) the conservative approach of allowing the arbitration of consumer disputes but under specific restrictions, which in turn can be categorized into two groups: (i) the procedural restrictions approach and (ii) the substantive restrictions approach. Subsection (3) then outlines the framework within the European Union.

1. Liberal Approach

240. The first approach is the liberal approach, which is applied in the US (generally), Switzerland (in international matters), China, and Singapore.

The United States

241. In the US, the Supreme Court has strongly supported the arbitration of consumer disputes. When read together, important decisions of the Court provide the general rule that the FAA preempts state laws prohibiting the arbitration of consumer disputes, even where an arbitration clause waives the consumers' rights to launch/join any class action or class arbitration, and even if the cost of consumer's individually arbitrating a federal statutory claim exceeds the potential recovery.[374]

242. Given the large number of federal statutes that protect consumers' rights, the arbitrability of a consumer dispute should be examined under the relevant statute under which the dispute has arisen. For instance:

- The Supreme Court, in *CompuCredit Corp v. Greenwood* (2012), held that consumer disputes arising under the Credit Repair Organizations Act, 15 USC

372. European Union (Withdrawal) Act 2018 (amended 2020), ss. 2 and 3.
373. The Insolvency (Amendment) (EU Exit) Regulations 2019, The Insolvency (Amendment) (EU Exit) (No. 2) Regulations 2019, and The Insolvency (Amendment) (EU Exit) Regulations 2020.
374. *Allied-Bruce Terminex v. Dobson*, 513 US 265 (1995) at 274-75, 277, 281; *AT&T Mobility v. Concepcion*, 131 S Ct 1740 (2011) at 1746–1747, 1753; *American Exp Co v. Italian Colors Rest*, 133 S Ct 2304 (2013) at 2308, 2312.

§1679-1679j are arbitrable,[375] and in *Green Tree Fin Corp Ala v. Randolph* (2000), the Court held that claims brought under the Truth in Lending Act, 15 USC §§ 1601-1667-f, are arbitrable.[376]

- In the Magnuson-Moss Warranty Act (MMVA)—the federal statute that governs warranties on consumer products—Congress expressed its policy to facilitate the informal settlement of consumer disputes (§ 110(a)(1)) and tasked the Federal Trade Commission (FTC) with regulating this mechanism (§ 110(a)(2)). However, the FTC rules prohibit any binding arbitration of disputes concerning written warranty claims arising under the MMVA.[377] The Courts of Appeals for three circuits have addressed the arbitrability of MMVA claims as follows:
  - The Courts of Appeals for the Fifth and Eleventh Circuits in *Davis v. Southern Energy Homes* (2002) and *Walton v. Rose Mobile Homes LLC* (2002) respectively, did not defer to the FTC regulations and enforced the arbitration agreements.[378]
  - However, the Court of Appeals for the Ninth Circuit in *Kolev v. Euromotors W/Auto Gallery* (2011), initially followed the FTC regulations but shortly after withdrew its decision.[379] There are, nevertheless, some federal courts at the district level that have deferred to the FTC regulations.[380]
- With respect to claims arising under the Fair Credit Reporting Act (FCRA), US courts have supported their arbitrability. For example, the Eleventh Circuit Court of Appeals in *Hearn v. Comcast Cable Communications* (2021) and the District Court of Middle District of Pennsylvania in *Comrey v. Discover Financial Services* (2021) found that the consumers' FCRA claims were within the scope of the arbitration provision in the agreements with the service providers.[381]
- However, some US statutes prohibit *pre-dispute* arbitration agreements, which are discussed below, under the Subsection "Substantive Restrictions."

Switzerland

243. In Switzerland, under Article 114(b) of the PILA, courts' jurisdiction over consumer disputes may not be waived in advance. However, commentators believe

375. *CompuCredit Corp v. Greenwood*, 132 S Ct 665 (2012) at 672–673.
376. *Green Tree Fin Corp Ala v. Randolph*, 531 US 79 (2000) at 82, 89, 90.
377. *Interpretations of Magnuson-Moss Warranty Act*, 16 CFR § 700.8; *Informal Dispute Settlement Procedures*, 16 CFR § 703.5.
378. *Davis v. Southern Energy Homes, Inc*, 305 F3d 1268 (11th Cir 2002) at 1272, 1277–1280; *Walton v. Rose Mobile Homes LLC*, 298 F3d 470 (5th Cir 2002) at 474–478.
379. *Kolev v. Euromotors W/Auto Gallery*, 658 F3d 1024 (9th Cir 2011) at 1205–1208, opinion withdrawn by 676 F3d 867 (9th Cir 2012).
380. *Rhode v. E & T Invs, Inc*, 6 F Supp 2d 1322 (MD Ala 1998) at 1333, n 6; *Browne v. Kline Tysons Imports, Inc*, 190 F Supp 2d 827 (ED Va 2002) at 833; *Rickard v. Teynor's Homes, Inc*, 279 F Supp 2d 910 (ND Ohio 2003) at 921; *but see Krusch v. TAMKO Bldg Prods*, 34 F Supp 3d 584 (MDNC 2014) at 594.
381. *Hearn v. Comcast Cable Communications, LLC*, 992 F3d 1209 (11th Cir 2021); *Comrey v. Discover Financial Services, Inc*, 806 F Supp 2d 778 (MD Penn 2011) at 785.

that Article 114 is not an impediment to the arbitration of *international* consumer disputes, as the provision is not located in Chapter 12 of the PILA that governs international arbitration.[382] As such, Swiss law does not impose any specific restriction on the arbitrability of consumer disputes in international matters.[383]

China

244. In China, Article 39(4) of the Law on the Protection of Consumer Rights and Interests provides that consumer disputes are arbitrable, without imposing any specific limitation. However, in free zones, as per an Opinion issued by the Supreme People's Court (2016), an e-commerce enterprise must remind consumers about the existence of the arbitration clause in the agreement.[384]

Singapore

245. Singapore has adopted a similar approach to China, as its statutory regime does not have any prohibition or limitation on the arbitration of consumer disputes. Sections 7(10), 7(11), and 35(3) of the Singapore Consumer Protection (Fair Trading) Act 2003 provide for the possibility of submitting consumer disputes to "dispute resolution schemes" as well as the "settlement of disputes," but these sections make no explicit reference to "arbitration." Likewise, no limitation on the arbitrability of consumer disputes has been reported in Singapore case law.[385]

2. Conservative Approach

246. The second approach is the conservative approach that consists in allowing the arbitration of consumer disputes while imposing specific restrictions, the nature of which could be procedural or substantive.

i. Procedural Restrictions Approach

247. This approach is to allow the arbitration of consumer disputes on the condition that certain procedural formalities are met. Among the jurisdictions that were studied, only Germany has adopted this approach. In German law, for an arbitration agreement to be valid in consumer disputes, section 1031(5) of the Code of Civil Procedure requires that it be in a separate document and be signed by both parties, or

382. Philippe Bärtsch & Angelina M Petti, "Chapter 3: The Arbitration Agreement" in Elliott Geisinger & Nathalie Voser, eds, *International Arbitration in Switzerland: A Handbook for Practitioners* (Kluwer Law International, 2013) 25 at 39; Daniel Girsberger & Nathalie Voser, *International Arbitration: Comparative and Swiss Perspectives*, 3rd ed (Schulthess, 2016) at paras. 442, 443.
383. It should be noted that an opposite view has been expressed too. *See Ibid.*
384. Supreme People's Court Opinions on the Provision of Judicial Safeguards for the Construction of Pilot Free Trade Zones (2016).
385. For example, the High Court's 2009 decision in *Merrill Lynch Pierce, Fenner & Smith Inc v. Prem Ramchand Harjani* indicates the possibility of arbitrating disputes between customers and banks. *Merrill Lynch Pierce, Fenner & Smith Inc v. Prem Ramchand Harjani* [2009] SLR(R) 16 (HC) at paras. 12, 14, 17, 18, 24, 25.

alternatively, the entire contract should be notarized. The requirements in section 1031(5) seem to be part of German public policy,[386] as the Federal Court of Justice in *BGH, 19.05.2011—III ZR 16/11* held that these are strict requirements that may not be waived, to the extent that failure to meet these requirements should prevent even the consumer from relying on the arbitration agreement. However, the rule does not apply if, as per section 1031(6) of the Code of Civil Procedure, the consumer participates in the arbitration proceeding without objecting to the validity of the arbitration agreement.

ii. Substantive Restrictions Approach

248. This approach imposes restrictions of a substantive nature on the arbitration of consumer disputes: either by imposing restrictions on the validity/enforceability of *pre-dispute* arbitration agreements or by categorizing arbitration provisions as "unfair" provisions. Six jurisdictions have taken this approach: France, England and Wales, Switzerland (in domestic disputes), Canada, Hong Kong, and the US (mainly with respect to disputes relating to financial products and services). Each jurisdiction will be discussed in turn.

France

249. French law imposes two types of restrictions on the arbitration of consumer disputes: one under the Civil Code and the other under the Consumer Code.

- Under the Civil Code (Article 2061—amended in 2016), pre-dispute arbitration agreements may not be enforced against a consumer. Thus, a pre-dispute arbitration clause with a consumer may only be invoked by the consumer.[387]
- Under the Consumer Code (Articles L212-1, L212-3, and L241-1), any clause in a contract "between professionals and consumers" that causes a significant imbalance between the rights and obligations of the parties is considered "unfair" and thus "unwritten" because the rule is of "public order." Further, under Article R212-2, arbitration clauses are *presumed* to be "unfair" unless proved otherwise by the professional.[388]

386. Hilmar Raeschke-Kessler, "Chapter 20: Germany" in James H Carter, ed, *The International Arbitration Review*, 6th ed (Law Business Research Ltd, 2015) 258 at 267.

387. Thomas Clay, "La réforme des articles du Code civil sur l'arbitrage en France" (2017) 35:1 ASA Bulletin 40 at 47; Jean-Christophe Honlet et al, "Chapter 16: France" in *The International Arbitration Review*, 8th ed (Law Business Research Ltd, 2017) 184 at 184.

388. The concept of "significant imbalance" between the rights and obligations of parties is already covered by the Consumer Code; nevertheless, Art. 1171 of the Civil Code, which was introduced in 2016, addresses the matter further concerning adhesion contracts. According to Art. 1171: "In an adhesion contract, any non-negotiable clause, determined in advance by one of the parties, that creates a significant imbalance between the rights and obligations of the contractual parties shall be deemed unwritten. The assessment of the significant imbalance concerns neither the main purpose of the contract nor to the adequacy of the price to the service." This article, in addition to protecting consumers, extends protection to business-to-business adhesion contracts. *See* Andrew Tetley, *Legal Revolution in France—Civil Law Reforms (or Napoleon's Second Coming)*, Reed Smith LLP Client Alerts (6 April 2016),

250. Prior to 2020, those restrictions did not apply to international arbitration, as per the numerous rulings of the Court of Cassation.[389] In addition, the task of deciding the "unfairness" of an arbitration clause was left to arbitrators.[390] As such, the French law approach was bifurcated: with respect to domestic consumer disputes, it would fall into the current group (Substantive Restrictions Approach), while with respect to international consumer disputes, it would fall into the Liberal Approach group (discussed previously).

251. However, the above approach changed in 2020, as the Court of Cassation took a significant step toward blurring the distinction between international and domestic consumer disputes. In *PwC Landwell-PricewaterhouseCoopers Tax & Legal Services v. [not indicated]* (2020), the Court of Cassation held that the arbitration clause in a contract between the Spanish arm of an international legal service provider and its French client was "unfair."[391] It rejected the argument that arbitrators should first decide the unfairness of an arbitration clause under Article 1448 of the Code of Civil Procedure (on the negative effect of the competence-competence principle).[392] The Court relied on the Council Directive 93/13/EEC of 5 April 1993 on Unfair Terms in Consumer Contracts (Articles 6 and 7)[393] and a relevant European Court of Justice's decision[394] to rule that Article 1448 of the Code of Civil Procedure may not make it excessively difficult for consumers to exercise their rights under the Directive, given that the Member States are under obligation to provide consumers with effective means to exercise those rights.[395]

---

online: https://www.reedsmith.com/Legal-revolution-in-France--civil-law-reforms-or-Napoleons-second-coming-04-04-2016/ (last visited 4 February 2021).

389. Regarding Art. 2061 of the Civil Code, *see M Zanzi v. J de Coninck et autres*, Court of Cassation (1st Civil Chamber), 5 January 1999, reported in (1999) 1999:2 Rev Arb 260, 261; *G El Assidi v. Société Nest et autres*, Court of Cassation (1st Civil Chamber), 12 May 2010, reported in (2010) 2010:2 Rev Arb 391. Regarding the restrictions in the Consumer Code, *see Renault v. Société V 2000 (Jaguar France)*, Court of Cassation (1st Civil Chamber), 21 May 1997, reported in (1997) 1997:4 Rev Arb 537; *Rado v. Société Painvewebber*, Court of Cassation (1st Civil Chamber), 30 March 2004, reported in (2005) 2005:1 Rev Arb 115.

390. *Renault v. Société V 2000 (Jaguar France)*, Court of Cassation (1st Civil Chamber), 21 May 1997, Decision No 95-11.428; *Pourdieu v. SAS Merril Lynch Pierce Fenner & Smith SAF*, Paris Court of Appeal, 2 April 2003, reported in (2005) 2005:1 Rev Arb 115; *Mattei et autres v. SAS Merril Pierce, Fenner & Smith SAF*, Paris Court of Appeal, 28 April 2004, reported in (2004) 2004:1 Rev Arb 115.

391. *PwC Landwell-PricewaterhouseCoopers Tax & Legal Services v. [not indicated]*, Court of Cassation (1st Civil Chamber), 30 September 2020, Decision No 18-19.241.

392. Article 1448 of the Code of Civil Procedure reads: "When a dispute relating to an arbitration agreement is brought before a State court, the latter declares itself incompetent unless the arbitral tribunal has not yet been seised and if the arbitration agreement is manifestly null or manifestly inapplicable of being performed." According to Art. 1506 of the same Code, Art. 1448 applies to international arbitration.

393. It is worth noting that the Directive is the same instrument based on which the rule on the unfairness of arbitration clauses was first introduced into the Consumer Code (then Art. L131-1).

394. *OTP Bank Nyrt. and OTP Faktoring Követeléskezelő Zrt v. Teréz Ilyés and Emil Kiss*, ECJ, Case No C-51/17, Judgment, 20 September 2018 at para. 89.

395. *PwC Landwell-PricewaterhouseCoopers Tax & Legal Services v. [not indicated]*, Court of Cassation (1st Civil Chamber), 30 September 2020, Decision No 18-19.241.

252. The full implications of the Court of Cassation's decision are not clear yet: some believe the Court has overturned its previous case law allowing arbitration of international consumer disputes,[396] while some disagree.[397] However, it is clear that the rule in the Consumer Code (about the unfairness of arbitration clauses)[398] is no longer limited to domestic arbitration matters and can be applied to international arbitration, *at least* with respect to matters where the consumer is protected by EU consumer law.[399] It remains to be seen whether French courts apply the new approach to international matters that do not involve EU consumer law.

England and Wales

253. In England and Wales, Schedule 2 to the Consumer Rights Act 2015—as amended by the Consumer Protection (Amendment etc.) (EU Exit) Regulations 2018—lists arbitration provisions under contract terms which *might* be regarded as *unfair*. The Act revoked the Unfair Terms in Consumer Contracts Regulations 1999[400] which had revoked the previous 1994 version. However, the three sets of Regulations share elements in terms of the definition of unfair terms in consumer contracts. The similar requirements across the three being: (i) *significant imbalance* in the parties' rights and obligations and (ii) lack of *good faith*. There is much discussion in English case law about the meaning of those terms.[401]

---

396. *See, e.g.*, Practical Law Arbitration, Quinn Emanuel Urquhart & Sullivan UK LLP, "Final Clap for Consumer Disputes in International Arbitration? (French Cassation Court)" published online at Practical Law a Thomson Reuters Legal Solution (21 October 2020): https://uk.practicallaw.thomsonreuters.com/w-027-9940?transitionType=Default&contextData=(sc.Default)&firstPage=true (last visited 3 February 2021).
397. *See, e.g.*, Armand Terrien, "Arbitration of Consumer Disputes in France: Get Thee Behind Me Competence-Competence?" Kluwer Arbitration Blog (12 November 2020), online: http://arbitrationblog.kluwerarbitration.com/2020/11/12/arbitration-of-consumer-disputes-in-france-get-thee-behind-me-competence-competence/ (last visited 3 February 2021).
398. Discussed above, para. 251.
399. *See* Antoine Cottin & Florian Renaux, "2020 in Review: Arbitration-related Developments in France" Kluwer Arbitration Blog (31 January 2021), online: https://arbitrationblog.kluwerarbitration.com/2021/01/31/2020-in-review-arbitration-related-developments-in-france/ (last visited 3 February 2021).
400. Consumer Rights Act 2015, Schedule 4, para. 34.
401. *See, e.g., Director General of Fair Trading v. First National Bank Plc* [2001] UKHL 52 at para. 17, [2001] 3 WLR 1297 (HL) (it should be noted that although the case concerned a provision for interest in a consumer credit agreement and not arbitration, the decision is relevant to arbitration because the House of Lords defined the two key elements in the definition of "unfairness"—being "significant imbalance" and lack of "good faith"—under the 1994 Unfair Terms in Consumer Contracts Regulations. Under the 1994 Regulations, an arbitration provision, too, could be found "unfair"); *Bryen & Langley Ltd v. Boston* [2005] EWCA Civ 973 at para. 45, 2005 WL 1767579 (elaborating on the definition of unfair terms); *Mylcrist Builders Ltd v. Buck* [2008] EWHC 2172 (TCC) at paras. 51, 53, 59, 2008 WL 3996507 (relying on the two foregoing decisions and holding that the arbitration clause in a builder's standard terms was not binding on the customer, as it was unfair under the Unfair Terms in Consumer Contracts Regulations 1999 because it would cause a significant imbalance in the parties' rights and obligations to the customer's detriment by preventing her from taking legal action other than arbitration).

Switzerland

254. In Switzerland, as explained earlier, there is no specific restriction on the arbitrability of consumer disputes in international matters.[402] However, that is not the case for domestic consumer disputes. Article 35 of the Swiss Civil Procedure Code does not allow *pre-dispute* waiver of courts' jurisdiction. As such, parties can enter into an arbitration agreement only after a dispute arises.

Canada

255. In Canada, the province of Québec and two of the common law provinces (Ontario and Alberta) provide for the invalidity of *pre-dispute* arbitration agreements through their Consumer Protection Acts.[403] Further, the Civil Code of Québec imposes another restriction on the arbitration of consumer disputes. Article 3149, in the part of the Civil Code that covers the international jurisdiction of Québec courts, prohibits any waiver of courts' jurisdiction in consumer disputes. In *Dell Computer Corp v. Union des Consommateurs* (2007), the Supreme Court of Canada held that the restriction in Article 3149 applies only when a "foreign element" is involved.[404] The Court defined a "foreign element" as a "point of contact that is legally relevant to a foreign country which means that the contact must be sufficient to play a role in determining whether a court has jurisdiction"—such as when there is a "fact, event or transaction that is so closely connected with a foreign system of law as to necessitate recourse to that system," but the mere fact that an arbitration proceeding is governed by the rules of a foreign institution would not qualify it as a "foreign element."[405]

256. In British Columbia (the third common law province of Canada), a consumer dispute may not be submitted to arbitration where the claimant acts as a *public interest plaintiff* (usually in a class action), whereas, if the claimant is the one who has suffered damages and does not act as a public interest plaintiff, the dispute is arbitrable. The Business Practices and Consumer Protection Act (BPCPA) of British Columbia includes two provisions that provide two different causes of action. Section 171(1) of the BCPCPA allows a person who has *suffered damages* as a result of a violation of the Act to bring an action, while section 172(1) allows nearly *anyone*, whether or not affected by the consumer transaction violating the BCPCA, to bring an action. In *Seidel v. Telus Communications Inc* (2011), the Supreme Court of Canada ruled that claims brought under section 171(1) are private claims and may be submitted to arbitration, while claims brought under section 172(1) are public interest remedies that could be lodged

---

402. *See* above, para. 243.
403. Consumer Protection Act of Québec, s. 11.1; Consumer Protection Act of Ontario, ss. 7, 8; Consumer Protection Act of Alberta, s. 16. It should be noted that the Consumer Protection Act of Alberta is the result of the 2017 amendments to Alberta's former consumer-related legislation (Fair Trading Act), which provided for more severe restrictions on arbitration of consumer disputes. Under s. 16 of the Fair Trading Act, arbitration of consumer disputes was prohibited *unless* the Minister would approve the arbitration agreement. An example of application of s. 16 was the decision of the Alberta Court of Appeal in *Young v. National Money Mart Co*, 2013 ABCA 264 at paras. 16–20, 556 AR 173.
404. *Dell Computer Corp v. Union des Consommateurs*, 2007 SCC 34 at para. 3, 284 DLR (4th) 577.
405. *Ibid.*, at paras. 25–28, 52 (internal citations omitted).

by any person.[406] Thus, the Court held that such claims are non-arbitrable and any class action waiver in the arbitration clause would be void.[407] More recently, in *Williams v. Amazon* (2020), which was before the BC Supreme Court, even the defendant conceded that, as a result of *Seidel*, the consumer claims portion of the dispute could not be referred to arbitration.[408]

257. With respect to consumers' privacy rights, the Supreme Court of Canada has taken an even more restrictive approach to arbitration and forum selection clauses. In *Douez v. Facebook* (2017)—which was brought by a Facebook user against that company with respect to the use of her personal information—the Supreme Court of Canada refused to enforce the forum selection clause in Facebook's mandatory Terms of Use.[409] The Court ruled as follows: although section 4 of the BC Privacy Act does not include a "clear and specific language" to override the parties' forum selection clause and although the clause itself was valid, it could not be enforced because there were "strong public policy reasons" against the enforcement of that otherwise valid clause.[410] Those public policy reasons included the existence of "a consumer contract of adhesion," "the grossly uneven bargaining power between the parties and the importance of adjudicating quasi-constitutional privacy rights in the province."[411]

Hong Kong

258. In Hong Kong, under section 15(1) of the Control of Exemption Clause Ordinance Cap 71 (CECO) the general rule is that, for an arbitration agreement to be enforceable, it should be signed by the consumer after the dispute arises. If it is a *pre-dispute* arbitration agreement, only the consumer may invoke the arbitration clause. However, under section 15(2) of the CECO, the restriction applies only to cases that involve negligence liability, liability arising in contracts with standard terms, unreasonable indemnity clauses, and "miscellaneous contracts under which goods pass."

259. However, Hong Kong courts have taken a pro-arbitration approach in this regard by not interpreting the term "consumer" broadly. For example, in *Fung Hing Chiu Cyril & Anor v. Henry Wai & Co* (2018), the Hong Kong Court of First Instance referred the

406. *Seidel v. Telus Communications Inc*, 2011 SCC 15 at paras. 7, 10, 31–34, 37, 43–45, [2011] 1 SCR 531.
407. *Ibid.*
408. *Williams v. Amazon.com, Inc*, 2020 BCSC 300 at paras. 1–2, 4, 70–71, 80, 82, 86, 4 BLR (6th) 271.
409. *Douez v. Facebook, Inc*, 2017 SCC 33, 411 DLR (4th) 434. Although *Douez* concerns forum selection clause and not arbitration, the Supreme Court's reasoning in relation to the importance of public policy considerations makes the case relevant to the arbitrability of consumer disputes in BC law.
410. *Ibid.*, at paras. 1–4, 28–29, 31, 33, 38, 41–50.
411. *Ibid.* Three years after *Douez*, the BC Court of Appeal, in *Schuppener v. Pioneer Steel Manufacturers* (2020), held that *Douez* does not support the position that the mere existence of a forum selection clause in a standard consumer contract would raise public policy concerns. According to the Court of Appeal, it was "the gross inequality of bargaining power" between the parties that led to raising the public policy concerns, and that the existence of a standard contract only served as a "contextual factor in assessing inequality of bargaining power." *Schuppener v. Pioneer Steel Manufacturers Limited*, 2020 BCCA 19 at paras. 6, 12–14.

parties (a law firm and its former clients) to arbitration based on the pre-dispute arbitration clause in their retainer agreement, in a dispute regarding outstanding fees.[412] The Court held that the claimants could not be considered a "consumer" of legal services under the CECO and, thus, the pre-dispute arbitration clause was enforceable.[413] According to the Court, the determination that a client of legal services is a "consumer" depends on the facts of each case because the CECO protects only "weaker or less sophisticated parties dealing as consumers, who may have contract conditions imposed on them by counter-parties who are in a stronger bargaining position."[414] This, the Court found, was not the situation in the case at bar because the claimants were sophisticated persons with extensive business-related backgrounds and had more than one month to review the agreement.[415] The Court listed the following examples as clients of legal services who might be considered "consumer" under the CECO: "alone, desperate widow being ousted from her home and seeking legal advice," "an injured employee on legal aid seeking recovery of damages from his employer, who may have little bargaining power in the terms of obtaining legal assistance," or "[a]n individual client instructing solicitors to prepare a will, or to act in divorce proceedings."[416]

260. The Court, in the same case, also rejected the argument that the arbitration clause was contrary to public policy for limiting the courts' supervisory power over solicitors and firms.[417] According to the Court, despite the existence of a public policy interest for courts to exercise control over solicitors (as officers of the court), there are competing and stronger public policy interests in enforcing arbitration agreements and respecting Hong Kong's obligations under the New York Convention.[418] Furthermore, referring the matter to arbitration, the Court continued, does not amount to courts losing control over firms and solicitors because a client can later submit their complaints, along with the arbitrator's findings, to courts.[419]

The United States

261. In the US (as explained earlier), there is generally no restriction on the arbitrability of consumer disputes.[420] However, given the large number of federal statutes protecting consumers' rights, the arbitrability of a consumer dispute should be examined according to the relevant statute under which the dispute arises. Some of these statutes hold *pre-dispute* arbitration agreements to be invalid.

262. For instance, under the Dodd-Frank Wall Street Reform and Consumer Protection Act (2010) § 1414(e) (amending § 129C of the Truth in Lending Act), lenders may not

412. *Fung Hing Chiu Cyril & Anor v. Henry Wai & Co (a firm)*, [2018] 3 HKC 375 at paras. 1, 7, 15, 16, 52, [2018] HKCFI 31.
413. *Ibid.*, at paras. 36, 40, 45.
414. *Ibid.*, at para. 40.
415. *Ibid.*, at paras. 43–45.
416. *Ibid.*, at paras. 43, 47.
417. *Ibid.*, at para. 35.
418. *Ibid.*, at paras. 21, 33.
419. *Ibid.*, at para. 26.
420. *See* above, para. 241.

incorporate pre-dispute arbitration clauses into residential mortgage loans or in extension of credit under an open-end consumer credit plan that is secured by the principal dwelling of the consumer. Also, under 15 USC § 1226(a)(2), with respect to "motor vehicle franchise contracts,"[421] only post-dispute arbitration agreements are valid and the agreement must be in writing.

263. Furthermore, with respect to disputes relating to financial products and services, the Consumer Financial Protection Bureau (CFPB) was tasked under § 1028 of the Dodd-Frank Act to submit a report to Congress on the use of pre-dispute arbitration agreements against consumers and was authorized to adopt necessary regulations. The CFPB submitted its report to Congress in 2015,[422] and in 2017 issued its final rule, prohibiting consumer financial product/service providers from relying on pre-dispute arbitration agreements to stop consumers from launching/joining a class action in court.[423] However, the CFPB rule did not take effect because the then Republican-controlled House of Representatives exercised its authority under the Congressional Review Act[424] to pass a resolution nullifying the CFPB rule.[425] In addition, Congress enacted the Economic Growth, Regulatory Relief and Consumer Protection Act in 2018, which exempted smaller banks from the application of the Dodd-Frank Act by increasing the applicability threshold of that Act.[426]

264. Given that, in the US, an arbitration agreement waiving any class proceeding in consumer matters is enforceable due to the preemptive effect of the FAA,[427] the CFPB rule—had it been implemented—would have acted as an exception to the authority of the FAA[428] and was likely to result in the total removal of arbitration clauses from

421. The term "motor vehicle franchise contract" is defined as "a contract under which a motor vehicle manufacturer, importer, or distributor sells motor vehicles to any other person for resale to an ultimate purchaser and authorizes such other person to repair and service the manufacturer's motor vehicles." 15 USC § 1226(a)(1)(B).
422. CFPB, *Arbitration Study: Report to Congress, pursuant to Dodd–Frank Wall Street Reform and Consumer Protection Act § 1028(a)* (2015), online: http://files.consumerfinance.gov/f/201503_cfpb_arbitration-study-report-to-congress-2015.pdf (last visited 15 June 2022).
423. Arbitration Agreements, 82 Fed Reg 33428 (10 July 2017) § 1040.4.(a)(1), online: https://www.gpo.gov/fdsys/pkg/FR-2017-07-19/pdf/2017-14225.pdf (it was supposed to be codified at 12 CFR pt 1040), online: https://www.federalregister.gov/documents/2017/11/22/2017-25324/arbitration-agreements (last visited 15 June 2022).
424. Congressional Review Act, 5 USC §§ 801-808 (allowing Congress to review and overrule a new federal regulation), online: http://uscode.house.gov/view.xhtml?path=/prelim@title5/part1/chapter8&edition=prelim (last visited 15 June 2022).
425. Joint Resolution, HR J Res 111, 115th Cong (2017) (enacted) Pub L 115–74, online: https://www.congress.gov/115/plaws/publ74/PLAW-115publ74.pdf (last visited 15 June 2022).
426. Economic Growth, Regulatory Relief and Consumer Protection Act, Pub L 115–174 (2018) § 401(a), online: https://www.govinfo.gov/content/pkg/PLAW-115publ174/pdf/PLAW-115publ174.pdf (last visited 15 June 2022).
427. According to the Supreme Court's decision in *AT&T Mobility LLC v. Concepcion*, 131 S Ct 1740 (2011) at 1746–1747, 1753.
428. According to the CFPB: "Nor does the Bureau believe that the rule creates any uncertainty as to the scope of preemption under the Federal Arbitration Act, since the Supreme Court has been quite clear that Congress can authorize exceptions to the FAA by statute as Congress did in s. 1028 [of the Dodd-Frank Act]." Arbitration Agreements, 82 Fed Reg 33428 (10 July 2017) at 33309, online: https://www.gpo.gov/fdsys/pkg/FR-2017-07-19/pdf/2017-14225.pdf (last visited 15 June 2022).

covered financial agreements because—as a commentator explains—"without the 'carrot' of a class arbitration waiver, a company has no incentive to offer, much less to cover the costs of, individual consumer arbitration."[429]

265. There are federal rules limiting consumer arbitration that went through a similar roller coaster. For example, the Centers for Medicare & Medicaid Services (CMS)—which is part of the US Department of Health and Human Services—published in 2016 its final rule prohibiting the use of pre-dispute arbitration clauses in long-term care facilities agreements.[430] The American Health Care Association and a group of nursing homes challenged the rule in court,[431] as a result of which the CMS suspended the enforcement of the rule.[432] The rule was then revised in 2019 and the prohibition against pre-dispute arbitration clauses was lifted.[433] However, the revised rule precludes long-term care facilities from requiring the residents or their representatives to enter into arbitration agreements "as a condition of admission to, or as a requirement to continue to receive care at, the facility."[434] The revised rule was again challenged by long-term-care facilities, but the Court of Appeals for the Eight Circuit upheld it.[435]

266. Likewise, in 2016, the Federal Communication Commission (FCC) published its rule titled Protecting the Privacy of Customers of Broadband and Other Telecommunications Services, which imposes significant restrictions on the use of consumers' information by internet service providers.[436] In the rule, the FCC asserted that:

> [W]e continue to have serious concerns about the impact on consumers from the inclusion of mandatory arbitration requirements as a standard part of many contracts for communications services. The time has come to address this

429. Ramona L Lampley, "The CFPB Proposed Arbitration Ban, the Rule, the Data, and Some Considerations for Change" Business Law Today (May 2017), online: https://commons.stmarytx.edu/cgi/viewcontent.cgi?referer=&httpsredir=1&article=1070&context=facarticles (last visited 15 June 2022); Manatt Phelps & Phillips LLP, "CFPB Launches New Battle: Proposal to Ban Arbitration Clauses Blocking Group Action" (29 October 2015), online: https://www.manatt.com/insights/newsletters/financial-services-law/cfpb-launches-new-battle-proposal-to-ban-arbitrat#Article1 (last visited 15 June 2022).
430. Medicare and Medicaid Programs; Reform of Requirements for Long-Term Care Facilities, § 483.70, 81 Fed Reg 68688 (2016), online: https://www.gpo.gov/fdsys/pkg/FR-2016-10-04/pdf/2016-23503.pdf (last visited 15 June 2022).
431. *American Health Care Association v. Burwell*, 217 F Supp 3d 921 (ND Missi 2016).
432. CMS, *Memorandum* (16 December 2016), online: https://www.cms.gov/Medicare/Provider-Enrollment-and-Certification/SurveyCertificationGenInfo/Downloads/Survey-and-Cert-Letter-17-12.pdf (last visited 15 June 2022).
433. Medicare and Medicaid Programs; Revision of Requirements for Long-Term Care Facilities: Arbitration Agreements, 84 Fed Reg 34718, online: https://www.govinfo.gov/content/pkg/FR-2019-07-18/pdf/2019-14945.pdf (last visited 15 June 2022). The final version of the rule has been codified in 42 CFR 483.70(n), online: https://www.ecfr.gov/current/title-42/chapter-IV/subchapter-G/part-483/subpart-B/section-483.70 (last visited 15 June 2022).
434. 42 CFR 483.70(n)(1).
435. *Northport Health Services of Arkansas, LLC v. US Department of Health and Human Services*, 14 F4th 856 (8th Cir 2021) at 867.
436. Protecting the Privacy of Customers of Broadband and Other Telecommunications Services, 81 Fed Reg 87274 (2016), online: https://www.govinfo.gov/content/pkg/FR-2016-12-02/pdf/2016-28006.pdf (last visited 15 June 2022).

> important consumer protection issue in a comprehensive way. Therefore, we will initiate a rulemaking on the use of mandatory arbitration requirements in consumer contracts for broadband and other communications services, acting on a notice of proposed rulemaking in February 2017.[437]

However, Congress nullified the FCC rule in 2017.[438]

267. This book does not discuss US states' arbitration laws and, as such, it should be noted that not all state courts have strictly followed the Supreme Court's favorable stand on the arbitration of consumer disputes. Some state courts have distinguished the case before them from Supreme Court precedents. For example, the Supreme Court of California in *McGill v. Citibank* (2017), held that a pre-dispute arbitration agreement waiving a consumer's statutory right to seek public injunctive relief in any forum under the California Consumers Legal Remedies Act, the Unfair Competition Law, or the False Advertising Law violated California public policy and, given that this rule in California law is not preempted by the FAA, ruled that the agreement was unenforceable.[439] Subsequently, the Court of Appeals for the Ninth Circuit has ruled (in at least three cases) that the FAA does not preempt California's *McGill* rule, and in two of those cases, the US Supreme Court denied the petition for writ of certiorari.[440]

3. Framework Within the European Union

268. In addition to the approaches discussed in previous sections, the relevant legal framework operative within the EU (including France and Germany) should now be discussed.

269. The framework, which was introduced by Directive 2013/11/EU[441] and Regulation (EU) No 524/2013,[442] enables consumers to access out-of-court dispute resolution mechanisms on a voluntary basis and without jeopardizing their right to seek remedy before courts.[443] Therefore, the framework introduced by the Directive and the Regulation does not involve arbitration in the sense of a mechanism that provides for a final and binding award. Under Article 2 of the Regulation, which is directly applicable in EU Member States, the European Commission oversees the operation of an online dispute resolution platform (called the ODR Platform) for disputes between consumers and online traders established within the EU. Further,

---

437. *Ibid.*, at 87318.
438. SJ Res 34, 115th Cong (2017), online: https://www.congress.gov/115/bills/sjres34/BILLS-115sjres34enr.pdf (last visited 15 June 2022).
439. *McGill v. Citibank*, 393 P3d 85 (Cal Sup Ct 2017).
440. *Blair v. Rent-A-Center, Inc*, 928 F3d 819 (9th Cir 2019); *McArdle v. AT&T Mobility LLC*, 772 Fed Appx 575 (9th Cir 2019) cert denied, 140 S Ct 2827 (2020); *Tillage v. Comcast Corporation*, 772 Fed Appx 569 (9th Cir 2019), cert denied, 140 S Ct 2827 (2020).
441. Directive 2013/11/EU of the European Parliament and of the Council of 21 May 2013 on Alternative Dispute Resolution for Consumer Disputes.
442. Regulation (EU) No 524/2013 of the European Parliament and of the Council of 21 May 2013 on Online Dispute Resolution for Consumer Disputes.
443. Article 1 of Directive 2013/11/EU and Recital 26 of Regulation (EU) No 524/2013.

under Article 14(1), all such traders must provide an electronic link to the ODR Platform on their website.

270. Prior to Brexit, the same mechanism was also applicable in the UK as an EU Member State. After Brexit, the UK revoked the above Regulation through the Consumer Protection (Amendment etc.) (EU Exit) Regulations 2018; consequently, consumers in the UK can no longer access the ODR Platform. However, the situation is different with respect to the Directive. Before Brexit, it had been transposed into UK law through the Alternative Dispute Resolution for Consumer Disputes (Competent Authorities and Information) Regulations 2015 and then, after Brexit, it remained part of the UK domestic law but was amended by the Consumer Protection (Amendment etc.) (EU Exit) Regulations 2018. The UK regulations set up the competent authorities to certify ADR schemes and set out the standards that ADR providers must meet in order to be certified.

D. CORPORATE LAW

271. All jurisdictions studied for this book allow the arbitration of corporate disputes, but not necessarily to the same extent. As will be explained below, the US, France, Switzerland, and the Canadian provinces of Ontario and Alberta have all taken liberal approaches to the arbitration of corporate disputes, while other jurisdictions apply some restrictions. In two of the civil law jurisdictions (China and Germany), the restrictions concern the arbitrability of corporate disputes, whereas in the majority of common law jurisdictions that apply some restrictions, those restrictions concern the remedies a tribunal may award. As such, the discussion in this section is divided into three subsections: (1) Jurisdictions that Have Liberal Approaches; (2) Jurisdictions Limiting the Arbitrability of Corporate Disputes; and (3) Jurisdictions Limiting the Arbitral Remedies in Corporate Disputes.

1. Jurisdictions That Have Liberal Approaches

272. This group includes the US, France, Switzerland, and the Canadian provinces of Ontario and Alberta. Their approaches are considered liberal because their legislative framework, together with their case law, allow for a remarkable range of corporate disputes to be arbitrated without imposing any specific restrictions.

The United States

273. In the US, where corporate law is mainly a state matter,[444] Delaware is a significant jurisdiction because more than 90% of "all US initial public offerings are

444. This is despite an increase in federal laws and regulations affecting corporate governance. Faith Stevelman, "Regulatory Competition, Choice of Forum, and Delaware's Stake in Corporate Law" (2009) 34 Del J Corp L 57 at 58. It should be noted that "when corporations make public offerings, they engage in interstate commerce, thus making it possible for them to use the

entities registered with Delawar,"[445] and it is home to more than two-thirds of all Fortune 500 companies.[446]

274. From the legislative perspective, §§ 102(b), 109(b), and 115 of the Delaware General Corporation Law (DGCL) are relevant. These three provisions apply to the contents of a certificate of incorporation and bylaws, and their broad scope allows corporations to insert an arbitration provision in any of those corporate documents. However, § 115 was added to the DGCL in 2015,[447] which provides that "no provision of the certificate of incorporation or the bylaws may prohibit bringing [internal corporate claims] in the courts of this State." According to § 115, "internal corporate claims" include "claims in the right of the corporation, (i) that are based upon a violation of a duty by a current or former director or officer or stockholder in such capacity, or (ii) as to which this title confers jurisdiction upon the Court of Chancery." Also relevant is the Delaware Limited Liability Act, where § 18-109(d) expressly allows managers and members to include an arbitration provision in their limited liability company (LLC) agreement.

275. Delaware courts had strongly supported the arbitrability of corporate disputes up until 2015—when § 115 was added to the DGCL. For example, in *Douzinas v. American Bureau of Shipping, Inc* (2006), the Court of Chancery held that fiduciary claims brought by minority members of an LLC against a managing member should be referred to arbitration pursuant to the arbitration provision in their LLC agreement.[448] In so holding, the Court of Chancery followed the Delaware Supreme Court's 1999 decision in *Elf Atochem North America, Inc v. Jaffari*, where that Court held that fiduciary duty claims by an LLC member were within the scope of the arbitration provision in an LLC agreement.[449] The *Douzinas* Court of Chancery also distinguished the case before it and the *Elf* decision from a later decision of the Delaware Supreme Court in *Parfi Holding AB v. Mirror Image Internet Inc* (2002),[450] where the Supreme Court ruled against compelling the arbitration provision in an underwriting agreement for fiduciary claims brought by minority shareholders. In *Douzinas*, the Court of Chancery reasoned that, in *Parfi*, the arbitration provision was contained in an underwriting agreement which, unlike the constituting agreement of a corporation, would not cover fiduciary duty claims.[451] Commentators had even argued that a

FAA." Garry D Hartlieb, "Enforceability of Mandatory Arbitration Clauses for Shareholder-Corporation Disputes" (2014) 4:1 Mich Bus Entp L Rev 131 at 160 DOI: 10.3663 9/mbelr.4.1.enforceability.

445. Delaware Division of Corporations, *2020 Annual Report Statistics*, online: https://corpfiles.delaware.gov/Annual-Reports/Division-of-Corporations-2020-Annual-Report.pdf (last visited 15 June 2022).

446. *Ibid.*

447. 80 Del Laws, c 40, § 5 (2015), online: https://legis.delaware.gov/SessionLaws/Chapter?id=15571 (last visited 9 June 2022).

448. *Douzinas v. American Bureau of Shipping, Inc*, 888 A2d 1146 (Del Ch 2006).

449. *Elf Atochem North America, Inc v. Jaffari*, 727 A 2d 286 (Del 1999).

450. *Parfi Holding AB v. Mirror Image Internet, Inc*, 817 A2d 149 (Del 2002) at 155–158 (holding that minority shareholders' claims against majority shareholder for breach of fiduciary duty may not be referred to arbitration pursuant to the arbitration provision in an underwriting agreement).

451. *Douzinas v. American Bureau of Shipping, Inc*, 888 A2d 1146 (Del Ch 2006) at 1148–1150.

board-adopted bylaw—mandating arbitration of stockholder disputes and eliminating the right to pursue such claims on a class action basis—was likely to be enforceable,[452] because of the Supreme Court decision in *American Express Co v. Italian Colors Restaurant* (2013)[453] when read together with the Delaware Court of Chancery decision in *Boilermakers Local 154 Retirement Fund v. Chevron Corp* (2013).[454]

276. However, with the addition of § 115 to the DGCL[455] the Delaware law approach to the arbitrability of "internal corporate claims" is no longer clear. In *Salzberg v. Sciabacucchi* (2021), which concerned the validity of forum selection clauses in favor of federal courts, the Delaware Supreme Court noted in a footnote that:

> Much of the opposition to [forum selection clauses in favor of federal courts] seems to be based upon a concern that if upheld, the 'next move' might be forum provisions that require arbitration of internal corporate claims. Such provisions, at least from our state law perspective, would violate Section 115 [of the DGCL] which provides that, 'no provision of the certificate of incorporation or the bylaws may prohibit bringing such claims in the courts of this state.'[456]

277. Future cases in Delaware courts will show how much § 115 has in fact rolled back the arbitrability of corporate disputes in Delaware, and whether the prohibition in § 115 is preempted by the FAA.[457]

278. Apart from the not-so-arbitration-friendly developments in Delaware, courts in other US states have long enforced arbitration clauses of shareholders' agreements with respect to corporate disputes, including claims as to breach of fiduciary duty, corporate waste, diversion of assets by a corporate officer and stockholder, failure to account, refusal to permit inspection of corporate records, minority shareholder oppression, conversion and conspiracy.[458]

France

279. France has express legislative provisions that deal with the arbitrability of corporate disputes, as well as remarkably liberal case law dealing with the matter.

452. Claudia H Allen, "Bylaws Mandating Arbitration of Stockholder Disputes?" (2015) 39 Del J Corp L 751 at 753–756.
453. *American Express Co v. Italian Colors Restaurant*, 133 S Ct 2304 (2013) (holding that an arbitration agreement waiving any class arbitration is enforceable, even where the costs of consumers' individually arbitrating a federal statutory claim exceed the potential recovery).
454. *Boilermakers Local 154 Retirement Fund v. Chevron Corp*, 73 A3d 934 (Del Ch 2013) (upholding the statutory and contractual validity of the bylaws adopted by Chevron Corporation and FedEx Corporation requiring that stockholder class actions, derivative actions, and other intra-corporate disputes be litigated exclusively in Delaware).
455. Discussed above, in the current Chapter, para. 274.
456. *Salzberg v. Sciabacucchi*, 227 A3d 102 (Del 2021) at 113, n 169.
457. The preemptive effect of the FAA has been discussed above, para. 88.
458. *See, e.g.*, *Siegel v. Ribak*, 249 NYS2d 903 (NY Sup 1964); *Denihan v. Denihan*, 506 NYS2d 39 (NY App Div 1986); *Ehrlich v. Stein*, 533 NYS2d 517 (NY App Div 1988); *Breakstone v. Breakstone Homes, Inc*, 999 So2d 731 (Fla Dist Ct App 2009); *Edenbaum v. Moore*, 2012 WL 33938 (NJ Super Ct App Div 2012); *Baty v. Bowen, Miclette & Britt, Inc*, 423 SWd 427 (Tex App 2013) at 429, 433, 442.

Under Article L721-3 of the Commercial Code, which has a broad scope, disputes in relation to commercial companies are arbitrable. This includes matters such as disputes amongst partners/shareholders, disputes between partners/shareholders and their company, disputes between the company and its directors, and disputes in relation to the transfer of corporate minority shares.[459]

280. According to French case law, even disputes as to the dissolution of a company may be submitted to arbitration and the tribunal may appoint a liquidator. In 1967, in *Veuve Lemaitre v. Deshayes et autre*, the Court of Cassation held that a broad arbitration clause in the articles of association of a French company should be enforced when there is a dispute as to the dissolution of the company if two conditions are met: (i) the clause is broad enough to cover all disputes between its members as well as between the members and the company, and (ii) the clause does not contain any waiver of or restriction on the member's rights to ask for the dissolution of the company.[460] In 1993, the Colmar Court of Appeal in *Marin et autre v. Marin* held that a domestic arbitral tribunal that decided a dispute between two equal shareholders as to the dissolution of a company—on the basis of the arbitration clause in the articles of association—and that appointed a liquidator had not acted in violation of public policy rules.[461]

281. However, in holding that the award was not contrary to any public policy rule, the Colmar Court of Appeal observed the following relevant points about the facts: (i) the total number of shareholders was very limited; and (ii) the company that was dissolved was given the chance to appoint an arbitrator and participate in the arbitration proceedings.[462] This last point brings us to a more recent case. The 2015 decision of the Paris Court of Appeal in *Société Coralsa Corp Alimentaria SA v. Société Ingelco* suggests that an arbitral tribunal may decide on the dissolution and liquidation of a company, provided that the company participates in the arbitration proceeding and is given the opportunity to be heard.[463]

Switzerland

282. Following the 2020 amendment of Chapter 12 of the PILA, Article 178(4) has been added to the Act, which explicitly allows for an arbitration provision to be included in

459. Philippe Fouchard, "La laborieuse réforme de la clause compromissoire par la loi du 15 mai 2001" (2001) 3 Rev Arb 397 at para. 34.
460. *Veuve Lemaitre v. Deshayes et autre*, Court of Cassation, Commerciale Chamber, 30 January 1967, Decision No 64.13-692.
461. *Marin et autre v. Marin*, Colmar Court of Appeal, 21 September 1993, Decision No 5378/92 (reasoning that although Art. 51 of Decree of 23 March 1967 [now Art. R210-15 of the Commercial Code] provides that dissolving a company is within the jurisdiction of the Commercial Court, this rule operates only to clarify the Commercial Court's jurisdiction as against other courts and does not exclude arbitration).
462. *Ibid.*
463. *Société Coralsa Corp Alimentaria SA, société de droit cubain v. Société Ingelco, société de droit panaméen*, Paris Court of Appeal, 20 January 2015, reported in (2015) 33:4 ASA Bulletin 938 at 938–939, 941–942. *See* Matthieu de Boisséson & Marie-Isabelle Barretto Delleur, "Note: Coralsa Corporation Alimentaria SA (Coralsa) v. Ingelco SA, Court of Appeal of Paris, Case No. RG n° 12/16039 and 13/17333, 20 January 2015" (2015) 12:48 Revista Brasileira de Arbitragem 181 at 184.

articles of association. Also, the amendments to the Code of Obligations (effective as of 2023) have added three new articles to the Code: 697n, 764(2), and 797a. The added articles expressly allow three types of Swiss entities (namely, companies limited by shares, partnerships limited by shares, and limited liability companies) to include an arbitration clause in their articles of association.[464] However, the arbitration will be governed by Part III of the Civil Procedure Code, and not Chapter 12 of the PILA.[465] Furthermore, the arbitration clause in the articles of association "*shall* in any event ensure that persons who may be *directly* affected by the legal consequences of the arbitral award are notified of the instigation and conclusion of the proceedings and may participate in appointing the arbitral tribunal and in the proceedings as an intervening party."[466] In response to these developments, the Swiss Arbitration Centre issued the Supplemental Swiss Rules for Corporate Law Disputes as additional rules to the Centre's arbitration rules.[467]

283. Even prior to the above developments, the Swiss Federal Supreme Court, in *BGE 136 III 107, 8 December 2009* (a domestic matter), had noted that generally an arbitration clause in the articles of association of a company was valid for disputes between the company and its board members and/or shareholders. And more than a decade prior to that decision, in *BGE 124 III 83, 19 December 1997*, which concerned a dispute as to the shareholders' right of first refusal, the Federal Supreme Court had held that an arbitration clause in the articles of association of a company was valid. Commentators were also of the opinion that disputes as to the nullity of partnerships and companies and decisions taken in shareholders' general meetings were all matters that were generally arbitrable, but the company/partnership had to be a party to the arbitration.[468]

Canada (Provinces of Alberta and Ontario)

284. The Canadian federal and provincial legislation relevant to corporate matters (excepting the province of Ontario) have no specific provisions on the arbitrability of corporate disputes.[469] Therefore, it has fallen to the case law of each province to

464. In French, online: https://www.fedlex.admin.ch/eli/cc/27/317_321_377/fr (last visited 28 April 2023); English translation, online: https://www.fedlex.admin.ch/eli/cc/27/317_321_377/en (last visited 28 April 2023).
465. *Ibid.*, at Arts. 697n(2), 764(2), 797a.
466. *Ibid.*, at Arts. 697n(3), 764(2), 797a (emphasis added).
467. Federal Act on the Amendment of the Swiss Civil Code (Part Five: The Code of Obligations) (1911, consolidated version as of February 2023).
468. *See, e.g.*, Paolo Michele Patocchi, "National Report for Switzerland (2018-2020)" in Jan Paulsson & Lise Bosman, eds, *ICCA International Handbook on Commercial Arbitration* (Kluwer Law International, 2020) 1 at 32; Elliott Geisinger, "Implementing the New York Convention in Switzerland" (2008) 25:6 J Int'l Arb 691 at 701 DOI: 10.54648/joia2008056; Marc Blessing, "The New International Arbitration Law in Switzerland: A Significant Step Towards Liberalism" (1988) 5:2 J Int'l Arb 9 at 25 DOI: 10.54648/joia1988014; Mariella Orelli, "Commentary on Chapter 12 PILS, Article 177 [Arbitrability]" in Manuel Arroyo, ed, *Arbitration in Switzerland: The Practitioner's Guide*, (Kluwer Law International, 2018) 61 at para. 4.
469. For federal laws, *see* Canada Business Corporations Act, RSC 1985, c C-44; Canada Corporations Act, RSC 1970, c C-32. For Alberta, *see* Business Corporations Act, RSA 2000, c

develop principles in relation to the arbitrability of corporate disputes. The discussion in the following paragraphs demonstrates that the two provinces of Alberta and Ontario have developed a liberal approach to the arbitrability of corporate disputes, in that they even regard oppression claims as arbitrable.[470]

285. In Alberta, until the 2010s, the King's Bench had been reluctant to regard oppression claims as arbitrable. For example, in *Scozzafava v. Prosperi* (2003), the Court refused to enforce an arbitration agreement for an oppression claim.[471] However, in the 2010s, the King's Bench liberalized its approach to the arbitrability of corporate disputes and, more specifically, oppression claims. In *Murphy v. Cahill* (2013), the Court rejected an application to appoint an interim receiver-manager in accordance with the oppression claim provisions of the Business Corporations Act of Alberta, and held that the parties' management dispute within the company should be referred to arbitration on the basis of the arbitration provision in their unanimous shareholder agreement.[472] Likewise, in *Black Fluid Inc v. Opulence Clothing Inc* (2014), the Court noted that shareholders of a corporation may include an arbitration provision in their unanimous shareholder agreement, to address a future deadlock situation that might arise.[473]

286. In Ontario, unlike other provinces, the Business Corporations Act expressly allows shareholders to include an arbitration clause in their unanimous shareholder agreement as a mechanism to resolve disputes pertaining to the agreement. Further, in *Woolcock v. Bushert* (2004), the Ontario Court of Appeal held that claims of oppression, punitive damages, wrongful dismissal, and inducing the company to breach the employment contract with its director were all within the scope of the arbitration clause of the shareholder agreement and should be referred to arbitration under the Arbitration Act of Ontario.[474] The *Woolcock* decision also clarified that oppression claims are generally considered to be arbitrable in Ontario.[475]

287. However, it should be noted that the liberal approach to oppression claims preferred by the Ontario Court of Appeal in cases such as *Woolcock* was not always

B-9; Companies Act, RSA 2000, c C-21. For British Columbia, *see* Business Corporations Act, SBC 2002, c 57. For Québec, *see* Business Corporations Act, CQLR c S-31.1; Companies Act, CQLR c C-38.

470. The provinces of Québec and British Columbia are discussed in the third group "Jurisdictions with Restrictions on Remedies."
471. *Scozzafava v. Prosperi*, 2003 ABQB 248 at paras. 66, 68, [2003] 6 WWR 351.
472. *Murphy v. Cahill*, 2013 ABQB 335 at paras. 1–13, 568 AR 80.
473. *Black Fluid Inc v. Opulence Clothing Inc*, 2014 ABQB 138 at para. 38, 4 Alta LR (6th) 414.
474. *Woolcock v. Bushert* (2004), 246 DLR (4th) 139 (Ont CA) at paras. 20–33, [2004] OJ No 4498.
475. The *Woolcock* decision was not the first time that Ontario courts allowed the arbitration of oppression claims. For example, in *Kints v. Kints* (1998), the Ontario Court (General Division) stayed the proceeding pursuant to Art. 7(1) of the Arbitration Act of Ontario in favor of arbitration of the oppression claims. *Kints v. Kints*, [1998] OJ No 3244, 1998 CarswellOnt 3188. The Ontario Court of Appeal affirmed the *Woolcock* approach in *Haas v. Gunasekaram*, 2016 ONCA 744, [2016] OJ No 5286.

favored by the Ontario Superior Court of Justice—at least not until the 2010s. This Court had held, in different decisions, that for statutory claims under the Business Corporations Act of Ontario to be arbitrable, the parties' agreement had to be explicit about encompassing the determination of statutory obligations and remedies.[476] This meant that arbitral tribunals would have jurisdiction over a wide range of corporate disputes, including oppression claims, but the arbitration clause had to be clear and explicit about covering statutory obligations and remedies.[477]

288. However, this changed in the 2010s when the Ontario Superior Court of Justice aligned its approach with the liberal approach of the Ontario Court of Appeal in that the Superior Court no longer requires the arbitration clause to be clear and explicit about oppression claims.[478]

2. Jurisdictions Limiting the Arbitrability of Corporate Disputes

289. Among the jurisdictions studied for this text, only two jurisdictions (from the civil law camp) apply significant restrictions on the arbitrability of corporate disputes: China and Germany.

China (Mainland)

290. Prior to 2020, China had four major legislative texts that were applicable to foreign investors with a permanent presence in the country: the Company Law, the Chinese-Foreign Equity Joint Ventures Law, the Chinese-Foreign Contractual Joint Ventures Law, and the Law on Wholly Foreign-Owned Enterprises.[479] In 2020, the latter three laws were repealed when a new law (namely, the Foreign Investment Law) came into effect. However, according to Article 42 of the Foreign Investment Law, enterprises that were already established based on those three repealed laws "may retain their original organization forms and other aspects for five years." As such, some provisions of the three laws remain relevant until 2025.

291. Of those three laws, only the two that deal with joint ventures contain provisions on arbitration. First, Article 16 of the Chinese-Foreign Equity Joint Ventures Law allows for the arbitration of "any dispute" between the partners and the venture. However, the

---

476. *Pandora Select Partners LP v. Strategy Real Estate Investments Ltd* (2007), 27 BLR (4th) 299 (Ont Sup Ct) at paras. 1, 15–17, 20, 22, [2007] OJ No 993; *Armstrong v. Northern Eyes Inc* (2000), 48 OR (3d) 442 (Ont Sup Ct) at paras. 14, 17, 22, 36, 8 BLR (3d) 46.

477. *See* Byron Shaw, "The Arbitrability of Oppression Claims" (2011) 69:1 Advocate (Vancouver) 21 at 23.

478. *See, e.g.*, *Blind Spot Holdings Ltd v. Decast Holdings Inc*, 2014 ONSC 1760 at para. 28; *The Campaign for the Inclusion of People who are Deaf and Hard of Hearing v. Canadian Hearing Society*, 2018 ONSC 5445 at paras. 48–50, 58–59, 64, 65; *Randhawa v. Randhawa*, 2021 ONSC 3643 at paras. 4, 9, 12–13, 20, 24–30; *Pezo v. Pezo et al*, 2021 ONSC 5406 at paras. 1–3, 35, 38–39, 41, 49(ii), 49(iv)(2)(b), 50(ii), 50(v), 51–57.

479. *See* UK Institute of Export, *Doing Business in China Guide*, 2nd ed (International Market Advisor, 2015) at 109–111, online: http://www.china.doingbusinessguide.co.uk/media/880543/Doing_Business_in_China_Guide_PDF.pdf (last visited 5 February 2023); Ligang Song, Ross Garnaut & Cai Fang, *Deepening Reform for China's Long-term Growth and Development* (Australian National University Press 2014) at 533.

accompanying regulations to that law qualify the scope of matters that may be submitted to arbitration, limiting it to disputes that arise out of the "interpretation or execution of the agreement, contract or articles of association."[480] Second, Article 26 of the Chinese-Foreign Contractual Joint Ventures Law allows for the arbitration of disputes between Chinese and foreign partners as to the implementation of their "contractual joint venture contract and articles of association."

292. After the expiration of the five years (i.e., in 2025), all those enterprises will, under Article 31 of the Foreign Investment Law, be governed by the Company Law and the Partnership Enterprise Law. While the Company Law includes no provision allowing or prohibiting arbitration, the Partnership Enterprise Law expressly allows partners to include an arbitration provision in the partnership agreement (Article 103). It should be noted that the Foreign Investment Law and its accompanying regulations do not include any provision on dispute resolution mechanisms.

293. Chinese courts tend to take a conservative position on the arbitration of corporate matters that involve administrative issues.[481] This is because Article 3(2) of the Arbitration Law of the People's Republic of China expressly prohibits the arbitration of disputes that are within the jurisdiction of administrative authorities. The Supreme People's Court in *Expert Assets et al v. Huayuan Pharmaceutical* (2006) partially annulled an award and held that the tribunal had no jurisdiction to decide share distribution when the relevant administrative authority had already approved the share distribution among the shareholders.[482] The Court reasoned that the award would have affected the interests of other shareholders who were not party to the arbitration proceeding.[483]

294. Similarly, in *Vision Plus Image v. Sepaso Pharmaceutical* (2009), the Intermediate People's Court of Kaifeng refused to enforce an award on corporate matters, reasoning that the award would have interfered with decisions that had already been taken by relevant administrative authorities.[484] Taking a similar approach, the Intermediate People's Court of Huizhou in *Sichuangde Development et al v. Huayang Industrial et al* (2001) partially annulled an award that had ordered the parties to terminate the equity joint venture company's articles of association and dissolve the company.[485]

480. Regulations on the Implementation of the Law of the People's Republic of China on Chinese-Foreign Equity Joint Ventures (1983, last amended in 2019), Art. 97.
481. WunschARB, "Expert Assets et al. v. Huayuan Pharmaceutical (2006), Supreme People's Court of the People's Republic of China, [2006] 民四他字第2号 (SPC) & 京高法 [2005] 332号 (Beijing HPC), 7 March 2006, Chinese Court Decision Summaries on Arbitration" (WunschARB Sàrl; Kluwer Law International) at "Commentary" section.
482. *Expert Assets et al v. Huayuan Pharmaceutical*, Supreme People's Court of the People's Republic of China, [2006] 民四他字第2号 (SPC) & 京高法 [2005] 332 号 (Beijing HPC), 7 March 2006.
483. *Ibid.*
484. *Vision Plus Image v. Sepaso Pharmaceutical*, Intermediate People's Court of Kaifeng, [2009] 汴法执字第88号 (Kaifeng IPC), 15 May 2009.
485. *Sichuangde Development et al v. Huayang Industrial et al*, Intermediate People's Court of Huizhou, [2001] 惠中法经初字第 39号 (Huizhou IPC), 12 June 2001.

295. In 2009, the Supreme People's Court adopted a more liberal approach in *Yongxin Auto Components v. SK Central*, in which it rejected an application to annul an award on the liquidation and dissolution of an equity joint venture company.[486] However, in *Jiacheng Engineering v. VEM et al* (2011), the Court reverted to its previous conservative approach.[487]

296. It should also be noted that, despite the silence of Article 151 of the Company Law as to the arbitrability of shareholders' derivative claims, Chinese case law shows that shareholders filing a claim in their own name to recover for the company are bound by arbitration agreements between the company and third parties. For example, in *Nanhua Investment Company v. Foshan Gas Company* (2016), the Guangdong Higher People's Court held that the claimant—which had filed the lawsuit for Guanghua Company's interests—was bound by the arbitration clause between the latter and the respondent.[488]

Germany

297. The German approach to the arbitrability of corporate disputes is far more open than the Chinese approach. Nevertheless, it is not as liberal as the jurisdictions discussed in the first group (such as the US and France), as it applies noteworthy restrictions to the arbitration of corporate disputes.

298. In Germany, corporate disputes are generally considered to fall within the category of arbitrable matters, as they usually involve economic interests within the meaning of section 1030(1) of the Code of Civil Procedure.[489] For example, in *BGH, 19.07.2004—III ZR 65/03*, the Federal Court of Justice held that claims as to capital contribution in limited liability corporations (GmbH) are arbitrable. Further, in stock corporations (AG), disputes involving economic interests such as claims regarding the founder's liability (section 50 of the Stock Corporation Act), capital contribution (section 54) and distribution of profits (section 58(4)) are all arbitrable.[490]

299. However, the arbitrability of disputes as to the validity of shareholder resolutions in limited liability corporations (GmbH) was controversial until 2009, when the Federal

486. *Yongxin Auto Components v. SK Central*, Supreme People's Court of the People's Republic of China, [2009] 民四他字第 45 号 (SPC) & [2009] 浙商外他字第 2 号 (Zhejiang HPC), 29 October 2009.
487. *Jiacheng Engineering v. VEM et al*, Supreme People's Court of the People's Republic of China, [2011] 民四他字第13号 (SPC) & 京高法 [2011] 67 号 (Beijing HPC), 22 April 2011.
488. *Nanhua Investment Company v. Foshan Gas Company*, Guangdong Higher People's Court, [2016] 粤民终468, 18 April 2016.
489. Christian Duve, "Arbitration of Corporate Law Disputes in Germany" in Karl-Heinz Böckstiegel et al, eds, *Arbitration in Germany: The Model Law in Practice* (Kluwer Law International, 2015) 927 at para. 9. It should be noted that s. 130(1) of Code of Civil Procedure offers two criteria for arbitrability: "Any claim under property law may become the subject matter of an arbitration agreement. An arbitration agreement regarding non-pecuniary claims has legal effect insofar as the parties to the dispute are entitled to conclude a settlement regarding the subject matter of the dispute."
490. Christian Duve, "Arbitration of Corporate Law Disputes in Germany" in Karl-Heinz Böckstiegel et al, eds, *Arbitration in Germany: The Model Law in Practice* (Kluwer Law International, 2015) 927 at para. 16.

Court of Justice settled the matter. Disputes in relation to shareholder resolutions are regarded as not involving economic interests within the meaning of section 1030(1) of the Code of Civil Procedure and, as such, the parties' ability to resolve the subject matter by settlement agreement is decisive.[491] In 2009, the Federal Court of Justice in *BGH, 06.04.2009—II ZR 255/08* held that disputes concerning shareholder resolutions are arbitrable, but in order for an arbitration agreement to be valid, it must meet the following four conditions:

- first, unanimous consent of all shareholders to incorporate the arbitration clause in the articles of association or a separate agreement, to confer power on the tribunal to render an award with a *res judicata* effect;
- second, informing all shareholders and directors of the company about the institution and the progress of the arbitral proceedings, so as to provide them with the opportunity to join the proceedings;
- third, allowing all shareholders to participate in the designation of the arbitrators, unless a neutral third party appoints the arbitrators; and
- fourth, providing a mechanism to join all related disputes before the same tribunal.[492]

The Federal Court of Justice in *BGH, 06.04.2017—I ZB 23/16* extended its above decision to partnerships and limited partnerships.[493] Thus, for an arbitration clause to cover disputes relating to partnership resolutions, the clause must now satisfy the four requirements set out above.

300. Again, in limited liability corporations (GmbH), shareholders' right to request and receive information appear prima facie to be non-arbitrable, as section 51b of the Limited Liability Companies Act (GmbHG) refers to the rule in section 132(1) of the Stock Corporation Act, which provides that Regional Courts have exclusive jurisdiction over these matters. However, the explanatory section of the Bill of the Arbitration Law Reform Act (in relation to the 1998 reform in the Code of Civil Procedure) indicates that, where the Code of Civil Procedure vests exclusive jurisdiction in a court, the exclusivity of jurisdiction should not be considered a determining factor against the arbitrability of the matter, *unless* the court is a special court for specific disputes pertaining to the revocation or nullity of the rights granted through an administrative

491. *Ibid.*, at paras. 17–19.
492. Following the 2009 decision of the Federal Court of Justice, the German Arbitration Institution (DIS) issued a set of rules for corporate disputes as supplementary rules to the DIS Arbitration Rules. For the latest version, *see* Annex 5 to DIS Arbitration Rules 2018, online: https://www.disarb.org/en/tools-for-dis-proceedings/dis-rules (last visited 22 February 2021). Initially, the rules were developed for limited liability corporations (which are usually closely held companies) but commentators have considered these rules to be applicable in the broader context of the arbitration of class actions in Germany. Christian Borris, "Collective Arbitration: The European Experience—Germany and the DIS Supplementary Rules for Corporate Law Disputes (DIS-SRCoLD)" in Bernard Hanotiau & Eric A Schwartz, eds, *Class and Group Actions in Arbitration*, (Kluwer Law International; International Chamber of Commerce ICC, 2016) 80 at 80, 81, 84.
493. *BGH, 06.04.2017—I ZB 23/16.*

act of the government.[494] Those "exclusive jurisdiction" circumstances are not present in the case of shareholders' claims to receive information, as the Regional Courts are not special courts, nor do shareholders' claims involve the revocation of a right granted through an administrative act of the government. Thus, the Hamm Higher Regional Court, in *OLG Hamm 07.03.2000, BB 2000, 1159*, held that claims as to shareholders' rights to request and receive information are arbitrable.

301. In stock corporations (AG), the arbitrability of disputes as to shareholder resolutions is controversial. Under section 23(5) of the Stock Corporation Act, articles of association may contain provisions different from those in the Act only if the Act "explicitly so permits." Relying on this provision, it has been argued that disputes as to shareholder resolutions may not be submitted to arbitration, not only because there is no explicit permission given within the Stock Corporation Act for including an arbitration clause in the articles of association but also because section 246(3) gives the Regional Court exclusive jurisdiction over such disputes.[495] However, those arguing in favor of the arbitrability of disputes as to shareholder resolutions are of the view that section 23(5) has a number of objectives, including protecting the investors and minority shareholders, as well as providing for legal certainty, none of which would be jeopardized by an arbitration clause.[496] As such, they argue that, if the conditions for a multi-party arbitration that were set out by the Federal Court of Justice in *BGH, 06.04.2009—II ZR 255/08*[497] (about the arbitrability of disputes as to the validity of shareholder resolutions in limited liability corporations) are satisfied, disputes as to shareholder resolutions in stock corporations can also be submitted to arbitration.[498]

3. Jurisdictions Limiting the Arbitral Remedies in Corporate Disputes

302. All the common law jurisdictions that were the focus of this research regard corporate disputes as arbitrable. However, the majority of these jurisdictions impose restrictions on the remedies a tribunal may award in oppression claims. Therefore, other than the US and the Canadian provinces of Alberta and Ontario,[499] all common law jurisdictions are discussed in this third group. From the civil law camp, only Québec fits into this group.

303. In summary, the jurisdictions in this group hold the view that oppression claims are arbitrable, but tribunals may not grant statutory remedies suitable to oppression

494. Bill of the Arbitration Law Reform Act (12 July 1996), BT-Drs 13/5274 at 70, online (in original language): http://dipbt.bundestag.de/doc/btd/13/052/1305274.pdf (last visited 14 February 2021).
495. *See* Christian Duve, "Arbitration of Corporate Law Disputes in Germany" in Karl-Heinz Böckstiegel et al, eds, *Arbitration in Germany: The Model Law in Practice* (Kluwer Law International, 2015) 927 at paras. 37, 38.
496. *Ibid.*, at paras. 40, 43, 46.
497. Discussed above, para. 299.
498. Christian Duve, "Arbitration of Corporate Law Disputes in Germany" in Karl-Heinz Böckstiegel et al, eds, *Arbitration in Germany: The Model Law in Practice* (Kluwer Law International, 2015) 927 at paras. 40, 43, 46.
499. Discussed above, paras. 273–278, 284–287.

claims because those remedies are within the courts' exclusive jurisdiction. Clearly, such an approach leads to the bifurcation of proceedings: with the merits arbitrated first, and then an application for relief made to the courts. This approach has not been well received by some commentators and has been described as making the arbitration process "a paper tiger in the resolution of shareholder disputes"[500] as well as being "unnecessary and inconsistent with the principle that a multiplicity of proceedings should be avoided at all costs."[501]

England and Wales

304. The English law approach to the arbitrability of corporate disputes is most clearly set out in the 2011 decision of the Court of Appeal in *Fulham Football Club (1987) Ltd v. Richards*.[502] In that case, the Court of Appeal noted that "[a] dispute between members of a company or between shareholders and the board about alleged breaches of the articles of association or a shareholders' agreement is an essentially contractual dispute which does not necessarily engage the rights of creditors or impinge on any statutory safeguards imposed for the benefit of third parties."[503] Thus, the Court held that such disputes fall within the category of arbitrable matters.[504]

305. In the same case, the Court of Appeal held that a dispute as to whether there has been unfair prejudice under the Companies Act 2006 is arbitrable, but there are certain *restrictions as to the type of relief* a tribunal may award in such a case.[505] For example, according to the Court, an arbitral tribunal may not make a winding up order, as this power rests exclusively with courts.[506] The Court also noted that, in a winding up petition on just and equitable grounds under section 122(1)(g) of the Insolvency Act 1986, tribunals may decide the underlying dispute so as to determine whether it would be justified to present a winding up petition to courts.[507]

Hong Kong

306. Disputes between a company and its members that arise out of the articles of association of a company have been held to be arbitrable in Hong Kong. In *NG Kin, Kenneth v. The HK Football Association Ltd* (1994), the Court of First Instance held that an arbitration clause in the articles of association of a company incorporated in Hong Kong is a valid arbitration agreement by reason of section 23(1) of the former Companies Ordinance (Cap 32)—now section 86 of the Companies Ordinance (Cap

500. Rebecca Huang, "Shareholders Disputes: Arbitrator's Power to Grant Statutory Oppression Remedy" (2010) 36 Advocates' Q 457 at 427.
501. Byron Shaw, "The Arbitrability of Oppression Claims" (2011) 69:1 Advocate (Vancouver) 21 at 26.
502. *Fulham Football Club (1987) Ltd v. Richards* [2011] EWCA Civ 855, [2012] 2 WLR 1008 (CA) permission to appeal to the Supreme Court refused UKSC 2011/0187 (22 February 2012).
503. *Ibid.*, at para. 77.
504. *Ibid.*
505. *Ibid.*, at paras. 76, 77.
506. *Ibid.*
507. *Ibid.*, at para. 83.

622).[508] This section provides that, upon registration of the articles of association, the articles bind the company and all its members.

307. However, in *Quiksilver Greater China Ltd v. Quiksilver Glorious Sun JV Ltd* (2014), the Court of First Instance adopted a similar approach to that of the English Court of Appeal in *Fulham Football Club (1987) Ltd v. Richards* (2011),[509] holding that a tribunal may not make a winding up order but may determine whether presenting a winding up petition to courts would be justified.[510]

Singapore

308. The general view is that an arbitration clause in the articles of association of a company is, in principle, binding on all members of the company as well as the company itself, because section 39(1) of the Companies Act 1967 (prior to the 2014 amendments) provided that all members of a company and the company were bound by the articles of association as if they had individually signed it.[511] The 2014 amendments to the Companies Act, which came into force in 2016, replaced the term "articles of association" with "constitution." However, the 2014 amendments have not affected the arbitrability of corporate disputes, because "[t]he memorandum and articles of association of existing companies will be treated in law as their constitution, from 3 Jan 2016."[512]

309. As to the arbitrability of winding up petitions, the Court of Appeal in *Tomolugen Holdings Ltd v. Silica Investors Ltd* (2015) drew a clear distinction between minority oppression claims brought under section 216 of the Companies Act and disputes over the liquidation of an insolvent company that arise upon insolvency.[513] The Court held that the former are arbitrable, whereas the latter are not.[514] According to the Court, section 216 minority oppression claims are different in nature from disputes over the liquidation of an insolvent company.[515] First, because section 216 claims "almost always arise in the context of a *solvent* company" and, second, because section 216 claims do not involve the same public policy considerations as disputes over insolvency claims.[516] The Court of Appeal explained that section 216 was not enacted

508. *NG Kin, Kenneth v. The HK Football Association Ltd*, [1994] HKCFI 153, HCA 2383/1994 (3 June 1994) at 4–7.
509. Discussed above, paras. 304–305.
510. *Quiksilver Greater China Ltd v. Quiksilver Glorious Sun JV Ltd and Another*, [2014] HKCFI 1304, HCCW 364/2013 (25 July 2014) at paras. 12, 14, 18, 19.
511. Michael Hwang & Rajesh C Muttath, "Arbitration in Company Matters" (2001) 5 IBLJ 555 at 557.
512. Singapore Accounting and Corporate Regulatory Accounting (ACRA) website, "Phase 2 of Companies (Amendment) Act 2014—Frequently Asked Questions," online: https://www.acra.gov.sg/legislation/legislative-reform/companies-act-reform/companies-amendment-act-2014/two-phase-implementation-of-companies-amendment-act-2014/faqs-phase-2-of-companies-amendment-act-2014-frequently-asked-questions (last visited 10 April 2023).
513. *Tomolugen Holdings Ltd and another v. Silica Investors Ltd* [2016] 1 SLR 373 (CA) at paras. 82, 84, 88, 95–106.
514. *Ibid.*
515. *Ibid.*
516. *Ibid* (emphasis added).

to protect the public interest, but rather was intended to protect "the commercial expectations" of members of a company and, as such, if members of the company have initially agreed to arbitrate their disputes, courts should honor that agreement.[517]

310. The Court of Appeal's ruling in *Tomolugen* is particularly important because the Court rejected the position that the arbitrability of a dispute must be linked to the tribunal's power to grant the specific relief being sought.[518] In this regard, the Court of Appeal ruled that: "it is beyond the powers of an arbitrator to liquidate a company [as a relief under section 216]," but "it just does not follow from the limitations which might apply to an arbitrator's powers [concerning the relief sought] that the dispute itself is thus unsuitable for resolution by arbitration."[519] It should be noted that in *Tomolugen*, the Court of Appeal adopted an approach similar to that of the English Court of Appeal in *Fulham Football Club v. Richards* (2011)[520] and the Hong Kong Court of First Instance in *Quiksilver Greater China Ltd v. Quiksilver Glorious Sun JV*.[521]

311. Two years after *Tomolugen*, the Court of Appeal in *L Capital Jones Ltd v. Maniach Pte Ltd* (2017) reasserted its position that minority oppression claims are arbitrable in principle.[522] However, the Court clarified that there might be minority oppression claims involving specific features (i.e., features other than being a minority oppression claim) such as abuse of the judicial process that raise public policy concerns and thus render those claims inarbitrable.

312. Another corporate matter that has been addressed by Singapore courts is the issue of the alter ego of a company. The High Court in *Aloe Vera of America, Inc v. Asianic Food (S) Pte Ltd* (2006) relied on a passage in *Halsbury's Laws of Singapore*[523] on arbitrability and held that a dispute as to whether a person is the alter ego of a company "is an issue which does not have a public interest element. It normally arises in a commercial transaction in which one party is trying to make an individual responsible for the obligations of a corporation ... [S]uch an issue can in an appropriate case be decided by arbitration."[524]

Canada (Provinces of British Columbia and Québec)

313. The Canadian federal and provincial legislation relevant to corporate matters (excepting the province of Ontario) have no specific provision on the arbitrability of

517. *Ibid.*
518. *Ibid.*, at para. 82.
519. *Ibid.*
520. *Fulham Football Club (1987), Ltd v. Richards* [2011] EWCA Civ 855. Discussed above, paras. 304–305.
521. *Quiksilver Greater China Ltd v. Quiksilver Glorious Sun JV Ltd and Another*, [2014] HKCFI 1304. Discussed above, para. 307.
522. *L Capital Jones Ltd and another v. Maniach Pte Ltd* [2017] SGCA 3 at paras. 26–32.
523. *Halsbury's Laws of Singapore*, vol 2 (LexisNexis, 2003) at para. 20.149.
524. *Aloe Vera of America, Inc v. Asianic Food (S) Pte Ltd and Another* [2006] 3 SLR(R) 174 (HC) at para. 72.

corporate disputes.[525] Therefore, it has fallen to the case law of each province to develop principles in relation to the arbitrability of corporate disputes. The discussion in the following paragraphs demonstrates that, like Alberta and Ontario,[526] the provinces of British Columbia and Québec regard oppression claims as arbitrable. Nevertheless, the possibility of bifurcation of proceedings in British Columbia has long caused pro-arbitration commentators to encourage courts to further develop the law in favor of arbitration.[527]

314. In British Columbia, the relevant case law indicates that oppression claims are arbitrable, in that tribunals may make findings of oppression. However, they may not grant relief that is within the exclusive jurisdiction of courts, such as the winding-up of a company. In *ABOP LLC v. Qtrade Canada Inc* (2007), the BC Court of Appeal upheld the lower court's decision to stay court proceedings in favor of arbitration of a corporate shareholder's oppression claim under the Canada Business Corporation Act (CBCA) and pursuant to the arbitration clause in the shareholders' agreement.[528] The BC Court of Appeal affirmed the lower court's ruling that although a finding of oppression and granting of suitable relief rest within the exclusive jurisdiction of the court, the arbitral tribunal will establish the facts and, if it finds that there is any foundation for the shareholder's oppression claim, the shareholder may then return to the court to seek relief.[529] The BC Court of Appeal held that referring the shareholder to pursue its oppression claim in arbitration did not debar the shareholder from a statutory remedy under the CBCA.[530]

315. In Québec, the 21st century has seen a major shift in the Court of Appeal's approach to the arbitrability of oppression claims,[531] which is mainly due to the Supreme Court of Canada's decision in *Desputeaux v. Éditions Chouette* (2003).[532] First, in *Acier Leroux Inc v. Tremblay* (2004), the Québec Court of Appeal relied on the *Desputeaux* case to hold that oppression claims arising under the CBCA are

525. For federal laws, *see* Canada Business Corporations Act, RSC 1985, c C-44; Canada Corporations Act, RSC 1970, c C-32. For British Columbia, *see* Business Corporations Act, SBC 2002, c 57. For Québec, *see* Business Corporations Act, CQLR c S-31.1; Companies Act, CQLR c C-38.
526. Discussed above, paras. 284–287.
527. *See, e.g.,* Rebecca Huang, "Shareholders Disputes: Arbitrator's Power to Grant Statutory Oppression Remedy" (2010) 36 Advocates' Q 457 at 466–68; Byron Shaw, "The Arbitrability of Oppression Claims" (2011) 69:1 Advocate (Vancouver) 21 at 26.
528. *ABOP LLC v. Qtrade Canada Inc,* 2007 BCCA 290 at paras. 1, 11–12, 16–23, 72 BCLR (4th) 34.
529. *Ibid.*
530. *Ibid.*
531. For the approach of the Court of Appeal in the 20th century, *see, e.g., Borenstein v. Trans-American Investment and Development Co Ltd,* [1970] CS 192 (Qc CS), 1969 CarswellQue 101; *Oeufs Trois-Rivières ltée v. Entreprises Labler Inc,* 1990 CarswellQue 415 (Qc CA) at paras. 4, 5, 9, [1990] JQ no 16. Even at the beginning of the 21st century, the Québec Court of Appeal was still reluctant to allow the arbitration of oppression claims. *See, e.g., Camirand v. Rossi,* [2003] JQ no 3320 (Qc CA), 2003 CanLII 74899 at paras. 7–12, 28–30, 33.
532. *Desputeaux v. Éditions Chouette (1987) Inc,* 2003 SCC 17 at paras. 22, 40, 42, [2003] 1 SCR 178 (holding, inter alia, that the intention behind statutory provisions providing for a court's jurisdiction over a subject matter is not to exclude arbitration of the matter, but rather is to identify which court within the judicial system has jurisdiction over that matter and therefore "it cannot be assumed to exclude arbitral jurisdiction unless it *expressly* so states").

arbitrable.[533] Then, in *Investissement Charlevoix Inc v. Gestion Pierre Gingras Inc* (2010), the same Court ruled that the judicial liquidation of a company may be submitted to arbitration but that the *remedy* provided for in the Québec Winding-Up Act can only be ordered by a judge.[534]

316. Although the Québec Court of Appeal ruled that the matters in those two cases were arbitrable in principle, it ultimately refused to enforce the arbitration clauses. This raises the question of whether the Court of Appeal was comfortable referring oppression claims to arbitration in practice. In the first case (the *Acier Leroux* case), part of the Court's reasoning for refusing to refer the parties to arbitration was that the shareholder's oppression claim did not require the interpretation or application of the shareholders' agreement, and therefore it did not fall within the scope of the arbitration clause.[535] In the second case (*Investissement Charlevoix*), the Court set out three reasons for not referring the matter to arbitration:

- First, "the parties [were] completely deadlocked and that no arbitral award concerning the obligation and method of voluntary liquidation of the Company within the meaning of articles 1 et seq of the Act [the Winding-Up Act], [would] be subject to voluntary execution."[536]
- Second, the remedy provided for in the Winding-Up Act can only be exercised by a judge because "no arbitrator seized of a voluntary winding-up application would have the power to appoint one or more liquidators (article 5 of the Act), nor to provide for their replacement, if necessary, without the consent of the shareholders, or without going to the Superior Court in the absence of agreement (article 8)."[537]
- Third, it was necessary that the remedy for a judicial liquidation be exercised by the Superior Court "because of the urgency of a situation that [had] been deteriorating for more than seven years and [because of] the interest of the parties themselves and third parties."[538]

317. On its face, the Québec Court of Appeal's position in both *Acier Leroux* and *Investissement Charlevoix* was that oppression claims are arbitrable and that it was only due to the specific circumstances of those cases that the Court of Appeal refused to enforce the arbitration agreements. Yet, careful consideration of the Court of Appeal's line of reasoning indicates that the identified circumstances are not peculiar to those two cases. In fact, those circumstances are nearly always present in an oppression claim where a shareholder seeks to wind up a company: there is usually a deadlock between the parties as a result of long-standing conflict, the remedies are typically within the exclusive jurisdiction of the court, and third-party rights are often

533. *Acier Leroux Inc v. Tremblay*, [2004] RJQ 839 (Qc CA) at paras. 5, 30, 32–36, 39, 41–45.
534. *Investissement Charlevoix Inc v. Gestion Pierre Gingras Inc*, 2010 QCCA 1229 at paras. 57–59, 60–64, 67, [2010] JQ No 6183.
535. *Acier Leroux Inc v. Tremblay*, [2004] RJQ 839 (Qc CA) at para. 41.
536. *Ibid.*, at para. 62.
537. *Ibid.*, at para. 63
538. *Ibid.*, at para. 67.

involved. The question which courts of other Canadian jurisdictions have tried to answer in these types of claims has been whether, despite all of these circumstances being present, oppression claims should be arbitrable.

318. As a result of the Québec Court of Appeal's ambiguous approach to oppression claims (which continued up until 2015, when the Court eventually clarified its approach), inconsistencies developed in the decisions of Québec's trial court (Superior Court). For example, on the one hand, in *Johnson v. Kensington Capital Partners Ltd* (2009), the Superior Court enforced the arbitration clause of a shareholders' agreement against a shareholder who had requested a court order to purchase his shares in the company, due to alleged oppressive conduct of the respondents.[539] On the other hand, in *Heeg v. Hitech Piping Ltd* (2009), the same Court refused to enforce the arbitration clause with respect to the oppression claims because "the recourse and relief sought [were not] clearly stipulated in the arbitration provision."[540] Similarly, in *Dupuis v. Hébert* (2012), the Superior Court refused to enforce an arbitration agreement in relation to oppression claims.[541]

319. Eventually, in 2015, the Court of Appeal clarified its approach to the arbitrability of oppression claims. In *Ferreira v. Tavares* (2015), the Court ruled as follows: while oppression remedy claims are in essence arbitrable, for such claims to be submitted to arbitration, the parties' agreement must *waive their right to go to court* and *grant the arbitrator the power to issue injunctive relief orders*.[542] The Court held the same position in *Jack v. Jack* (2018) and *AEC Symmaf Inc v. Poirier* (2018).[543]

E. FAMILY/DOMESTIC RELATIONS LAW

320. In the field of family law (or "domestic relations," as it is known in the US), the authors focused on four matters: divorce, spousal support, child support, and custody.[544] Research shows that the majority of the jurisdictions that were the focus of this research have adopted a conservative approach to the arbitrability of disputes in

539. *Johnson v. Kensington Capital Partners Ltd*, 2009 QCCS 1861 at paras. 1-2, 4, 8-9, 20-23, 35, [2009] QJ No 4007.
540. *Heeg v. Hitech Piping (HTP) Ltd*, 2009 QCCS 4043 at paras. 1, 3, 6, 8, 79, 81-90.
541. *Dupuis v. Hébert*, 2012 QCCS 6189, [2012] JQ no 15972.
542. *Ferreira v. Tavares*, 2015 QCCA 844 at paras. 1, 5, 12-14, 29.
543. *Jack v. Jack*, 2018 QCCA 788; *AEC Symmaf Inc v. Poirier*, 2018 QCCA 916 at paras. 4-10.
544. This book does not discuss religious/faith-based arbitration (defined as a voluntary arbitration that is conducted based on religious principles). Although the topic may seem to be relevant to the field of family law/domestic relations, religious arbitration fits more appropriately within discussions on "governing law" rather than "arbitrability." The topic may also be discussed from an "arbitrability" perspective (when discussing, for instance, whether religious entities such as a church have the capacity to enter into arbitration agreements—for the purpose of religious arbitration—with their employees) but even when viewed from that perspective, the topic seems to be more relevant to the issue of subjective arbitrability than objective arbitrability. Commentators have also discussed the broader issue of accommodating religious beliefs in secular societies, but that issue, too, is beyond the scope of this book. It is more appropriately addressed within the scope of discussions on public policy concerns that arise at the enforcement stage.

this field of law, to the point that family law/domestic relations is the only field (among the nine fields of law focused on in this text), where the majority of jurisdictions restrict the arbitration of related disputes. This does not come as a surprise given the public policy considerations at stake, including the frequent involvement of children in family disputes and the importance of "family" as a core unit of society.

321. In jurisdictions such as France, Québec (Canada) and China, there is an express legislative prohibition on the arbitration of family/domestic relations matters.[545] However, in many jurisdictions, the applicable legislative prohibition is indirect, for example, the rule that divorce may only be granted through a judicial decree and that courts have exclusive jurisdiction on such matters,[546] or the rule that the parties may not in this context waive their right of recourse to courts.[547]

322. The following three points provide an overview of the arbitrability of family law/domestic relations disputes. First, none of the jurisdictions allows parties to refer the matter of divorce to arbitration, except Singapore (and then only with respect to court-ordered arbitrations in family court matters that deal with Islamic law) and the US state of Indiana.[548] Second, in respect of financial matters (such as spousal support and child support), only the US, the common law provinces of Canada, Switzerland (in international matters), and Germany (in matters of spousal support) allow the arbitration of these disputes. Third, as concerns custody disputes, only the common law provinces of Canada and some states of the US allow these disputes to be arbitrated.

545. French Civil Code, Art. 2060; Québec Civil Code, Art. 2639; Chinese Arbitration Law, Art. 3. It should be noted that the Chinese Civil Code, which came into force in 2021, repealed and replaced a number of relevant legislative texts, including the Marriage Law, the Inheritance Law, and the Adoption Law. However, the Civil Code does not include any provision that contradicts the arbitrability provisions of the Arbitration Law with respect to family and inheritance disputes.

546. German Civil Code, s. 1564; German Act on Proceedings in Family Matters and in Matters of Non-Contentious Jurisdiction (FamFG), ss. 121, 122; Hong Kong Matrimonial Causes Ordinance (Cap 179), s. 3.

547. English Matrimonial Causes Act 1973, s. 34; English Civil Partnership Act 2005, Schedule 5; English Child Support Act 1991, s. 9; Hong Kong Matrimonial Proceedings and Property Ordinance (Cap 192), s. 14(1).

548. In the US, the law of domestic relations is traditionally considered a matter of state law rather than federal law (this is known as the "domestic relations exception" to federal courts' jurisdiction). State legislatures and courts play a pivotal role in forming the law of domestic relations and, as such, the approach to the arbitrability of domestic relations matters may vary from one state to another. However, it should be noted that in past decades, Congress and federal courts have become increasingly involved in the field of domestic relations, particularly in child welfare matters. Linda D Elrod, "The Federalization of Family Law" (2009) 36:3 Human Rights Magazine, online: https://www.americanbar.org/groups/crsj/publications/human_rights_magazine_home/human_rights_vol36_2009/summer2009/the_federalization_of_family_law/ (last visited 15 June 2022); Maureen McBrien & Patricia A Kindregan, "The Domestic Relations Exception to Federal Diversity Jurisdiction" in *Massachusetts Practice Series: Family Law and Practice with Forms*, 4th ed, vol 1 (Thomson Reuters, 2017) at §13:2; Meredith Johnson Harbach, "Is the Family a Federal Question?" (2009) 66 Wash & Lee L Rev 131.

323. Thus, the arbitration of family/domestic relations matters seems to be mainly a North American concept. The tendency in North American jurisdictions to provide access to arbitration in this field of law may be explained by the fact that their judicial systems have historically been overburdened with such cases. For example, in Canada, 29% of cases in civil courts initiated in 2019/2020 concerned family law disputes.[549] In the US, while nationwide numbers for the domestic relations caseload are not high,[550] some states report a remarkably high caseload. For example, in Florida, domestic relations cases filed in 2015 constituted 38.2% of the total of all circuit court filings (including criminal matters).[551]

324. The non-arbitrability of family law disputes in other jurisdictions does not mean that those jurisdictions do not allow for out-of-court settlement mechanisms in family disputes. Under the Swiss Civil Procedure Code, Article 297(2), the court may ask parents to use mediation in matters relating to their children. It is believed that family mediation constitutes a considerable part of mediation practice in Switzerland.[552] Likewise, in Hong Kong, mediation is encouraged in family disputes and the judiciary has issued a number of Practice Directions encouraging parties to settle their disputes out of courtrooms.[553] In Québec, despite the non-arbitrability of family disputes, such disputes may be submitted to mediation but, under Article 616 of the Code of Civil Procedure, the mediator must be a certified family mediator.

325. The following subsections elaborate on the arbitrability of: (1) Divorce; (2) Financial Matters (Spousal Support and Child Support); and (3) Custody disputes.

549. Statistics Canada has reported that for 2019/2020, the total number of initiated civil court cases was 454,372, of which 131,001 were family cases. That means approximately 29% of the total initiated civil court cases. Statistics Canada, *Table 35-10-0112-01 (Civil Court Cases, by Level of Court and Type of Case, Canada and Selected Provinces and Territories)*, released 25 March 2021, online: https://www150.statcan.gc.ca/t1/tbl1/en/tv.action?pid=3510011201.

550. The domestic relations caseload in the US for the year 2020 was 7.08% of all incoming cases. Website of Court Statistics Project, tab "Court Statistics," sub-tab "Explore the Data," section "CSP Stat," subsection "Overview Trial Courts," online: https://www.courtstatistics.org/csp-stat-nav-cards-first-row/csp-stat-overview, compare "Grand Total" with "Total Domestic Relations." The "Court Statistic Project" is a joint project of the US Conference of State Court Administrators and the US Bureau of Justice Statistics (BJS).

551. Florida Courts website, tab "Resources & Services," sub-tab "Court Improvement," sub-tab "Family Courts," sub-tab "Family Court Basics," sub-tab "Family Court Tool Kit: Basics," sub-tab "Family court jurisdiction and filings data," online http://www.flcourts.org/core/fileparse.php/573/urlt/family-court-filings-2017.pdf.

552. Isaak Meier, "Chapter 14: Mediation and Conciliation in Switzerland" in Nadja Alexander, ed, *Global Trends in Mediation, Global Trends in Dispute Resolution* (Kluwer Law International, 2006) 371 at para. 14.3.1.

553. *See, e.g.*, Practice Direction 15.10 (Family Mediation), Practice Direction 15.11 (Financial Dispute Resolution Pilot Scheme), Practice Direction 15.13 (Children's Dispute Resolution Pilot Scheme), and Practice Direction SL9 (Pilot Scheme on Private Adjudication of Financial Disputes in Matrimonial and Family Proceedings).

1. Divorce

326. Divorce (a matter involving a change of marital status) could be considered the exemplar of non-arbitrable disputes. Nearly all jurisdictions studied for this book retain a judicial monopoly on divorce adjudication. The exceptions are Singapore (only with respect to court-ordered arbitrations in Islamic law matters)[554] and the US state of Indiana.[555] The discussion in this subsection contains three Segments: (i) Jurisdictions with an Express Legislative Ban; (ii) Jurisdictions with an Indirect Legislative Ban; and (iii) Other Jurisdictions.

i. Jurisdictions with an Express Legislative Ban

327. Some jurisdictions have an express legislative ban on the arbitrability of divorce matters: France, Québec, China (Mainland), and a number of states within the US. Article 2060 of the French Civil Code expressly rules out the arbitrability of disputes as to the status and capacity of persons, as well as matters relating to divorce and judicial separation. Likewise, Article 2639 of the Québec Civil Code—to the extent it applies to divorce in the absence of overriding federal provisions—provides that matters related to the "status of a person" and "family matters" fall within the category of non-arbitrable matters. Similarly, Article 3 of the Chinese Arbitration Law categorically excludes the arbitration of disputes as to marriage.

328. In the US, states such as North Carolina and New Jersey have express legislative prohibitions on the arbitrability of divorce matters. Section 50-41 of the North Carolina Family Law Arbitration Act provides for the arbitrability of "all issues arising from a marital separation or divorce, except for the divorce itself." Similarly, Rule 5:1-5 of the Rules Governing the Courts of the State of New Jersey on the arbitration of family disputes expressly excludes the arbitrability of "the entry of the final judgment of annulment or dissolution of relationship."

ii. Jurisdictions with an Indirect Legislative Ban

329. Germany and Hong Kong both have an indirect legislative ban on the arbitrability of divorce matters. Under section 1030(1) of the German Code of Civil Procedure, if a claim is a non-pecuniary matter, it can be submitted to arbitration only if the parties are allowed to conclude a settlement regarding the subject matter. Even though divorce entails economic consequences, it is not a pecuniary matter. Therefore, for divorce to be arbitrable, couples must be able to enter into a settlement regarding the matter. However, couples may not dissolve a marriage by settlement agreement in German law

554. Discussed below, para. 335.
555. Indiana Arbitration Act § 34-57-5-2 allows the arbitration of not only all incidental matters to the dissolution of a marriage (such as support and custody) but also the dissolution of a marriage. It should be noted that the authors have not researched the laws of all 50 US states, and, as such, there might be other US states that allow the arbitration of the dissolution of a marriage.

because, under section 1564 of the Civil Code, divorce decrees may only be issued by judicial decision and, further, under sections 121 and 122 of the Act on Proceedings in Family Matters and in Matters of Non-Contentious Jurisdiction (FamFG), courts have exclusive jurisdiction in the dissolution/annulment of a marriage.[556] As such, these matters are not arbitrable.

330. In Hong Kong, under section 3 of the Matrimonial Causes Ordinance (Cap 179), "courts shall have jurisdiction in proceedings for divorce." The term "shall" has been generally interpreted as granting Hong Kong courts exclusive jurisdiction over a matter. In *Paquito Lima Buton v. Rainbow Joy Shipping Limited Inc* (2008), the Final Court of Appeal construed the term "shall" as implying the exclusive jurisdiction of courts in statutory claims brought under the Employees' Compensation Ordinance (Cap 282).[557]

iii. Other Jurisdictions

331. In the other jurisdictions under study (England and Wales, the US [other than the states discussed above], the common law provinces of Canada, and Switzerland), although no doubts have been expressed as to the non-arbitrability of divorce matters, the prohibition is not expressed (even indirectly) in statutes or case law.[558] In these jurisdictions, the non-arbitrability of divorce is usually expressed in scholarly commentaries or can be inferred from reading relevant statutes together.

332. In England and Wales, commentators believe that divorce, as it pertains to the legal status of a relationship, may not be submitted to arbitration.[559]

333. In Canada,[560] in the common law provinces, it is not possible for arbitrators to grant a divorce. In the province of Ontario, according to the website of the Ontario

556. Stephanie Uta Gilfrich, *Schiedsverfahren im Scheidungsrecht: eine rechtvergleichende Untersuchung* (Mohr Siebeck, 2007) at 33–34, 36; Rolf Trittmann & Inka Hanefeld, "Commentary on the German Arbitration Law (10th Book of the German Code of Civil Procedure) § 1030" in Karl-Heinz Böckstiegel et al, eds, *Arbitration in Germany: The Model Law in Practice*, 2nd ed (Kluwer Law International, 2015) 94 at para. 21.
557. *Paquito Lima Buton v. Rainbow Joy Shipping Limited Inc*, [2008] HKCFA 30 at paras. 3–4, 7, 48, 50–55, FACV 26/2007 (28 April 2008).
558. The Swiss Federal Supreme Court in *Case No 4A_12/2017, 19 September 2017* noted that an arbitral tribunal may not decide a petition for divorce.
559. Julian D M Lew & Oliver Marsden, "Arbitrability" in Julian D M Lew et al, eds, *Arbitration in England, with Chapters on Scotland and Ireland* (Kluwer Law International, 2013) at para. 19.33.
560. It should be noted that in Canada, family law falls partly under federal jurisdiction and partly under provincial jurisdiction. The main federal family law is the Divorce Act, which applies to married couples who have divorced or who have applied for divorce. The Divorce Act sets out rules about divorce, child support, spousal support, and custody after divorce. Provincial laws about child support, spousal support, and custody for children apply when an unmarried couple separates, or when a married couple separates but they have not applied for a divorce. Department of Justice website, tab "Family Law," sub-tab "Divorce and Separation," sub-sub-tab "About Divorce and Separation," online: http://www.justice.gc.ca/eng/fl-df/divorce/sd.html (last visited 1 December 2021).

Attorney General, an arbitrator "cannot grant a divorce or annul a marriage."[561] In the province of British Colombia, commentators consider it "obvious" that an arbitrator does not have the authority to issue a divorce decree.[562]

334. In the US, for those states that do not have an express legislative ban on the arbitrability of divorce matters,[563] non-arbitrability may be inferred from the fact that some states do not even allow the arbitrability of child custody disputes, and those states that allow it, do so only subject to specific standards for the judicial review of custody awards.[564] Therefore, divorce should a fortiori be considered non-arbitrable in those states.

335. In Singapore, there are two sets of legislative Acts that apply in relation to ending a marriage:

- for every person other than Muslims, family law is codified in the Women's Charter 1961; and
- for Muslims, family law is dealt with under the Administration of Muslim Law Act 1966.

With respect to the first group, the legislative history of the Singapore Arbitration Act shows that the drafters regarded "legitimacy of marriage" as non-arbitrable.[565] This view is still shared by commentators.[566] Regarding the second group, section 47(5) of the Administration of Muslim Law Act provides for a specific type of arbitration in divorce cases: if a wife requests a divorce but her husband disagrees, the Syariah Court[567] may appoint two arbitrators (called "hakam") and may, under section 50(3), instruct them on how to conduct the arbitration. Under section 50(6) and (7), the arbitrators may have the authority to pronounce the divorce, but they must report it to the Syariah Court for registration. Commentators on Singaporean law believe that, apart from the court-ordered arbitrations in Islamic law-related matters, arbitration is not yet "part of the legal framework" in family law disputes.[568]

561. Ontario Ministry of the Attorney General website, tab "Family Law," sub-tab "Family Arbitration," hyperlink "Overview," heading "What an arbitrator can decide," online: https://www.ontario.ca/page/family-arbitration#section-0 (last visited 2 November 2021).
562. *See, e.g.*, John-Paul Boyd, "Arbitration of Family Law Disputes in British Columbia" (2017) 36 CFLQ 139.
563. For discussion on the US states that have such bans, *see* above, para. 328.
564. Discussed below, paras. 378–382.
565. Review of Arbitration Act Committee, *Review of Arbitration Laws*, LRRD No 3/2001, online: https://www.sal.org.sg/sites/default/files/PDF%20Files/Law%20Reform/1993-08%20-%20Review%20of%20Arbitration%20Laws.pdf (last visited 10 April 2023).
566. Michael Hwang, Lawrence Boo & Eugene Thong, "National Report for Singapore (2018–2022)" in Lise Bosman, eds, *ICCA International Handbook on Commercial Arbitration* (Kluwer Law International, 2022) at sec 3.a (citing *Halsbury's Laws of Singapore*, vol 1(2) (LexisNexis, 2020 Reissue) at para. 20.002); David Joseph & David Foxton, *Singapore International Arbitration: Law & Practice* (LexisNexis, 2014) at para. 5.3.
567. The Syariah Court has jurisdiction "to hear and determine all actions and proceedings in which all the parties are Muslims or where the parties were married under the provisions of the Muslim law." Administration of Muslim Law Act 1966, s. 35(2).
568. Randolph Khoo & Hoon Shu Mei, "Family law in Singapore: overview" in *Family Law: A Global Guide From Practical Law* (Thomson Reuters, 2020) at question 34, online: http://ca.practicallaw.com/4-568-0826 (last visited 10 April 2023).

336. In Switzerland, the Federal Supreme Court, in *Case No 4A_12/2017, 19 September 2017*, noted that an arbitral tribunal may not decide a petition for divorce. It is also understood from the provisions of the Civil Procedure Code, such as Articles 274, 279, and 288(1), that only courts have jurisdiction to issue a divorce decree.[569] Commentators, too, are of the opinion that divorce is not arbitrable.[570]

2. Financial Matters (Spousal Support and Child Support)

337. The discussion in this subsection demonstrates that the majority of jurisdictions have taken a conservative approach by expressly prohibiting couples from waiving their right of access to courts in spousal and child support disputes. The first Segment discusses the few jurisdictions where financial matters are arbitrable. The second Segment discusses the jurisdictions where financial matters are non-arbitrable.

i. Jurisdictions Where Financial Matters Are Arbitrable

338. Of the ten jurisdictions studied, only the US and the common law provinces of Canada allow parties to arbitrate their spousal and child support disputes. Switzerland also allows arbitration in these matters, but only if the dispute is considered "international" under its laws. Similarly, Germany allows the arbitration of spousal support disputes but not of child support matters.

The United States

339. State courts have generally held that disputes as to financial aspects of domestic relations, including spousal support, child support, and property division are arbitrable. The following are examples. In New York, the Appellate Division of the Supreme Court in *Sheets v. Sheets* (1964) and the Court of Appeals in *Schneider v. Schneider* (1966) held that spousal support and child support disputes are arbitrable.[571] Three decades later, the Appellate Division of the New York Supreme Court in *Hampton v. Hampton* (1999) held that child support disputes are arbitrable.[572] In New Jersey, the Supreme Court in *Faherty v. Faherty* (1984) held that alimony and child support disputes are arbitrable.[573] In Pennsylvania, the Supreme Court in *Miller v.*

569. Article 274 reads: "Divorce proceedings are initiated by submitting a joint request for divorce or by filing an action for divorce." Article 279 reads: "(1) The court shall approve the agreement on the effects of the divorce if it is persuaded that the spouses have concluded the agreement of their own volition and after careful reflection, ... (2) The agreement is valid only when it has been approved by the court." Article 288(1) reads: "If the conditions for a divorce at joint request are fulfilled, the court shall decree the divorce and approve the agreement."

570. Daniel Girsberger & Nathalie Voser, *International Arbitration: Comparative and Swiss Perspectives*, 3rd ed (Schulthess, 2016) at para. 436; Bernhard Berger & Franz Kellerhals, International and Domestic Arbitration in Switzerland, 3rd ed (Hart, 2015) at para. 259.

571. *Sheets v. Sheets*, 254 NYS2d 320 (NY App Div 1964) at 322–324; *Schneider v. Schneider*, 216 NE2d 318 (NY 1966).

572. *Hampton v. Hampton*, 689 NYS2d 186 (NY App Div 1999) at 188.

573. *Faherty v. Faherty*, 477 A2d 1257 (NJ Sup Ct 1984) at 1262–1263.

Miller (1993) noted that spousal support and child support disputes are arbitrable.[574] In Michigan, the Court of Appeals in *Dick v. Dick* (1995) held that issues of property distribution and child support are arbitrable.[575] In Virginia, the Court of Appeals in *Bandas v. Bandas* (1993) affirmed the lower court's decision enforcing an arbitral award on spousal support and marital property.

340. In terms of legislative frameworks, one example is § 50-42 of the North Carolina Family Law Arbitration Act, which provides that spousal support and child support disputes are arbitrable.[576] Under § 50-42 of the Act, even pre-dispute arbitration agreements are valid unless the agreement was signed prior to the marriage *and* the dispute concerns, among other things, child support. However, the North Carolina Family Law Arbitration Act departs from some typical features of arbitration, for instance, by allowing for court modification of an award on alimony and child support in cases where there is a substantial change of circumstances (§§ 50-41, 50-56).

341. Other examples include arbitration laws of the states of Indiana and New Jersey. Under § 34-57-5-2 of the Indiana Family Law Arbitration Act, all matters incidental to the dissolution of a marriage (such as support disputes) may be submitted to arbitration. However, according to § 34-57-5-2, the parties must reduce their agreement to writing and file it with Indiana courts. Likewise, rule 5:1-5 of the Rules Governing the Courts of the State of New Jersey (on arbitration of family disputes) provides for the arbitrability of spousal support and child support disputes.

342. In 2005, the American Academy of Matrimonial Lawyers (AAML) issued a Model Family Law Arbitration Act. The AAML model law was not adopted by any state, but it was a contribution to the overall improvement of family law arbitration in the US. In 2016, the Uniform Law Commission issued the Uniform Family Law Arbitration Act (UFLAA).[577] However, it remains to be seen how the UFLAA will be received by state legislatures.[578]

Canada (Provinces of Alberta, British Columbia, and Ontario)

343. In the common law provinces of Canada, the arbitration of financial matters incidental to marriage and civil partnership is a well-recognized practice. In the province of Alberta, the Family Law Act has no provision on arbitration, but Alberta courts have supported the arbitration of financial matters relevant to family disputes. There are multiple decisions by the King's Bench of Alberta, including *Seneviratne v.*

574. *Miller v. Miller*, 620 A2d 1161 (Pa Super Ct 1993) at 1163–1166.
575. *Dick v. Dick*, 534 NW2d 185 (Mich Ct App 1995) at 188, 190.
576. The section reads: "all issues arising from a marital separation or divorce, except for the divorce itself."
577. Online: https://www.uniformlaws.org/committees/community-home/librarydocuments?communitykey=ddf1c9b6-65c0-4d55-bfd7-15c2d1e6d4ed&tab=librarydocuments (last visited 15 June 2022).
578. To find out which states have adopted the UFLAA, *see* the enactment-status map on the website of the Uniform Law Commission, online: https://www.uniformlaws.org/committees/community-home?CommunityKey=ddf1c9b6-65c0-4d55-bfd7-15c2d1e6d4ed (last visited 15 June 2022).

Seneviratne (1998),[579] *Metcalfe v. Metcalfe* (2006),[580] *Dawson v. Dawson* (2016),[581] *Kawchuk v. Kovacs* (2016),[582] *Driscoll v. Hautz* (2018),[583] and *Aldred Estate (Re)* (2020).[584] These decisions—either directly or indirectly—support the arbitration of financial matters in matrimonial disputes such as spousal support, child support, and the division of matrimonial property. Likewise, the Alberta Court of Appeal in *Murray v. Murray* (2007) held that, when the divorcing spouses' separation and property agreement contains an arbitration clause, they may not litigate their dispute as to financial disclosure before the courts.[585] However, it should be noted that, in all of these decisions, the arbitration agreements were *post-dispute* agreements.

344. In the province of British Columbia (BC), relevant laws and regulations allow for the arbitration of family law disputes (including financial matters), but there are restrictions. The new Arbitration Act (enacted in 2020) does *not* apply to family law disputes. Rather, new provisions on arbitration have been added to the BC Family Law Act, which now governs the arbitration of family law disputes independently from the Arbitration Act. Under sections 19.2(2) and (3) of the Family Law Act, pre-dispute arbitration agreements are unenforceable unless: a court order under the same Act provides otherwise or that the parties' arbitration agreement concerns the implementation of a court order, an arbitration award, or a settlement agreement under the Act.

345. Also, the regulation under the BC Family Law Act contains two provisions that, when read together, limit the scope of arbitrable family matters in BC. Under rule 5(1) of the Family Law Act Regulation, only "family dispute resolution professionals" (FDRPs) are allowed to sit as arbitrator in family disputes. Further, under rule 5(3), FDRPs may only arbitrate three types of disputes: parenting arrangements, contact with a child, and child support. Given that FDRPs are the only arbitrators in family disputes, and can only decide the above three types of disputes, one might conclude that those disputes are the only arbitrable matters in BC family law and, consequently, that disputes as to spousal support or distribution of matrimonial property are non-arbitrable. However, it is not exactly clear that such a conclusion would be correct given BC case law and other applicable legislative Acts.

346. For example, under the BC Family Maintenance Enforcement Act, section 1(1), a maintenance order is defined as "a provision for the payment of maintenance in an order, judgment or *family law arbitration award* that is enforceable in British Columbia" (emphasis added). Further, in *SMR v. RSB* (2003), the BC Court of Appeal held that the parties' dispute as to the husband's maintenance obligation should be submitted to arbitration on the basis of the arbitration clause in their separation

579. *Seneviratne v. Seneviratne*, 1998 ABQB 289, 60 Alta LR (3d) 311.
580. *Metcalfe v. Metcalfe*, 2006 ABQB 798 at paras. 3-6, 20, 54, 55, 70 Alta LR (4th) 268.
581. *Dawson v. Dawson*, 2016 ABQB 167 at paras. 1-5, 11, 22, 29, 30, 55, [2016] AJ No 287.
582. *Kawchuk v. Kovacs*, 2016 ABQB 118, [2016] AJ No 223.
583. *Driscoll v. Hautz*, 2018 ABCA 272 at paras. 1-4, 13.
584. *Aldred Estate (Re)*, 2020 ABQB 469 at paras. 4-9, 31, 57-58, 62.
585. *Murray v. Murray*, 2007 ABCA 113 at paras. 2, 3, 9-11, 404 AR 123.

agreement.[586] Also, the BC Court of Appeal, in *McMillan v. McMillan* (2016), upheld the lower court's decision to refuse to set aside an arbitral award on the distribution of matrimonial property, which was rendered on the basis of the arbitration clause in their minutes of settlement.[587]

347. In the province of Ontario, under section 1 of the Arbitration Act, the following may be submitted to arbitration: matters which could be dealt with in a marriage contract, separation agreement, a cohabitation agreement, or a paternity agreement under Part IV of the Ontario Family Law Act. Section 59.4 of the Ontario Family Law Act provides only for the enforceability of *post-dispute* arbitration agreements. However, according to section 59.7(2) of the Ontario Family Law Act, the limitation in section 59.4 is not applicable where a separation agreement, court order, or family arbitration award provides for the arbitration of possible future disputes that relate to the ongoing management or implementation of that agreement, order, or award. It should also be noted that, under section 59.6(1), for a family arbitration agreement to be enforceable, the parties must have received "independent legal advice" before entering into the agreement.

348. Ontario courts have been supportive of the arbitrability of financial disputes in family law-related matters. For example, in *Borschel v. Borschel* (2020), the Ontario Superior Court rejected challenges to the validity and enforceability of two arbitral awards that covered a host of issues such as child and spousal support, equalization of the net family property, disclosure, preservation of assets, and insurance issues.[588]

349. There are training requirements for a family arbitrator in Ontario.[589] This is pursuant to Rule 3 of the Ontario Family Arbitration Regulation, O Reg 134/07 which reads: "Every arbitrator who conducts a family arbitration shall have received the training approved by the Attorney General for the arbitrator or class of arbitrators, as set out on the Ministry's website."

350. It should be noted that the Ontario Superior Court in *Blustein v. Blustine* (2011) held that the provisions of the Ontario Family Law Act have not converted family arbitration to statutory arbitration and, as such, courts may not conduct judicial review of family arbitration awards under administrative law standards.[590]

Germany and Switzerland

351. In Germany, section 1030(1) of the Code of Civil Procedure provides that the general rule for arbitrability is that claims involving an economic interest are arbitrable.

---

586. *SMR v. RSB*, 2003 BCCA 412 at paras. 1, 3, 8, 10–14, 20, 34, 41 RFL (5th) 159.
587. *McMillan v. McMillan*, 2016 BCCA 441, 406 DLR (4th) 398. The BC Court of Appeal in the first paragraph of its decision noted that "[t]his is the first appeal to reach this court involving the decision of an arbitrator to which the Family Law Act, S.B.C. 2011, c. 25 ('FLA') and concomitant amendments to the Arbitration Act, S.B.C. 1996, c. 55 apply."
588. *Borschel v. Borschel*, 2020 ONSC 4395 at paras. 1, 18, 16, 38, 70.
589. Ontario Ministry of the Attorney General website, tab "Family Law," sub-tab "Family Arbitration," hyperlink "Overview," heading "What an arbitrator can decide," online: https://www.ontario.ca/page/family-arbitration#section-0 (last visited 1 December 2021).
590. *Blustein v. Blustine*, 2011 ONSC 1888 at paras. 2, 4–7, 5 RFL (7th) 41.

Therefore, spousal support and property division disputes are generally considered arbitrable, as they involve economic interests.[591]

352. In Switzerland, if the couple's financial dispute is considered to be an international dispute that falls within the scope of the PILA,[592] their dispute is arbitrable under Article 177(1) of the PILA.[593]

ii. Jurisdictions Where Financial Matters Are Non-Arbitrable

353. The majority of jurisdictions do not allow couples to limit their right of access to courts for spousal or child support disputes. This includes France, Québec, England and Wales, China (Mainland), Hong Kong, Singapore, Switzerland (in domestic disputes), and Germany (for child support disputes).

France, Québec, and China

354. France, Québec, and China have banned the arbitration of family law disputes (including financial matters).[594]

England and Wales

355. In relation to financial matters between a married couple, section 34 of the Matrimonial Causes Act 1973 prohibits spouses from agreeing to restrict court jurisdiction over a request for an order containing financial arrangements. For partners in a civil partnership, schedule 5 of the Civil Partnership Act 2004 provides similar provisions. Likewise, section 9(4) of the Child Support Act 1991 declares void any provision in a maintenance agreement that restricts the right of access to court for a child-related maintenance assessment.

356. In the leading case of *Hyman v. Hyman* (1929), the House of Lords stated that "the power of the court to make provision for a wife on the dissolution of her marriage is a necessary incident of the power to decree such a dissolution, conferred not merely in the interests of the wife, but of the public, and that the wife cannot by her own covenant preclude herself from invoking the jurisdiction of the court or preclude the

591. Stephanie Uta Gilfrich, *Schiedsverfahren im Scheidungsrecht: eine rechtvergleichende Untersuchung* (Mohr Siebeck, 2007) at 60, 61; Daniela Kreidler-Pleus, "Family law in Germany: Overview" published online at Practical Law a Thomson Reuters Legal Solution (1 September 2020) at question 34: https://ca.practicallaw.thomsonreuters.com/8-575-0676?transitionType =Default&contextData=(sc.Default)&firstPage=true (last visited 24 February 2021); Wendy Kennett, "It's Arbitration, But Not As We Know It: Reflections on Family Law Dispute Resolution" (2016) 30:1 Int'l J L Pol'y & Fam 1 at 6 DOI: 10.1093/lawfam/ebv017.

592. International arbitrations that have their seat in Switzerland are governed by Chapter 12 of the PILA: provided that, under Art. 176(1), at the time of the conclusion of the arbitration agreement, at least one of the parties has neither its domicile nor habitual residence in Switzerland.

593. Mariella Orelli, "Commentary on Chapter 12 PILS, Article 177 [Arbitrability]" in Manuel Arroyo, ed, *Arbitration in Switzerland: The Practitioner's Guide,* (Kluwer Law International, 2018) 61 at para. 13.

594. French Civil Code, Art. 2060; Québec Civil Code, Art. 2639; Chinese Arbitration Law, Art. 3.

court from the exercise of that jurisdiction."[595] The *Hyman* case supports the interpretation that a request for an order for financial arrangements may not be submitted to arbitration.

357. The UK Supreme Court in *Radmacher v. Granatino* (2010) elaborated on the public policy rationale underpinning section 34 of the Matrimonial Causes Act 1973 and its history:

> They [the agreements that are the subject matter of section 34] *relieved the couple of the duty to live together*: this meant that neither was guilty of the matrimonial offence of desertion and neither could petition for or enforce a decree of restitution of conjugal rights. They might also make provision for the wife and any children. *In return* she might agree not to go to court for a maintenance order. However, in the leading case of *Hyman v Hyman* [1929] AC 601 it was firmly established that such agreements could not oust the statutory powers of the courts to award financial provision should the couple divorce. ... [T]he rule in *Hyman v Hyman* [was] confirmed, by the Maintenance Agreements Act 1957 ... The provisions in the 1957 Act were later amended in two significant respects by the Matrimonial Proceedings and Property Act 1970 and are now consolidated in the Matrimonial Causes Act 1973, ss 34 to 36.[596]

358. This interpretation by the Supreme Court indicates that the prohibition contained in section 34 of the Matrimonial Causes Act 1973 was not designed to bar arbitration. As such, it is uncertain whether the prohibition in section 34 and similar provisions also applies to submitting such financial requests to arbitral tribunals. Nevertheless, in *Fulham Football Club (1987) Ltd v. Richards* (2011), the Court of Appeal—when explaining the concept of non-arbitrability in English law—identified section 34 of the Matrimonial Causes Act 1973 as one of the statutory limitations on arbitration.[597]

359. One might conclude that the literature set out above (on the non-arbitrability of financial matters) conflicts with Article 2.2(b) of the Family Law Arbitration Financial Scheme Arbitration Rules, adopted by the Institute of Family Law Arbitrators (IFLA),[598] which provides for the arbitration of disputes that arise under Part II of the Matrimonial Causes Act 1973 (where section 34 is located). The Family Law Arbitration Financial Scheme Arbitration Rules also foresee the possibility of referring a request for an order containing financial arrangements to arbitrators instead of courts. However, the IFLA has noted that:

> Under English family law the parties *cannot* reach an agreement which excludes the power that the court has to make its own orders. However, it is highly likely that Courts will endorse Awards and Determinations made under the IFLA Schemes. In financial cases the parties will *need to apply to the court for an order*

595. *Hyman v. Hyman* [1929] AC 601 at 614.
596. *Radmacher v. Granatino* [2010] UKSC 42 at paras. 144, 145.
597. *Fulham Football Club (1987) Ltd v. Richards* [2011] EWCA Civ 855 at para. 41.
598. The IFLA is a "not for profit organisation, created by the Chartered Institute of Arbitrators (CIArb), the Family Law Bar Association, and the family lawyers" group Resolution, in association with the Centre for Child and Family Law Reform." Online: http://ifla.org.uk (last visited 28 October 2022).

> *in the same or similar terms as the Award or Determination.* The President of the Family Division, Sir James Munby, has recognised an IFLA arbitration Award in an important decided case which, it can safely be assumed, other judges will follow.[599]

Hong Kong

360. Under section 14(1) of the Matrimonial Proceedings and Property Ordinance (Cap 192), while spouses can enter into a maintenance agreement, any contractual term that restricts the parties' right to apply to a court for an order containing financial arrangements—defined under section 14(2) to include both spousal maintenance and child maintenance—is void. A 2013 speech by the Hong Kong Secretary for Justice on dispute resolution in family disputes explains the Hong Kong approach to arbitration of family disputes:

> [W]hilst mediation is popular in the matrimonial context, the use of arbitration is far less popular. Instead, arbitration is more popular in other contexts such as commercial claims and construction disputes. However, interesting development is taking place in England. ... Whilst it may be premature to pass any judgment on whether arbitration is a suitable means of ADR in the matrimonial context, it does provide fruit for thought, and it would certainly be worthwhile to keep an eye on it so as to see what can be done in Hong Kong.[600]

Singapore

361. There are two legislative Acts that apply in relation to ending a marriage: for everyone other than Muslims, family law is codified in the Women's Charter 1961; and for Muslims, family law falls under the Administration of Muslim Law Act 1966.

362. Under the Women's Charter, while parties may mediate disputes under section 139H(2), there is no reference to arbitration. Under section 116, any settlement by the parties "for the payment of a capital sum in settlement of all future claims to maintenance" is not effective unless the court approves such a settlement. Other relevant legislative Acts such as the Children and Young Persons Act 1993, the Guardianship of Infants Act 1934, or the Family Justice Act 2014 have no provisions relating to arbitration. Thus, commentators have concluded that, in Singapore, apart from the court-ordered arbitrations in Islamic law-related matters,[601] arbitration is not yet "part of the legal framework" in family law disputes.[602]

---

599. IFLA website, tab "what is arbitration," sub-tab "FAQs," question "Outcomes and their enforcement," online: http://ifla.org.uk/what-is-arbitration/faqs/ (last visited 28 October 2022) (emphasis added).
600. Hong Kong Department of Justice, Press Releases and Speeches: *Speech by the Hon Rimsky Yuen, SC, JP, Secretary for Justice at the Hong Kong Family Law Association on Tuesday, 12 March 2013 "Family Issues, Dispute Resolution and Related Matters"* online: https://www.doj.gov.hk/en/community_engagement/press/20130312_pr.html (last visited 9 March 2023).
601. Discussed above, para. 335.
602. Randolph Khoo & Hoon Shu Mei, "Family law in Singapore: overview" in *Family Law: A Global Guide From Practical Law* (Thomson Reuters, 2020) at question 34, online: https://uk.

Germany

363. Under section 1030(1) of the Code of Civil Procedure (ZPO), the general rule is that claims involving economic interest are arbitrable. However, commentators have argued that child support disputes, despite involving economic interests, are inarbitrable.[603]

364. Section 1030(3) of the ZPO provides that any other German law containing a provision on the non-arbitrability of a matter remains unaffected by the general rule on arbitrability. One such provision is section 1822(12) of the Civil Code, which provides that a guardian may not arbitrate a dispute in their capacity as guardian without first obtaining the Family Court's approval to do so, unless "the object of the dispute or of the uncertainty can be assessed in money and does not exceed the value of 3,000 euros, or the settlement corresponds to a judicial settlement suggestion made in writing or recorded by the court."

Switzerland

365. As discussed above, family law disputes involving financial interests that fall within the scope of application of the PILA may be submitted to arbitration.[604] Where the PILA does not apply, arbitration is governed by the Civil Procedure Code. Under articles 279, 280, and 282 of the Civil Procedure Code, parties may reach an agreement on the effects of divorce, including maintenance payments and the division of withdrawal benefits from occupational pension funds, but any such agreement must be approved by the competent court in order to be valid. Given that such agreements need court approval for validity, these matters appear not to fall within the category of rights that one may freely waive and, as such, they are not arbitrable under Article 354 of the Civil Procedure Code. However, certain commentators have expressed the opposite view that matrimonial property disputes are arbitrable under Swiss law.[605]

3. Custody

366. Like divorce, custody is a subject matter as to which states are generally reluctant to legislate in favor of arbitration. In fact, other than the common law provinces of Canada and some states in the US, the jurisdictions studied do not allow parties to waive their right of access to courts in custody disputes. This subject matter will be discussed below in two Segments: (i) Jurisdictions Where Custody Disputes Are Arbitrable; and (ii) Jurisdictions Where Custody Disputes Are Non-arbitrable.

---

practicallaw.thomsonreuters.com/4-568-0826?transitionType=Default&contextData=(sc.Default)&firstPage=true (last visited 10 April 2023).

603. *See, e.g.*, Stephanie Uta Gilfrich, *Schiedsverfahren im Scheidungsrecht: eine rechtvergleichende Untersuchung* (Mohr Siebeck, 2007) at 49, 57–59.

604. Discussed above, para. 352.

605. Daniel Girsberger & Nathalie Voser, *International Arbitration: Comparative and Swiss Perspectives*, 3rd ed (Schulthess, 2016) at para. 436.

i. Jurisdictions Where Custody Disputes Are Arbitrable

367. Of the jurisdictions that were studied, only the common law provinces of Canada and several US states consider custody disputes to be arbitrable.

Canada (Alberta, British Columbia, Ontario)

368. In Alberta, the Family Law Act has no provision on arbitration. However, the Registered Parenting Coordinator and Arbitrators (RPCAs)—who are appointed either by court order or parties' agreement—have decision-making authority by means of arbitration under the Arbitration Act of Alberta in relation to parties' disputes about parenting.[606] RCPAs' decisions are binding but they may be appealed to Alberta courts.[607]

369. Alberta courts have taken a favorable approach in relation to the arbitrability of non-financial matters, including child custody, access to children, and parenting. In *Metcalfe v. Metcalfe* (2006), the King's Bench allowed a partial appeal on points of law from an arbitral award in relation to, inter alia, custody and access to children, and held that the award should be sent back to the arbitrator to rectify errors.[608] The decision indicates the Court's underlying assumption that these disputes are arbitrable. Also in *Dawson v. Dawson* (2016), the King's Bench refused to set aside an arbitral award covering, among other things, the parties' custody and parenting disputes.[609]

370. In British Columbia (BC), laws and regulations allow the arbitration of family law disputes including non-financial matters, but such arbitration is subject to severe restrictions. The BC Arbitration Act comprehensively addresses the requirements necessary for the arbitration of family law disputes. For example, under section 2(2), an arbitration agreement is invalid if it removes the jurisdiction of a court for disputes arising under the federal Divorce Act or the BC Family Law Act. In addition, under section 2.1, only *post-dispute* arbitration agreements are valid, unless a court order made in accordance with the BC Family Law Act allows for an agreement or where the parties' agreement meets the requirements set out in section 6(1)(b) of the BC Family Law Act.[610] Furthermore, section 2(2.1) of the Arbitration Act makes it mandatory for arbitrators to consider the best interests of the child—as set out in section 37 of the BC

606. Alberta Family Mediation Society website, tab "FAQ," hyperlink "What is Parenting Coordination?" online: https://afms.ca/faq/ (last visited 29 October 2021).
607. Alberta Family Mediation Society website, tab "Resources," section "Articles," hyperlink "Parenting Coordination Information for Parents and Lawyers," online: https://afms.ca/wp-content/uploads/2017/07/PC_info_for_parents_and_lawyers.pdf (last visited 29 October 2021).
608. *Metcalfe v. Metcalfe*, 2006 ABQB 798 at paras. 3–6, 20, 54, 55, 70 Alta LR (4th) 268.
609. *Dawson v. Dawson*, 2016 ABQB 167 at paras. 1–5, 11, 22, 29, 30, 55, [2016] AJ No 287.
610. Section 6(1)(b) of the BC Family Law Act reads: "Subject to this Act, 2 or more persons may make an agreement respecting (i) a matter that may be the subject of a family law dispute in the future, (ii) the means of resolving a family law dispute or a matter that may be the subject of a family law dispute in the future, including the type of family dispute resolution to be used, or (iii) the implementation of an agreement or order."

Family Law Act—when deciding parenting arrangements, guardianship, or contact with a child.

371. The Regulation made under the BC Family Law Act contains two relevant provisions. Under rule 5(1) of the Family Law Act Regulation, only "family dispute resolution professionals" (FDRPs) may sit as arbitrator in family disputes and, under rule 5(3), they may only arbitrate three types of disputes: parenting arrangements, contact with a child, and child support.

372. In terms of custody disputes, it is interesting to note that, in *Stonier v. Stonier* (2004), the BC Court of Appeal observed that "[i]t is well-settled law that an agreement between the parents concerning the custody of their children cannot oust the jurisdiction of the court to determine the issue of custody."[611] However, this position no longer reflects BC's approach to the arbitrability of custody disputes. Amendments to the BC Arbitration Act (effective as of 2013) incorporate a number of provisions relating to the arbitration of family disputes, including section 2(2.1) that makes it mandatory for arbitrators to consider the best interests of the child—as set out in section 37 of the BC Family Law Act—when deciding parenting arrangements, guardianship, and contact with a child.

373. There is yet to be a court decision in BC that decides the question of arbitrability of custody disputes, but there are decisions where the court has referred to arbitral awards in custody disputes. For instance, in *Thomson v. Thomson* (2016), the BC Supreme Court decided to make changes in the terms of an arbitral award on custody and access to the parties' child, following allegations by both parties about the other's non-compliance with the award.[612] The *Thomson* decision indicates that the Court assumed the custody dispute was arbitrable.

374. In Ontario, under section 1 of the Arbitration Act, the following may be submitted to arbitration: matters which could be dealt with in a marriage contract, separation agreement, cohabitation agreement, or paternity agreement under Part IV of the Ontario Family Law Act. Section 59.4 of the Ontario Family Law Act only provides for the enforceability of *post-dispute* arbitration agreements. However, according to section 59.7(2), the limitation in section 59.4 is not applicable where a separation agreement, court order, or family arbitration award provides for the arbitration of possible future disputes relating to the ongoing management or implementation of that agreement, order, or award.

375. According to the website of the Ontario Attorney General, an arbitrator "cannot grant a divorce, annul a marriage or declare someone to be or not to be someone else's child. Only a court can make that kind of order."[613] The same source also sets out the

611. *Stonier v. Stonier*, 2004 BCCA 307 at para. 21, 4 RFL (6th) 220.
612. *Thomson v. Thomson*, 2016 BCSC 904, [2016] BCJ No 1031.
613. Ontario Ministry of the Attorney General website, tab "Family Law," sub-tab "Family Arbitration," hyperlink "Overview," heading "What an arbitrator can decide," online: https://www.ontario.ca/page/family-arbitration#section-0 (last visited 2 November 2021).

training requirements for a family arbitrator in Ontario.[614] These requirements are imposed pursuant to Rule 3 of the Ontario Family Arbitration Regulation, O Reg 134/07 which reads: "Every arbitrator who conducts a family arbitration shall have received the training approved by the Attorney General for the arbitrator or class of arbitrators, as set out on the Ministry's website."

376. Ontario courts have strongly supported the arbitrability of family disputes. In *Shoval v. Shoval* (2005), the Ontario Superior Court held that allegations by a parent as to physical and sexual abuse of the child by the other parent are matters that are related to the custody issue and should be submitted to arbitration on the basis of the arbitration clause in the parties' separation agreement, regardless of the fact that such allegations may be of a quasi-criminal nature.[615] Similarly, in *Reati v. Racz* (2016), the same Court dismissed a father's appeal from an arbitral award on custody and relocation that permitted the mother to relocate their child to the US to take up the employment she was offered.[616] However, if an Ontario court believes that submitting a custody dispute is not in the best interests of the child, it may refuse to incorporate the parties' agreed arbitration clause of their minutes of settlement into its final order, as the Superior Court did in *Wainwright v. Wainwright* (2012).[617]

377. It should be noted that the Ontario Superior Court in *Blustein v. Blustine* (2011) held that the provisions of the Ontario Family Law Act have not converted family arbitration into statutory arbitration and, as a result, courts may not conduct judicial review of family arbitration awards as a matter of administrative law.[618]

The United States

378. A number of states (e.g., North Carolina, New Jersey, and Indiana) have enacted liberal laws in favor of arbitration of domestic relations matters that cover custody disputes as well. North Carolina was the first US state to adopt a comprehensive arbitration law that applies to domestic relations. Under § 50-41 of the North Carolina Family Law Arbitration Act, "all issues arising from a marital separation or divorce, except for the divorce itself" may be submitted to arbitration. According to § 50-42, even pre-dispute arbitration agreements are valid unless the agreement was signed prior to the marriage *and* the parties' dispute concerns child support or custody.[619] Likewise, Rule 5:1-5 of the Rules Governing the Courts of the State of New Jersey, and

614. *Ibid.*, hyperlink "Find an arbitrator," hyperlink "Learn more about the required training for family arbitrators," online: https://www.ontario.ca/page/training-family-arbitrators (last visited 2 November 2021).
615. *Shoval v. Shoval*, 2005 CarswellOnt 2383 (Ont Sup Ct) at paras. 10–14, 17, [2005] OJ No 2401.
616. *Reati v. Racz*, 2016 ONSC 1967, [2016] OJ No 1674.
617. *Wainwright v. Wainwright*, 2012 ONSC 2686 at paras. 31, 126, 128, 134, 135, 139, 140, 148–152, 156, 157, 21 RFL (7th) 415.
618. *Blustein v. Blustine*, 2011 ONSC 1888 at paras. 2, 4–7, 5 RFL (7th) 41.
619. However, in order to accommodate the nuances of domestic relations, the North Carolina Family Law Arbitration Act departs from some typical features of arbitration. For instance, by allowing court modification of an award on child custody, among others, in case of substantial change of circumstances (§§ 50-41, 50-56).

§ 34-57-5-2 of the Indiana Family Law Arbitration Act provide for the arbitrability of custody disputes.

379. However, not all US states allow couples to submit their custody disputes to arbitration. In fact, disagreement exists among state courts as to whether child custody disputes are arbitrable and if so, what standard of review courts should apply in judicial review of such awards. Some states, such as Pennsylvania, New Jersey, and Michigan, allow custody disputes to be arbitrated but each state has adopted a different standard of review for these arbitral awards.[620]

380. In Pennsylvania, the Supreme Court in *Miller v. Miller* (1993) held that child custody disputes are arbitrable but that the "award shall [not] be binding on a court if such award is challenged by one of the parties as not being in the best interests of the child."[621] This will then result in de novo review of the award.

381. In New Jersey, the Supreme Court in *Faherty v. Faherty* (1984) noted that arbitration of custody disputes could be "more beneficial to the children of this state than the present system of courtroom confrontation," but held that any award concerning children may be subject to "special review" by courts, providing generally for de novo review.[622] More than two decades later, the New Jersey Supreme Court in *Fawzy v. Fawzy* (2009) held that child custody issues are arbitrable, and declined to adopt the Pennsylvania approach taken in the *Miller* decision.[623] Instead, the Court provided for de novo review of arbitral awards on child custody.[624] The New Jersey Supreme Court explained that the standard of review applied in its earlier decision in *Faherty* was based on the consideration of whether there is any *harm* to the child rather than whether the award satisfies the best *interest* of the child.[625] According to the Court, the New Jersey standard of review is a "hybrid model" that provides for two scenarios: first, if there is no claim of harm to the child, the standard of review is a limited review based on New Jersey's version of the Uniform Arbitration Act.[626] Second, if there is a claim of harm to the child, *and* a prima facie case is established, the court will first examine the alleged harm and if it finds no harm, the standard remains the same as scenario one.[627] However, if the court finds harm, then "the presumption in favor of the parents' choice of arbitration will be overcome and it will fall to the court to decide what is in the child's best interests."[628]

382. In Michigan, the Court of Appeals in *Dick v. Dick* (1995) held that child custody disputes may be submitted to arbitration.[629] However, the Michigan Supreme Court in

620. For discussion on the states that do not consider custody disputes to be arbitrable, *see* below, para. 390.
621. *Miller v. Miller*, 620 A2d 1161 (Pa Super Ct 1993) at 1163–1166.
622. *Faherty v. Faherty*, 477 A2d 1257 (NJ Sup Ct 1984) at 1261–1263.
623. *Fawzy v. Fawzy*, 973 A2d 347 (NJ Sup Ct 2009) at 360–362.
624. *Ibid.*
625. *Ibid.*
626. *Ibid.*
627. *Ibid.*
628. *Ibid.*
629. *Dick v. Dick*, 534 NW2d 185 (Mich Ct App 1995) at 188, 190.

Harvey v. Harvey (2004) held that, when an award on child custody reaches a court, it should review the award de novo and the court may "modify or vacate an arbitration award that is not in the best interests of the child."[630]

ii. Jurisdictions Where Custody Disputes Are Non-Arbitrable

383. Other than the North American jurisdictions discussed in the previous Subsection, none of the jurisdictions studied allows parties to submit custody disputes to arbitration. This group of jurisdictions includes France, Québec, England and Wales, Germany, Switzerland, China, Hong Kong, Singapore, and some states in the US.

384. France, Québec, and China have categorically banned the arbitration of family law disputes, which applies to custody disputes as well.[631]

385. In England and Wales, the relevant legislative Acts[632] contain no provision that relates to the arbitrability of custody disputes and, to date, no specific case law has been reported on the matter. However, given the non-arbitrability of financial matters (spousal and child maintenance disputes) in English law,[633] and the fact that custody is often considered to be more sensitive than financial matters (in the sense of the public interests involved), it seems unlikely that English law considers custody disputes to be arbitrable.[634]

386. In Germany, under section 1030(1) of the Code of Civil Procedure, non-pecuniary claims are arbitrable only if the parties are allowed to conclude a settlement regarding the subject matter. Child custody disputes do not involve economic interests within the meaning of section 1030(1), and nor are they considered to be matters about which parents may enter into a settlement agreement.[635] Therefore, such disputes are not arbitrable.[636] Under sections 86(1)(2) and 156(2) of the Act on Proceedings in Family Matters and in Matters of Non-Contentious Jurisdiction (FamFG), parents may reach an "agreement regarding contact with or surrender of the child," but this agreement would be enforceable only if it is approved and recorded by the competent court.

387. In Switzerland, given the non-arbitrability of spousal and child support disputes (in domestic matters),[637] it seems unlikely that custody disputes would be arbitrable.

630. *Harvey v. Harvey*, 680 NW2d 835 (Mich Sup Ct 2004) at 839.
631. French Civil Code, Art. 2060; Québec Civil Code, Art. 2639; Chinese Arbitration Law, Art. 3.
632. *See, e.g.*, Arbitration Act 1996; Family Law Act 1996; Matrimonial Causes Act 1973; Civil Partnership Act 2004; Child Support Act 1991; Marriage Act 1949; Marriage (Same Sex Couples) Act 2013.
633. *See* above, paras. 355–359.
634. *See* Audley Sheppard, "English Arbitration Act" in Loukas A Mistelis, ed, *Concise International Arbitration*, 2nd ed (Kluwer Law International, 2015) 977 at 1104.
635. Stephanie Uta Gilfrich, *Schiedsverfahren im Scheidungsrecht: eine rechtvergleichende Untersuchung* (Mohr Siebeck, 2007) at 39, 40, 47.
636. Daniela Kreidler-Pleus, "Family law in Germany: Overview" published online at Practical Law a Thomson Reuters Legal Solution (1 September 2020) at question 34: http://ca.practicallaw.com/8-575-0676?source=relatedcontent (last visited 24 February 2021).
637. *See* above, para. 365. However, in international disputes where the PILA applies, family disputes involving financial matters are arbitrable. *See* above, para. 317.

388. In Hong Kong, the relevant legislative Acts, namely the Matrimonial Causes Ordinance (Cap 179), the Matrimonial Proceedings and Property Ordinance (Cap 192), and the Separations and Maintenance Orders Ordinance (Cap 16), do not contain any provisions on the arbitrability of custody disputes. Further, provisions contained within these ordinances that address court power in relation to custody matters do not make it clear whether courts' jurisdiction is exclusive.[638] In this regard, initial reports on arbitration in Hong Kong (namely, the 1986 report by Kaplan and Greig[639] as well as the 1999 report by Kaplan and Morgan[640]) explained that:

> [S]ince the marital status and grounds for divorce involve questions of public policy, an arbitration award purporting to recognize or annul a marriage or to grant a divorce would be ineffective. For the same reason, an award that purported to affect the custody or support of a child would also be ineffective.

However, more recent reports (namely, the 2013 report by Kaplan and Morgan[641] as well as the 2022 report by Moser and Morgan[642]) no longer include the aforementioned paragraph in their section on the arbitrability of family disputes. Nevertheless, given the inarbitrability of spousal/child maintenance disputes,[643] it seems unlikely that Hong Kong law allows for the arbitration of custody disputes.

389. In Singapore, there are two sets of legislative Acts that apply in relation to ending a marriage: (i) for everyone other than Muslims, family law has been codified in the Women's Charter 1961; and (ii) for Muslims, family law falls under the Administration of Muslim Law Act 1966. Neither of these two laws contains a provision on the arbitrability of custody disputes. Further, other relevant legislative Acts such as the Children and Young Persons Act 1993, the Guardianship of Infants Act 1934, and the Family Justice Act 2014, have no provisions that relate to arbitration. Thus, commentators believe that, apart from the court-ordered arbitrations in Islamic law matters for divorce,[644] contractual arbitration is not yet "part of the legal framework" in family law disputes in Singapore.[645]

638. *See, e.g.*, Matrimonial Causes Ordinance (Cap 179), ss. 48, 48A; Matrimonial Proceedings and Property Ordinance (Cap 192), s. 19(1); Separations and Maintenance Orders Ordinance (Cap 16), s. 5.
639. Neil Kaplan & Robert T Greig, "National Report for Hong Kong (1986) [Archived]" in Albert Jan van den Berg ed, *ICCA Yearbook Commercial Arbitration*, vol 11 (Kluwer Law International, 1986) at 9.
640. Neil Kaplan & Robert Morgan, "National Report for Hong Kong (1999) [Archived]" in Jan Paulsson, ed, *ICCA International Handbook on Commercial Arbitration* (Kluwer Law International, 1999) at 22.
641. Neil Kaplan & Robert Morgan, "National Report for Hong Kong (2013) [Archived]" in Jan Paulsson & Lise Bosman, eds, *ICCA International Handbook on Commercial Arbitration* (Kluwer Law International, 2013).
642. Michael J Moser & Robert Morgan, "National Report for Hong Kong (2021 through 2022)" in Lise Bosman, ed, *ICCA International Handbook on Commercial Arbitration* (Kluwer Law International, 2022) at 30, 31.
643. *See* above, para. 360.
644. Discussed above, para. 335.
645. Randolph Khoo & Hoon Shu Mei, "Family law in Singapore: overview" in *Family Law: A Global Guide From Practical Law* (Thomson Reuters, 2020) at question 34, online: http://ca.practicallaw.com/4-568-0826 (last visited 10 April 2023).

390. In the US, some state jurisdictions allow for the arbitration of custody disputes, and some of these jurisdictions apply a range of restrictions on arbitration of custody disputes, including mandating court review of awards.[646] However, not all US states allow parties to submit their custody disputes to arbitration. For example, the Appellate Division of the New York Supreme Court in *Glauber v. Glauber* (1993) held that custody disputes are not arbitrable.[647] After a decade, in *Hirsch v. Hirsch* (2004)[648] and in *Schechter v. Schechter* (2009), the same Court confirmed the inarbitrability of custody disputes on the grounds that "the court's role as parens patriae must not be usurped."[649]

F. INTELLECTUAL PROPERTY LAW

391. This Section discusses the status of arbitrability in relation to (1) copyright, (2) patent, and (3) trademark disputes. The discussion in this section shows that jurisdictions have generally adopted a favorable approach to the arbitrability of intellectual property (IP) disputes. Nevertheless, in respect of patent and trademark *validity* disputes, most jurisdictions have exercised caution. Germany and China have preferred to stay closer to the conservative end of the spectrum by not allowing patent and trademark validity disputes to be submitted to arbitration. In those jurisdictions where validity disputes are arbitrable, arbitrators may generally decide the matter only in personam and not in rem. As such, annulment disputes (that affect the society at large) have remained within courts' exclusive jurisdictions.

1. Copyright

392. All jurisdictions that were the focus of this research have adopted a favorable approach to the arbitrability of copyright disputes: some more assertively than others. In this regard, the authors have categorized the jurisdictions into three groups. The first group includes jurisdictions that have expressly authorized copyright disputes to be submitted to arbitration. The second group includes jurisdictions that have indirectly allowed for the arbitration of copyright disputes. And in the third group are jurisdictions where commentators have inferred such authorization from the relevant applicable sources. Accordingly, the discussion here contains three Segments: (i) Express Authorization; (ii) Indirect Authorization; and (iii) Inferred Authorization.

646. Discussed above, paras. 378–382.
647. *Glauber v. Glauber*, 600 NYS2d 740 (NY App Div 1993) at 742–743.
648. *Hirsch v. Hirsch*, 774 NYS2d 48 (NY App Div 2004) at 49; *Schechter v. Schechter*, 881 NYS2d 151 (NY App Div 2009).
649. It should be noted that prior to the *Glauber* case, child custody disputes were considered to be arbitrable in New York. The Appellate Division in *Sheets v. Sheets* (1964) and the Court of Appeals in *Schneider v. Schneider* (1966) held custody matters to be arbitrable, but also that any award "would still be subject, in a direct proceeding affecting the child alone, to the supervisory power of the court," which meant that the award would bind the parents but only insofar as it would not adversely affect the "substantial interest" of the child. *Sheets v. Sheets*, 254 NYS2d 320 (NY App Div 1964) at 322–324; *Schneider v. Schneider*, 216 NE2d 318 (NY 1966).

393. It is worth noting that, within each group, there are jurisdictions from both the civil law and common law camps. As such, belonging to a specific legal tradition does not seem relevant to a jurisdiction's approach to the arbitrability of copyright disputes.

i. Express Authorization

394. The majority of jurisdictions expressly authorize the submission of copyright disputes to arbitration: through legislation, case law, or an announcement by a relevant authority. This majority consists of seven (out of nine) jurisdictions: the US, Canada, France, Switzerland, China (Mainland), Hong Kong, and Singapore.

395. The US Code, Title 17 (on copyrights) § 1321(d) provides for the arbitrability of copyright infringement disputes. Section 1321(d) was added to Title 17 in 1998,[650] but even prior to that, copyright disputes were held to be arbitrable. For example, the Court of Appeals for the Second Circuit in *Kamakazi Music Corp v. Robbins Music Corp* (1982) held that copyright infringement disputes are arbitrable, even while noting that validity disputes involve public interest concerns.[651] Later—and still prior to § 1321(d) being added to Title 17—the same Court in *Saturday Evening Post Co v. Rumbleseat Press, Inc* (1987), held that copyright validity disputes are arbitrable in cases where copyright is an issue raised in the arbitration of a contract dispute.[652]

396. In Canada, the case law has supported the arbitrability of copyright disputes, while legislative Acts are mainly silent on the matter. The federal Copyright Act has no provision on the arbitrability of disputes arising under the Act. The Federal Courts Act provides the Federal Court with *exclusive* jurisdiction over, among other things, disputes as to the registration of any copyright as well as over "all cases in which it is sought to ... have any entry in any register of copyrights." However, the Supreme Court of Canada in *Desputeaux v. Éditions Chouette* (2003) held that disputes as to the ownership of copyrights are arbitrable between the disputing parties and that the purpose of section 41.24 of the Copyright Act (providing for concurrent jurisdiction of federal and provincial courts) is to define the subject-matter jurisdiction of courts over copyright disputes and was not intended to exclude arbitration.[653]

397. Moreover, in the province of Québec, the legislative Act governing the relationship between self-employed artists and their promoters (namely, An Act Respecting the Professional Status of Artists in the Visual Arts, Arts and Crafts and Literature, and Their Contracts with Promoters) recognizes the validity of an arbitration clause in contracts that involve copyright (section 37).

---

650. Pub L No 105-304 § 502, 112 Stat 2860 (1998) at 2905, online: http://uscode.house.gov/statviewer.htm?volume=112&page=2905# (last visited 16 June 2022).
651. *Kamakazi Music Corp v. Robbins Music Corp*, 684 F2d 228 (2d Cir 1982).
652. *Saturday Evening Post Co v. Rumbleseat Press, Inc*, 816 F2d 1191 (2d Cir 1987) at 1198–1199.
653. *Desputeaux v. Éditions Chouette (1987) Inc*, 2003 SCC 17 at paras. 40, 42, 49, 56–58, 61, 62, [2003] 1 SCR 178.

398. In France, Article L331-1 of the Intellectual Property Code provides for the arbitrability of disputes in relation to copyrights.

399. In Switzerland, the Copyright Act has no provisions that address the arbitrability of copyright disputes. Only Articles 54 and 58 discuss an entity called the Federal Arbitration Commission for the Exploitation of Copyrights and Related Rights, which is "responsible for approving the tariffs of the collective rights management organisations" and, therefore, the Act does not refer to "arbitration" in terms of the meaning given to that term in this book. However, Swiss law has taken a very liberal approach to the arbitrability of validity disputes. Pursuant to the 1975 decision of the Swiss Federal Institute of Intellectual Property, arbitral tribunals may decide disputes that go to the validity of patents,[654] which may empower them to decide copyright matters as well. The decision reads: "a final and enforceable award rendered by an arbitral tribunal seated in Switzerland finding the invalidity of a Swiss patent shall constitute a valid basis for cancelling the patent from the Swiss patent registry."[655] The Swiss Federal Institute of Intellectual Property "registers the awards rendered as the basis for entries in the register, provided that the award is accompanied by a certificate of enforceability" that is issued by the competent Swiss court in accordance with Article 193 of the PILA and Article 356 of the Civil Procedure Code.[656]

400. In China, copyright disputes are arbitrable under Article 60 of the Copyright Law of the People's Republic of China which reads: "A dispute over copyright may be settled by mediation or be submitted to arbitration before a copyright arbitration institution under a written arbitration agreement concluded between the parties concerned, or under the arbitration clause in the copyright contract." However, the 2014 decision of the Supreme People's Court in *AMSC Suzhou v. Sinovel* creates challenges to a plain reading of Article 60 of the Copyright Law.[657] In that case, while

654. Revue Suisse de la Propriété Industrielle et du Droit d'Auteur (1976) at 36–38 (as cited in Robert Briner, "The Arbitrability of Intellectual Property Disputes with Particular Emphasis on the Situation in Switzerland" [Presentation delivered at the Worldwide Forum on the Arbitration of Intellectual Property Disputes, 3–4 March 1994], WIPO Publication No 728(E) at para. 2.2.2), online: http://www.wipo.int/amc/en/events/conferences/1994/briner.html (last visited 10 March 2021). *See* Marc Blessing "Arbitrability of Intellectual Property Disputes" (1996) 12:2 Arb Int'l 191, n 15 DOI: 10.1093/arbitration/12.2.191; Paolo Michele Patocchi, "National Report for Switzerland (2018-2020)" in Jan Paulsson & Lise Bosman, eds, *ICCA International Handbook on Commercial Arbitration* (Kluwer Law International, 2020) 1 at 31.

655. As quoted in Jacques de Werra, "New Developments of IP Arbitration and Mediation in Europe: The Patent Mediation and Arbitration Center Instituted by the Agreement on a Unified Patent Court" (2014) Revista Brasileira de Arbitragem 17 at 20, n 12.

656. Robert Briner, "The Arbitrability of Intellectual Property Disputes with Particular Emphasis on the Situation in Switzerland" [Presentation delivered at the Worldwide Forum on the Arbitration of Intellectual Property Disputes, 3–4 March 1994], WIPO Publication No 728(E) at para. 2.2.2), online: http://www.wipo.int/amc/en/events/conferences/1994/briner.html (last visited 10 March 2021); Swiss Federal Institute of Intellectual Property, Newsletter, "Entry into force of the Swiss Code of Civil Procedure (CPC) und arbitral decisions" (6 January 2011), online: (6 January 2011), online: https://www.ige.ch/fileadmin/user_upload/andere/Juristische_Infos/nl_archiv/2011/e/newsletter_jurinfo_1-2011_e.pdf (last visited 10 March 2021).

657. *AMSC Suzhou v. Sinovel*, Supreme People's Court of the People's Republic of China, (2013) Min Ti Zi No 55, 26 January 2014.

the Court did not hold the copyright dispute to be inarbitrable, it construed the scope of the arbitration clause so narrowly that eventually the dispute could not be submitted to arbitration.[658] According to the Court, although the disputed software was included in the purchase contract that contained the arbitration clause, the software's code, which had been illegally copied, did not fall within the scope of the contract.[659]

401. In Hong Kong, since 2017, the legislative framework has provided a clear and liberal approach to the arbitration of IP disputes, including copyright matters.[660] In 2017, section 103D was added to the Arbitration Ordinance (Cap 609), expressly allowing IP disputes to be submitted to arbitration. Section 103B of the Ordinance defines IP rights to cover a wide range of matters, including copyrights, and section 103C defines "disputes" to cover any disputes over infringement, validity, ownership, or any other aspect of an IP right. In addition, the Hong Kong International Arbitration Centre (HKIAC) offers arbitration services for IP disputes.[661]

402. In Singapore, the 2019 amendments to the International Arbitration Act 1994 and the Arbitration Act 2001 expressly provide for the arbitration of IP disputes.[662] Under section 26B(1) of the International Arbitration Act and section 52B(1) of the Arbitration Act, IP disputes are arbitrable. Sections 26A(1) and 52A(1) of the Acts, respectively,

658. *Ibid.*
659. *Ibid.*
660. Prior to 2017, Hong Kong law's position on the matter was not very clear. There was no provision in the Copyright Ordinance (Cap 528) that would allow or prohibit the arbitration of copyright disputes. Commentators such as Neil Kaplan and Robert Morgan were of the opinion that IP disputes were generally not arbitrable in Hong Kong because they would affect third-party rights and because relevant legislative texts provided for courts' jurisdiction over these matters. However, where third-party rights were not involved—for example, in disputes over royalty rates—IP disputes could be settled through arbitration. *See* Neil Kaplan & Robert Morgan, "National Report for Hong Kong (2013) [Archived]" in Jan Paulsson & Lise Bosman, eds, *ICCA International Handbook on Commercial Arbitration* (Kluwer Law International, 2013) at 24, 25. It should be noted that the Copyright Ordinance established a tribunal called the Copyright Tribunal (s. 169), which has jurisdiction over several matters (s. 173). The Arbitration Ordinance may be applied in proceedings before the Copyright Tribunal (s. 174(2)), but its decisions can be appealed to the Court of First Instance (s. 176(1)).
661. HKIAC website, News, "HKIAC Introduces a Panel of Arbitrators for Intellectual Property Disputes" (14 March 2016), online: http://www.hkiac.org/news/panel-arbitrators-intellectual-property-disputes (last visited 9 March 2023).
662. Prior to 2019, the relevant legislative Acts in Singapore did not contain any provisions that would expressly allow or prohibit the arbitration of IP disputes. However, former s. 170 (now s. 478) of the Copyright Act made some references to arbitration by stating that "[n]othing in this Part [on the establishment and jurisdiction of Copyright Tribunals] shall affect the operation of any agreement or of any award made by an arbitrator." However, the history of the Arbitration Act 2001 shows that the drafters of the Act regarded disputes as to the *validity* of copyrights as not suitable for arbitration (*see* Review of Arbitration Act Committee, *Review of Arbitration Laws*, LRRD No 3/2001). This view was shared by many commentators, who did not necessarily distinguish between international and domestic disputes, but opposing views also existed in the scholarship. *See* David Joseph & David Foxton, *Singapore International Arbitration: Law & Practice* (LexisNexis, 2014) at para. 5.3; Michael Hwang et al "National Report for Singapore (2015) [Archived]" in Jan Paulsson & Lise Bosman, eds, *ICCA International Handbook on Commercial Arbitration* (Kluwer Law International, 2015) at 10 (citing *Halsbury's Laws of Singapore*, vol 1(2) (LexisNexis, 2003)); Lawrence Boo, "Arbitrability of Intellectual Property Disputes" (Presentation), International Association for the Protection of Intellectual Property (AIPPI), Forum 07/12, Forum Session 12 at 2.

define the term "intellectual property" to include a wide range of matters, including copyrights. And sections 26A(4) and 52A(3) of the Acts, respectively, define the term "dispute" to cover: "(a) a dispute over the enforceability, infringement, subsistence, validity, ownership, scope, duration or any other aspect of an IPR [intellectual property right]; (b) a dispute over a transaction in respect of an IPR; and (c) a dispute over any compensation payable for an IPR." However, the effect of such awards, under sections 26C(3) and 52C(3) of the Acts, does not extend to third-party rights—whether arising from a contract or by the operation of law.

ii. Indirect Authorization

403. England and Wales is the only jurisdiction that indirectly allows for the arbitrability of copyright disputes.[663] The Copyright, Designs and Patents Act 1988 does not include any provisions that address the arbitrability of copyright disputes. The Copyright Tribunal, established under section 23 of the Copyright Act 1956, is responsible for resolving "commercial licensing disputes between copyright owners or their agents (collecting societies) and people who use copyrighted material in their business."[664] Decisions of the Copyright Tribunal may be appealed on points of law to the High Court, under section 152(1) of the Copyright, Designs and Patents Act 1988.

404. Despite the fact that, to date, there has been no decision in English law that addresses the arbitrability of copyright disputes directly, there are a number of decisions—such as the King's Bench's decision in *Lobb Partnership Ltd v. Aintree Racecourse Co Ltd* (1999)[665] and the Chancery Division's decision in *EDO Corporation v. Ultra Electronics Limited* (2009)[666]—clearly indicating that the judges in these cases assumed that copyright disputes are arbitrable. Also, according to commentators, disputes brought under English law as to IP rights that are not subject to registration (such as copyright over literary or artistic works) are arbitrable.[667]

iii. Inferred Authorization

405. Germany is the only jurisdiction where neither legislative Acts nor case law have any provision that (even indirectly) addresses the arbitrability of copyright disputes.[668]

663. Prior to 2019, Singapore also fit into this category. However, as a result of changes to its relevant laws in 2019, Singapore now fits into the category of jurisdictions that expressly allow the arbitration of copyright disputes. *See* above, note 662 and the accompanying text.
664. *See* Copyright, Designs and Patents Act 1988, ss. 140, 149, together with Copyright Tribunal website, section "What we do," online: https://www.gov.uk/government/organisations/copyright-tribunal (last visited 28 October 2022).
665. *Lobb Partnership Ltd v. Aintree Racecourse Co Ltd*, 1999 WL 1805404 (1999).
666. *EDO Corporation v. Ultra Electronics Limited* [2009] EWHC 682 (Ch) at paras. 1-7, 16, 19, 40, 2009 WL 1062977.
667. Julian D M Lew & Oliver Marsden, "Arbitrability" in Julian D M Lew et al, eds, *Arbitration in England, with Chapters on Scotland and Ireland* (Kluwer Law International, 2013) at paras. 19.47, 19.48; Michael J Mustill & Stewart C Boyd, *Commercial Arbitration* (2001 Companion to the 2nd ed, Butterworths, 2001) at 73.
668. Prior to 2017, Hong Kong also fit into this category. However, as a result of changes to its relevant laws in 2017, Hong Kong now fits into the category of jurisdictions that expressly allow the arbitration of copyright disputes. *See* above, note 660 and the accompanying text.

However, commentators believe that copyright disputes (particularly infringement disputes) are arbitrable.

406. The German Act on Copyright and Related Rights does not include any provision on the arbitrability of IP disputes. Further, according to commentators, no specific case law on this issue has been reported.[669] Commentators believe that disputes as to the infringement of IP rights (including copyright) are arbitrable because they involve economic interests within the meaning of section 1030(1) of the Code of Civil Procedure.[670]

407. The German Patent and Trade Mark Office (DPMA)[671] has two arbitration boards, one of which is relevant to copyright disputes: the Arbitration Board established under the Act on Collective Management Organisations.[672] However, the functions of the board are directed more to mediation than arbitration.[673] Further, section 36a of the Act on Copyright and Related Rights discusses "arbitration boards" to be established by "authors' associations together with associations of users of works or individual users of works" in order to set the "joint remuneration agreements." However, those arbitration boards seem to have an administrative nature and are not typical arbitration tribunals.

2. Patent

408. This subsection is organized into two Segments: (i) Infringement Disputes; and (ii) Validity Disputes. The discussion will show that the majority of jurisdictions have adopted a favorable approach to the arbitrability of patent disputes, particularly infringement matters. Also, six jurisdictions[674] have *expressly* clarified their position (be it positive or negative) on the arbitrability of patent disputes: through legislation, case law, or an announcement by a relevant authority, while the position in three jurisdictions[675] could be inferred from the relevant applicable laws.[676]

669. Erik Schäfer, "Arbitration of Intellectual Property Related Disputes in Germany" in Karl-Heinz Böckstiegel et al, eds, *Arbitration in Germany: The Model Law in Practice*, 2nd ed (Kluwer Law International, 2015) 907 at paras. 18, 29.
670. Rolf Trittmann & Inka Hanefeld, "Commentary on the German Arbitration Law (10th Book of the German Code of Civil Procedure) § 1030" in Karl-Heinz Böckstiegel et al, eds, *Arbitration in Germany: The Model Law in Practice*, 2nd ed (Kluwer Law International, 2015) 94 at para. 13.
671. The DPMA is "is the centre of expertise in the field of industrial property protection in Germany." *See* DPMA website, tab "Our office," sub-tab "About Us," online: https://www.dpma.de/english/our_office/about_us/index.html (last visited 24 February 2021).
672. The board "mediates disputes between collective copyright management organisations and users of copyrighted works." DPMA website, tab "Our Office," sub-tab "About Us," sub-tab "Further Duties," sub-tab "CMOs, Copyright," sub-tab "Arbitration Board Under the Act on Collective Management Organisations," online: https://www.dpma.de/english/our_office/about_us/further_duties/cmos_copyright/arbitration_board_under_the_cmo_act/index.html (last visited 24 February 2021).
673. The reason is that the board "submits a settlement proposal to the parties," to which the parties can contest but if they choose not to, the proposal's "effect is similar to a court judgement." *Ibid*.
674. The six jurisdictions include the US, France, Canada, Switzerland, Hong Kong, and Singapore.
675. The three jurisdictions include England and Wales, Germany, and China.

i. Patent Infringement Disputes

409. Other than China (where the position is difficult to determine), other jurisdictions have all adopted a favorable approach to the arbitration of patent infringement matters.

410. Article 65 of the Patent Law of the People's Republic of China states that such disputes can be settled through "negotiation" or the parties "*may* either file a lawsuit with the people's court or request the Patent Administrative Department for settlement" (emphasis added). Some commentators are of the opinion that patent infringement disputes are arbitrable,[677] but others disagree.[678] Jingzhou Tao is of the opinion that "the arbitrability of patents ... is more complicated than that of copyrights and there is no generally accepted attitude toward their arbitrability, since those rights are granted through registration with the State."[679] According to a number of commentators:

> [A] claim of infringement appears to be arbitrable in theory. To date, there have not been any official interpretations or scholarly opinions that interpret the word 'may' here [article 65 of the Patent Law] as excluding arbitration as an alternative. In practice, however, a defense of invalidity by the alleged infringer removes the dispute from the jurisdiction of the arbitral tribunal. Thus, parties engaged in a dispute concerning patent validity or infringement have recourse only to the patent administration organs and the courts.[680]

411. In the US, the arbitration of patent infringement disputes is expressly allowed by US Code, Title 35 (on patents) § 294 which was added in 1982. The Court of Appeals for the Federal Circuit, in *Deprenyl Animal Health, Inc v. University of Toronto Innovations* (2002), held that *international* patent disputes are also arbitrable, reasoning that § 294 "is not limited to domestic arbitration, nor is there any compelling reason to so interpret its authorization of the arbitration of disputes over patent-related rights."[681] For an arbitral award rendered under § 294 to be enforceable in the US, a notice of the award has to be filed with the United States Patent and Trademark Office, in accordance with § 1.3335 of the Rules of Practice in Patent Cases.

---

676. This means that in those jurisdictions, neither their legislative Acts nor their case law has any provision that (even indirectly) discusses the arbitrability of patent disputes. However, commentators have inferred the prevalent approach in those jurisdictions from the relevant legal sources.
677. Lu Song, "National Report for China (2020 through 2022)" in Lise Bosman, ed, *ICCA International Handbook on Commercial Arbitration* (Kluwer Law International, 2022) at Chapter II.3.a; Jingzhou Tao, "Arbitration Law of the PRC" in Loukas A Mistelis, ed, *Concise International Arbitration*, 2nd ed (Kluwer Law International, 2015) 911 at 914.
678. Kenneth R Adamo, "Overview of International Arbitration in the Intellectual Property" (2011) 2 Global Bus L Rev 7 at 18; Aaron Pereira, "Licensing Technology to the Brics: The Case for ADR" (2009) 11 Cardozo J Conflict Resol 235 at 260.
679. Jingzhou Tao, *Arbitration Law and Practice in China*, 3rd ed (Kluwer Law International, 2012) at para. 171.
680. M A Smith et al, "Arbitration of Patent Infringement and Validity Issues Worldwide" (2006) 19 Harv J L & Tech 299 at 346.
681. *Deprenyl Animal Health, Inc v. University of Toronto Innovations Found*, 297 F3d 1343 (Fed Cir 2002) at 1357.

412. In addition, the AAA has specific arbitration rules for patent disputes. The AAA administers the arbitration of patent disputes in accordance with its Commercial Arbitration Rules and Mediation Procedures (2013, amended 2016)[682] as modified by its Resolution of Patent Disputes Supplementary Rules (2006).[683]

413. In Canada, the federal Patent Act has no provision on the arbitrability of patent disputes. However, Canadian courts have supported the arbitrability of patent infringement disputes. For example, in *University of Toronto (Governing Council) v. John N Harbinson Ltd* (2005), the Ontario Superior Court held that contractual claims relating to patents, such as when one of the parties claims damages for misinformation about the ownership of a patent in the license agreement, are arbitrable even if the relief that has been sought is under the Patent Act.[684]

414. In England and Wales, the Patent Act 1977 does not discuss the arbitration of patent disputes in general. According to commentators, disputes relating to "the exercise of a contractual registrable intellectual property right" such as royalties under a license agreement are arbitrable in English law. In 1978, in *Roussel-Uclaf v. GD Searle & Co Ltd (No2)*, the Chancery Division of the High Court stayed a patent infringement court proceeding in order to refer the dispute to arbitration.[685] That decision was reversed in 2008 by the Court of Appeal, but not on grounds relevant to this issue.[686] It should be noted that, although the English Patent Act 1977 has no general provision on the arbitration of patent disputes, under section 52, the comptroller may refer parties' disputes about the application of specific sections of the Act to arbitration. The Act has one provision (section 58(12)) that is similar to the provision in the First Schedule to Schedule 4 of the Copyright, Designs and Patents Act 1988, which allows a court to refer disputes concerning Crown use to arbitration.

415. In France, Article L615-17 of the Intellectual Property Code provides for the arbitrability of disputes in relation to patents. There are also court decisions in the 1980s and the 1990s that deal with the arbitrability of contractual disputes in relation to patents, whether as to the performance of the contract or its interpretation.[687]

---

682. Online: https://www.adr.org/sites/default/files/Commercial%20Rules.pdf (last visited 16 June 2022).
683. Online: https://www.adr.org/sites/default/files/Resolution%20of%20Patent%20Disputes%20Supplementary%20Rules.pdf (last visited 16 June 2022).
684. *University of Toronto (Governing Council) v. John N Harbinson Ltd* (2005), 78 OR (3d) 547 (Ont Sup Ct) at paras. 19–26, 46 CPR (4th) 175.
685. *Roussel-Uclaf v. GD Searle & Co Ltd (No 2)* [1978] FSR 95, [1978] 1 Lloyd's Rep 225.
686. [2008] EWCA Civ 1283 at paras. 2, 30–34, 39, 2008 WL 4937948.
687. *Société Cordons et Equipements v. Bretegnier*, Paris Court of First Instance, 30 June 1988, reported in (1994) 1994:3 Rev Arb 542 (enforcing an arbitration agreement in a dispute concerning the conditions of using a patent pursuant to contractual obligations, reasoning that it would not infringe public policy provisions and there was no sign of manifest nullity of the arbitration clause); *Société Deko v. G Dingler et Société Meva*, Paris Court of Appeal, 24 March 1994, reported in (1994) 1994:3 Rev Arb 515 at 518 (holding that the parties' dispute as to whether a product is within the scope of the patent license is a contractual dispute and is arbitrable because contractual disputes in relation to patents, whether as to the performance of the contract or interpretation thereof, are arbitrable: as there is no public interest involved).

416. As regards Unitary Patents,[688] the 2013 Agreement on the Unified Patent Court establishes two bodies: (i) the Unified Patent Court to be in charge of disputes that relate to Unitary Patents (Article 1), and (ii) the Patent Mediation and Arbitration Centre (Article 35(1)). Under Article 52(2), the judges of the Unified Patent Court are expected to "explore with the parties the possibility for a settlement, including through mediation, and/or arbitration, by using the facilities of the Centre referred to in article 35." This raises the question as to whether the drafters of the Agreement on the Unified Patent Court considered arbitration to be a suitable dispute resolution mechanism only *after* a dispute is submitted to the Unified Patent Court.[689] It is also not clear whether the Patent Mediation and Arbitration Centre has the "exclusivity to handle arbitration or mediation proceedings" as to Unitary Patent disputes, i.e., whether the parties may choose other arbitration institutions for their disputes relating to Unitary Patents.[690]

417. Although Article 32(1)(a) of the Agreement on the Unified Patent Court vests the Unified Patent Court with exclusive jurisdiction over infringement disputes, the function of Article 32(1) is understood to exclude national courts rather than arbitral tribunals, given that the second part of Article 32 states that national courts "remain competent" for matters "which do not come within the exclusive competence of the Court."[691]

418. In Switzerland, the Patents Act has no provision dealing with the arbitrability of patent disputes, and Article 26(1) of the Patent Court Act provides for the exclusive jurisdiction of the Federal Patent Court over both validity and infringement disputes. However, Swiss law has taken a liberal approach to the arbitrability of intellectual property disputes, even disputes that pertain to patent validity.[692] For example, in *BGE 140 III 134, 27 February 2014*, the Federal Supreme Court held that the patent infringement disputes that arose after the termination of a patent license agreement were within the arbitral tribunal's jurisdiction, despite the contractual provision in the license which seemed to limit the scope of the arbitration clause to pre-termination disputes.[693]

688. Unitary Patents have been defined as "European patents granted by the EPO [the European Patent Office] under the rules and procedures of the European Patent Convention, to which, at the patent proprietor's request, unitary effect is given for the territory of the EU Member States participating in the Unitary Patent system that have ratified the Agreement on a Unified Patent Court. It is expected that, initially, a Unitary Patent will cover the territory of at least 17 EU Member States. ... A Unitary Patent gives inventors uniform and territorially broad protection in the participating EU Member States. Uniform protection means that the scope of the right conferred by the Unitary Patent and its limitations are the same for all the participating states, as are the available legal remedies." EPO website, tab "Applying for a patent," sub-tab "European route," sub-tab "Unitary Patent & Unified Patent Court," section "Unitary Patent," hyperlink "FAQ," online: https://www.epo.org/applying/european/unitary/unitary-patent/faq.html (last visited 28 October 2022).

689. *See* Jacques de Werra, "New Developments of IP Arbitration and Mediation in Europe: The Patent Mediation and Arbitration Center Instituted by the Agreement on a Unified Patent Court" (2014) Revista Brasileira de Arbitragem 17 at 22, 23.

690. *Ibid.*, at 24, 25.

691. *Ibid.*, at 26.

692. *See* below, the discussion on patent validity disputes in Switzerland, paras. 429–430.

693. Federal Supreme Court, *BGE 140 III 134, 27 February 2014*.

419. In Hong Kong, since 2017, the legislative framework has provided a clear and liberal approach to the arbitration of IP disputes, including patent matters.[694] In 2017, section 103D was added to the Arbitration Ordinance (Cap 609), expressly allowing IP disputes to be submitted to arbitration. Section 103B of the Ordinance defines IP rights to cover a wide range of matters including patents, and section 103C defines "disputes" to cover infringement matters. In addition, the Hong Kong International Arbitration Centre (HKIAC) offers arbitration services for IP disputes.[695]

420. In Singapore, the 2019 amendments to the International Arbitration Act 1994 and the Arbitration Act 2001 expressly provide for the arbitration of IP disputes.[696] Under section 26B(1) of the International Arbitration Act and section 52B(1) of the Arbitration Act, IP disputes are arbitrable. Sections 26A(1) and 52A(1) of the Acts, respectively, define the term "intellectual property" to include a wide range of matters, including patents. And sections 26A(4) and 52A(3) of the Acts, respectively, define the term "dispute" to cover infringement disputes, among others.

ii. Patent Validity Disputes

421. The nine jurisdictions under study can be divided into two camps in relation to the arbitrability of patent validity disputes: (a) the arbitrability camp, which includes the majority of the jurisdictions (seven, to be exact) that regard such disputes as arbitrable,[697] and (b) the non-arbitrability camp, which includes the other two

694. Prior to 2017, Hong Kong law's position on the matter was not very clear. There was no provision in the Patents Ordinance (Cap 514) that would allow or prohibit the arbitration of patent disputes. There was a reference to arbitration in s. 62(4)(b) of the Ordinance, but this section provided no further detail. Commentators such as Neil Kaplan and Robert Morgan were of the opinion that IP disputes were generally not arbitrable in Hong Kong because they would affect third-party rights and because relevant legislative texts provided for courts' jurisdiction over these matters. However, where third-party rights were not involved—for example, in disputes over royalty rates—such disputes could be settled through arbitration. Neil Kaplan & Robert Morgan, "National Report for Hong Kong (2013) [Archived]" in Jan Paulsson & Lise Bosman, eds, *ICCA International Handbook on Commercial Arbitration* (Kluwer Law International, 2013) at 24, 25.

695. HKIAC website, News, "HKIAC Introduces a Panel of Arbitrators for Intellectual Property Disputes" (14 March 2016), online: http://www.hkiac.org/news/panel-arbitrators-intellectual-property-disputes (last visited 9 March 2023).

696. Prior to 2019, the relevant legislative Acts in Singapore did not contain any provisions that would expressly allow or prohibit the arbitration of IP disputes. The Patents Act provided only for court-ordered arbitration in disputes as to government use (s. 58(6)). However, patent *infringement* disputes were considered arbitrable based on the following analysis. Section 11(1) of the International Arbitration Act 2001 provides that a dispute is non-arbitrable where it would be contrary to "public policy" to refer it to arbitration, but the Act does not define "public policy." Looking at the legislative history of the Arbitration Act, one would notice that the final report issued in 2001 by the Review of Arbitration Act Committee had listed the matters that could involve public interest elements, which did not include patent infringement matters. *See* Review of Arbitration Act Committee, *Review of Arbitration Laws*, LRRD No 3/2001.

697. Including the US, Canada, France, England and Wales, Switzerland, Hong Kong, and Singapore.

jurisdictions where patent validity disputes are non-arbitrable.[698] The discussion shows that, within the arbitrability camp, only arbitrators in Switzerland may decide the matter in rem. Finally, (c) the question of whether Unitary Patents—that is, patents issued by the European Patent Office—are arbitrable is not yet settled.

(a) The Arbitrability Camp

422. This camp includes the US, Canada, England and Wales, France, Switzerland, Hong Kong, and Singapore.

423. In the US, the arbitration of patent validity disputes is expressly allowed by the US Code, Title 35 (on patents) § 294 which was added in 1982. The Court of Appeals for the Federal Circuit in *Deprenyl Animal Health, Inc v. University of Toronto Innovations Found* (2002), held that international patent disputes are also arbitrable, reasoning that § 294 "is not limited to domestic arbitration, nor is there any compelling reason to so interpret its authorization of the arbitration of disputes over patent-related rights."[699] For an arbitral award rendered under § 294 to be enforceable in the US, as alluded to earlier, a notice of the award has to be filed with the United States Patent and Trademark Office (USPTO), in accordance with § 1.3335 of the Rules of Practice in Patent Cases.

424. It should be noted that the existence of a valid arbitration agreement between the parties does not bar them from petitioning the US Patent Trial and Appeal Board (PTAB)[700] to institute inter partes review of a patent. In *In re MaxPower Semiconductor* (2021), the Court of Appeals for the Federal Circuit ruled that: (i) the PTAB is not bound by the parties' private contract, and (ii) § 294 of Title 35 neither deprives the PTAB of its authority to institute inter partes review nor does it task the PTAB to enforce arbitration agreements like courts.[701] The Court then held that any arbitration-related challenges can be raised after the PTAB issues its final written decisions.[702]

425. In Canada, the federal Patent Act has no provision addressing the arbitrability of patent disputes. The Federal Courts Act provides the Federal Court with *exclusive* jurisdiction over disputes as to "conflicting applications for any patent of invention or for any certificate of supplementary protection under the Patent Act" as well as over "all cases in which it is sought to impeach or annul any patent of invention." Barry Leon and Jana Stettner have expressed the following opinion regarding the arbitrability of patent disputes:

---

698. Including Germany and China (Mainland).
699. *Deprenyl Animal Health, Inc v. University of Toronto Innovations Found*, 297 F3d 1343 (Fed Cir 2002) at 1357.
700. The PTAB is "a tribunal within the United States Patent and Trademark Office (USPTO) that reviews rejections made by examiners in proceedings called ex parte appeals and decides patentability questions for issued patents raised by third parties in proceedings called AIA trials." The website of the US Patent and Trademark office https://www.uspto.gov/patents/patent-trial-and-appeal-board/about-ptab/new-ptab (last visited 11 June 2022).
701. *In re MaxPower Semiconductor, Inc*, 13 F4th 1348 (Fed Cir 2021) at 1350–1353.
702. *Ibid.*

> According to the reasoning in *Desputeaux*,[703] where the Federal Court and superior courts have *concurrent* jurisdiction and Parliament has not clearly excluded arbitration, disputes can also be determined by arbitration ... Even on patent matters where the Federal Court has *exclusive* jurisdiction, such as in conflicting applications for patents or proceedings to impeach or annul any patent, superior courts are not precluded from determining comparable issues *between disputing parties*, such as the validity of a patent. But *only the Federal Court can make a decision in rem* —that is, a decision binding beyond the disputing parties. The superior court's decisions in those kinds of cases cannot result in patents being expunged and cannot bind non-parties. *On the basis of the Supreme Court's reasoning in Desputeaux, an arbitral tribunal has jurisdiction, just as a provincial superior court has jurisdiction, to make binding patent decisions between the parties.*[704]

426. This opinion finds support in Canadian case law. In *Bansal v. Stringam* (2009), the Alberta Court of Appeal refused to review an arbitral award concerning the appellant's entitlement to a patent.[705] In *University of Toronto (Governing Council) v. John N Harbinson Ltd* (2005), the Ontario Superior Court held that, when the parties' dispute concerns impeaching or annulling any patent of invention, it may not be referred to arbitration.[706] However, the Court held that contractual claims relating to patents, such as when one of the parties claims damages for misinformation about the ownership of a patent in the license agreement, are arbitrable even if the relief sought falls under the Patent Act.[707]

427. In England and Wales, the Patent Act 1977 does not discuss the arbitration of patent disputes in general. However, in *Nokia Corp v. InterDigital Technology Corp* (2005), the Court of Appeal noted that it was reasonable for the arbitral tribunal to decide the general validity and strength of a patent because such a determination was relevant to the tribunal's considerations with respect to the issues in the case before it.[708] According to commentators, disputes "concerning the existence or validity of a registrable intellectual property right" are arbitrable, but tribunals' declarations in such awards have no impact on third parties.[709] A contrary view has also been expressed in relation to the arbitrability of patent validity disputes.[710]

---

703. The case where the Supreme Court of Canada held that disputes as to the ownership of copyrights are arbitrable between the disputing parties and that the effect of s. 41.24 of the Copyright Act (providing for concurrent jurisdiction of federal and provincial courts) is to define the subject-matter jurisdiction of courts over copyright disputes and is not intended to exclude arbitration. *Desputeaux v. Éditions Chouette (1987) Inc*, 2003 SCC 17 at paras. 40, 42, 49, 56–58, 61, 62, [2003] 1 SCR 178.
704. Barry Leon & Jana Stettner, "Court Should Have Declared IP Arbitrable" *The Lawyers Weekly* (15 December 2006) (emphasis added).
705. *Bansal v. Stringam*, 2009 ABCA 87 at paras. 2–5, 8–10, 448 AR 236.
706. *University of Toronto (Governing Council) v. John N Harbinson Ltd* (2005), 78 OR (3d) 547 (Ont Sup Ct) at paras. 19–26, 46 CPR (4th) 175.
707. *Ibid.*
708. *Nokia Corp v. InterDigital Technology Corp* [2005] EWCA Civ 614 at paras. 2, 6, 7, 12, 2005 WL 2290398.
709. Julian D M Lew & Oliver Marsden, "Arbitrability" in Julian D M Lew et al, eds, *Arbitration in England, with Chapters on Scotland and Ireland* (Kluwer Law International, 2013) at paras.

428. In France, Article L615-17 of the Intellectual Property Code provides for the arbitrability of disputes in relation to patents. Under Article L615-17, French courts have "exclusive jurisdiction to declare that a French patent ceases to produce its effects, in whole or in part." However, in *Liv Hidravlika DOO v. SA Diebolt* (2008), the Paris Court of Appeal held that a patent validity dispute is arbitrable if the issue is raised in the course of an arbitral proceeding in relation to contractual disputes about the patent, but the tribunal's decision in relation to patent validity would be limited to the parties.[711]

429. In Switzerland, the Patents Act does not deal with the arbitrability of patent disputes, but Article 26(1) of the Patent Court Act provides for the exclusive jurisdiction of the Federal Patent Court over validity disputes. However, Swiss law has taken a very liberal approach to the arbitrability of IP disputes, including disputes pertaining to patent validity. Pursuant to a 1975 decision of the Swiss Federal Institute of Intellectual Property, arbitral tribunals may decide disputes as to the validity of patents.[712] The decision reads: "a final and enforceable award rendered by an arbitral tribunal seated in Switzerland finding the invalidity of a Swiss patent shall constitute a valid basis for cancelling the patent from the Swiss patent registry."[713]

430. The Swiss Federal Institute of Intellectual Property "registers the awards rendered as the basis for entries in the register, provided that the award is accompanied by a certificate of enforceability" that is issued by the competent Swiss court in accordance with Article 193 of the PILA and Article 356 of the Civil Procedure Code.[714] However, claims pertaining to the registration of IP rights are not arbitrable in Swiss

19.47, 19.48; Michael J Mustill & Stewart C Boyd, *Commercial Arbitration* (2001 Companion to the 2nd ed, Butterworths, 2001) at 73.

710. H G Beal et al, eds, *Chitty on Contracts*, vol II (Sweet & Maxwell, 2012) at para. 32.020.

711. *Liv Hidravlika DOO v. SA Diebolt*, Paris Court of Appeal, 28 February 2008, reported in (2008) 2008:4 Rev Arb 712 at 714.

712. Revue Suisse de la Propriété Industrielle et du Droit d'Auteur (1976) at 36–38 (as cited in Robert Briner, "The Arbitrability of Intellectual Property Disputes with Particular Emphasis on the Situation in Switzerland" [Presentation delivered at the Worldwide Forum on the Arbitration of Intellectual Property Disputes, 3–4 March 1994], WIPO Publication No 728(E) at para. 2.2.2), online: http://www.wipo.int/amc/en/events/conferences/1994/briner.html (last visited 10 March 2021). *See* Marc Blessing "Arbitrability of Intellectual Property Disputes" (1996) 12:2 Arb Int'l 191, n 15 DOI: 10.1093/arbitration/12.2.191; Paolo Michele Patocchi, "National Report for Switzerland (2018-2020)" in Jan Paulsson & Lise Bosman, eds, *ICCA International Handbook on Commercial Arbitration* (Kluwer Law International, 2020) 1 at 31.

713. As quoted in Jacques de Werra, "New Developments of IP Arbitration and Mediation in Europe: The Patent Mediation and Arbitration Center Instituted by the Agreement on a Unified Patent Court" (2014) Revista Brasileira de Arbitragem 17 at 20, n 12.

714. Robert Briner, "The Arbitrability of Intellectual Property Disputes with Particular Emphasis on the Situation in Switzerland" [Presentation delivered at the Worldwide Forum on the Arbitration of Intellectual Property Disputes, 3–4 March 1994], WIPO Publication No 728(E) at para. 2.2.2), online: http://www.wipo.int/amc/en/events/conferences/1994/briner.html (last visited 28 February 2021); Swiss Federal Institute of Intellectual Property, Newsletter, "Entry into force of the Swiss Code of Civil Procedure (CPC) und arbitral decisions" (6 January 2011), online: (6 January 2011), online: https://www.ige.ch/fileadmin/user_upload/andere/Juristische_Infos/nl_archiv/2011/e/newsletter_jurinfo_1-2011_e.pdf (last visited 10 March 2021).

law, since such claims are not considered "adversarial proceedings" but rather "administrative proceedings" requiring government participation.[715]

431. In Hong Kong, since 2017, the legislative framework has provided a liberal approach to the arbitration of IP disputes, including patent matters. In 2017, section 103D was added to the Arbitration Ordinance (Cap 609), expressly allowing IP disputes to be submitted to arbitration. Section 103B of the Ordinance defines IP rights to cover a wide range of matters including patents, and section 103C defines "disputes" to cover validity and ownership disputes, among others. The 2017 amendments to the Arbitration Ordinance are notable developments in Hong Kong arbitration law because, prior to 2017, patent validity disputes were deemed inarbitrable: although the Patents Ordinance (Cap 514) did not expressly prohibit the arbitration of validity disputes, section 10 set out the appropriate proceedings and causes of action to challenge the validity of a patent, expressly providing that "[t]he validity of a patent may *not* be put in issue in *any other proceedings* and, in particular, no proceedings may be instituted (whether under this Ordinance or otherwise) seeking only a declaration as to the validity or invalidity of a patent" (emphasis added). Further, commentators such as Neil Kaplan and Robert Morgan considered that IP disputes, other than matters like disputes over royalty rates, were not arbitrable in Hong Kong because they would affect third-party rights and because legislative Acts provided for courts' jurisdiction over these matters.[716]

432. In Singapore, the 2019 amendments to the International Arbitration Act 1994 and the Arbitration Act 2001 expressly provide for the arbitration of IP disputes. Under section 26B(1) of the International Arbitration Act and section 52B(1) of the Arbitration Act, IP disputes are arbitrable. Sections 26A(1) and 52A(1) of the Acts, respectively, define the term "intellectual property" to include a wide range of matters, including patents. And sections 26A(4) and 52A(3) of the Acts, respectively, define the term "dispute" to cover validity and ownership disputes, among other things. Given that section 82(2) of the Patents Act 1994 expressly prohibits challenging the validity of a patent through any proceedings other than those set forth in that Act, both the International Arbitration Act (section 26G) and the Arbitration Act (section 52F) explicitly provide that the restriction in the Patents Act does not affect the arbitrability of patent validity disputes.[717] However, the effect of such arbitral awards, under

715. Bernhard Berger & Franz Kellerhals, International and Domestic Arbitration in Switzerland, 3rd ed (Hart, 2015) at paras. 226, 259.

716. Neil Kaplan & Robert Morgan, "National Report for Hong Kong (2013) [Archived]" in Jan Paulsson & Lise Bosman, eds, *ICCA International Handbook on Commercial Arbitration* (Kluwer Law International, 2013) at 24, 25.

717. Prior to 2019, patent validity disputes were considered inarbitrable in Singapore, without distinguishing between international and domestic disputes, although opposing views existed in the scholarship. There were two main grounds supporting the inarbitrability view: first, the prohibition in s. 82(2) of the Patents Act and, second, the legislative history of the Arbitration Act 2001, which shows the drafters of the Act did not consider patent validity disputes to be suitable for arbitration (Review of Arbitration Act Committee, *Review of Arbitration Laws*, LRRD No 3/2001). *See* David Joseph & David Foxton, *Singapore International Arbitration: Law & Practice* (LexisNexis, 2014) at para. 5.3; Michael Hwang et al, "National Report for Singapore (2015) [Archived]" in Jan Paulsson & Lise Bosman, eds, *ICCA International Handbook on*

sections 26C(3) and 52C(3) of the two arbitration Acts, does not extend to third-party rights—whether arising from a contract or by the operation of law.

(b) The Non-Arbitrability Camp

433. This camp includes Germany and China (Mainland).[718] In Germany, the Patent Act does not include provisions on the arbitrability of IP disputes. Further, according to commentators, no case law on this issue has been reported.[719] Section 65(1) of the Patent Act created the Federal Patent Court with jurisdiction to decide those actions for the revocation of patents. In addition, section 143(1) of the Patent Act vests the Civil Divisions of the Regional Courts with exclusive jurisdiction in patent litigation cases.

434. According to the explanatory section of the Bill of the Arbitration Law Reform Act (in relation to the 1998 reform in the Code of Civil Procedure), in matters where the Code of Civil Procedure vests exclusive jurisdiction in a court, the exclusivity of the court's jurisdiction should not be considered a decisive factor against the arbitrability of the matter *unless* the court is a special court for specific disputes pertaining to the revocation or nullity of the rights granted through an administrative act of the government, such as in the case of patents.[720] Therefore, disputes as to the validity of patents are generally considered to be non-arbitrable.[721] Nevertheless, the issue is not settled. Some commentators have argued in favor of the arbitrability of patent validity disputes, in those cases where the award affects only the parties and not any third party.[722]

435. The above discussion on Germany, however, seems to be applicable only to those cases where a German IP right is involved. If an arbitration proceeding in Germany concerns an IP right granted by another country, the rule is likely to be different. This issue has been discussed theoretically, with commentators arguing that there is no compelling reason why German courts should set aside or refuse to enforce an award as to the validity of an IP right registered in another country solely on the grounds that the validity issue may not be arbitrable under German law.[723]

Commercial Arbitration (Kluwer Law International, 2015) at 10 (citing *Halsbury's Laws of Singapore*, vol 1(2) (LexisNexis, 2003)); Lawrence Boo, "Arbitrability of Intellectual Property Disputes" (Presentation), International Association for the Protection of Intellectual Property (AIPPI), Forum 07/12, Forum Session 12 at 2.

718. Prior to 2019, Singapore also fit into this Camp. However, due to changes to its relevant laws in 2019, Singapore now fits into the Arbitrability Camp. *See* above, para. 432.
719. Erik Schäfer, "Arbitration of Intellectual Property Related Disputes in Germany" in Karl-Heinz Böckstiegel et al, eds, *Arbitration in Germany: The Model Law in Practice*, 2nd ed (Kluwer Law International, 2015) 907 at paras. 18, 29.
720. Bill of the Arbitration Law Reform Act, BT-Drs 13/5274 at 35, online (in original language): http://dipbt.bundestag.de/doc/btd/13/052/1305274.pdf (last visited 14 February 2021).
721. Stefan Michael Kröll, "National Report for Germany (2007)" in Jan Paulsson & Lise Bosman, eds, *ICCA International Handbook on Commercial Arbitration* (Kluwer Law International, 2020) at 17 [the 2020 Note by the editors confirms that the 2007 Report "continues broadly to reflect current arbitral practice in Germany"].
722. Erik Schäfer, "Arbitration of Intellectual Property Related Disputes in Germany" in Karl-Heinz Böckstiegel et al, eds, *Arbitration in Germany: The Model Law in Practice*, 2nd ed (Kluwer Law International, 2015) 907 at paras. 18, 22–30.
723. *Ibid.*, at paras. 31–34.

436. The German Patent and Trade Mark Office (DPMA)[724] has two arbitration boards, one of which is relevant to patent disputes: the Arbitration Board established under the Employee Inventions Act.[725] However, the functions of the board are directed more to mediation than arbitration.[726]

437. In China, given that administrative disputes are inarbitrable,[727] disputes as to the validity of patents are believed to be non-arbitrable because they involve administrative authorities.[728] Under articles 45 and 46 of the Patent Law of the People's Republic of China, patent validity disputes should be referred to the Patent Administration Department of the State Council (whose decisions are not final) and a party dissatisfied with the decision may file a suit in the People's Court. Consider the Supreme People's Court's 2020 decision in *Beijing Huayu Tongfang Chemical Technology Development v. Shandong Kangbao Bio-chemical Technology*.[729]

438. In that case, the parties had an arbitration agreement for "disputes arising out of the performance" of their underlying contract.[730] The respondent applied for a patent, using the claimant's technical documents and drawings without the latter's consent.[731] The claimant lodged a lawsuit before the Qingdao Intermediate People's Court on the basis that the respondent was not the rightful owner of the patent.[732] The Court ruled that, because of the arbitration clause, it did not have jurisdiction over the dispute.[733] The matter was referred to arbitration, but the Dong Ying Arbitration Commission took the position that it could not decide a patent ownership dispute.[734] The case eventually

724. The DPMA is "is the centre of expertise in the field of industrial property protection in Germany." *See* DPMA website, tab "Our office," sub-tab "About Us," online: https://www.dpma.de/english/our_office/about_us/index.html (last visited 24 February 2021).
725. The board deals with disputes between "an employee who has made an invention within the scope of his employment and his employer" and the objective is to determine an "appropriate compensation for the employee if the employer has filed a patent or utility model application for the employee's invention and exploits the invention. DPMA website, tab "Our Office," sub-tab "About Us," sub-tab "Further Duties," sub-tab "Arbitration Board—Employee Invention," online: https://www.dpma.de/english/our_office/about_us/further_duties/arbitration_board_employee_inventions/index.html (last visited 24 February 2021).
726. The reason is that it can only submit a settlement proposal to the parties. The parties are then free to "accept them as binding, but they may also object to the proposals or conclude a settlement outside the office." *Ibid.*
727. Article 3 of the Arbitration Law of People's Republic of China expressly excludes the arbitrability of administrative disputes.
728. Lu Song, "National Report for China (2020 through 2022)" in Lise Bosman, ed, *ICCA International Handbook on Commercial Arbitration* (Kluwer Law International, 2022) at Chapter II.3.a; Jingzhou Tao, "Arbitration Law of the PRC" in Loukas A Mistelis, ed, *Concise International Arbitration*, 2nd ed (Kluwer Law International, 2015) 911 at 914.
729. *Beijing Huayu Tongfang Chemical Technology Development Co, Ltd v. Shandong Kangbao Bio-chemical Technology Co, Ltd*, Supreme People's Court of China, [2020] Zhi Min Xia Zhong No 111, 19 May 2020.
730. *Ibid.*
731. *Ibid.*
732. *Ibid.*
733. *Ibid.*
734. *Ibid.*

reached the Supreme People's Court, which confirmed that the matter could not be arbitrated.[735]

(c) Unitary Patents[736]

439. It is not clear whether disputes as to the validity of Unitary Patents are arbitrable. The 2013 Agreement on the Unified Patent Court[737] establishes two bodies: first, the Unified Patent Court that is in charge of disputes over Unitary Patents (Article 1) and, second, the Patent Mediation and Arbitration Centre (Article 35(1)). Article 32(1) of the Agreement on the Unified Patent Court vests the Unified Patent Court with exclusive jurisdiction over validity disputes. However, the function of Article 32(1) is understood to exclude national courts rather than arbitral tribunals, given that the second part of Article 32 states that national courts "remain competent" for matters "which do not come within the exclusive competence of the Court."[738] Therefore, it seems possible that parties will be allowed to pursue arbitration outside the Unified Patent Court system.[739] Nevertheless, under Article 35(2), Unitary Patents "may not be revoked or

735. *Ibid.*
736. Unitary Patents have been defined as "European patents granted by the EPO [the European Patent Office] under the rules and procedures of the European Patent Convention, to which, at the patent proprietor's request, unitary effect is given for the territory of the EU Member States participating in the Unitary Patent system that have ratified the Agreement on a Unified Patent Court. It is expected that, initially, a Unitary Patent will cover the territory of at least 17 EU Member States. ... A Unitary Patent gives inventors uniform and territorially broad protection in the participating EU Member States. Uniform protection means that the scope of the right conferred by the Unitary Patent and its limitations are the same for all the participating states, as are the available legal remedies." EPO website, tab "Applying for a patent," sub-tab "European route," sub-tab "Unitary Patent & Unified Patent Court," section "Unitary Patent," hyperlink "FAQ," online: https://www.epo.org/applying/european/unitary/unitary-patent/faq.html (last visited 28 October 2022).
737. All EU Member States have signed the Agreement, except Spain and Poland. After Brexit, the UK withdrew its ratification of the Agreement in 2020. For the Agreement to enter into force, it needed to be ratified by 13 Member States, including "the three Member States in which the highest number of European patents had effect" (Art. 89), which includes Germany, France, and Italy (replacing the UK after Brexit). The three states have ratified the Agreement, and it will come into force in June 2023. It is worth noting that the process of ratification in Germany faced serious challenges. Following the German parliament's initial approval of the Agreement in 2017, the German Federal Constitutional Court, in March 2020, declared that the relevant legislation did not met the constitutional requirements and thus the approval was void. The German parliament's lower and upper houses passed the legislation anew, respectively in November and December 2020, which paved the way for the Unified Patent Court to open its door in 2022. However, the German government and President could not sign the legislation, as two new complaints were filed with the Constitutional Court. Eventually, the latter found the complaints inadmissible in July 2021, and Germany deposited its instrument of ratification in February 2023.
738. Jacques de Werra, "New Developments of IP Arbitration and Mediation in Europe: The Patent Mediation and Arbitration Center Instituted by the Agreement on a Unified Patent Court" (2014) Revista Brasileira de Arbitragem 17 at 26.
739. Ana Alba Betancourt, "Cross-Border Patent Disputes: Unified Patent Court or International Commercial Arbitration?" (2016) 32 Utrecht J Int'l Eur L 44 at 53 ("The use of the UPC Arbitration Centre is just one option open to the parties. If the parties want to solve their patent dispute through arbitration they may choose any arbitration institution or even an ad hoc procedure to manage it"); Susie Middlemiss & Laura Balfour (Slaughter and May), "Patent Litigation in the Unified Patent Court: Overview" published online at Practical Law a Thomson Reuters Legal Solution, at question 24 ("the parties can attempt to resolve the dispute

limited" in an arbitration proceeding. Yet, it is unclear whether arbitral tribunals are allowed to decide the dispute only between the parties with no effect on third parties.[740]

440. Even assuming that validity disputes as to Unitary Patents are arbitrable, other questions remain to be answered. Under Article 52(2), the judges of the Unified Patent Court are expected to "explore with the parties the possibility for a settlement, including through mediation, and/or arbitration, by using the facilities of the Centre referred to in Article 35." This raises the question, again, of whether the drafters of the Agreement on the Unified Patent Court considered arbitration to be a suitable dispute resolution mechanism only *after* a dispute is submitted to the Unified Patent Court.[741] It is also not clear, here again, whether the Patent Mediation and Arbitration Centre has "exclusivity to handle arbitration or mediation proceedings" as to Unitary Patent disputes, i.e., whether the parties may choose other arbitration institutions or mechanisms for their disputes relating to Unitary Patents.[742]

3. Trademark

441. This subsection is organized into two Segments: (i) Infringement Disputes; and (ii) Validity Disputes. The discussion shows that the majority of jurisdictions have adopted a favorable approach to the arbitrability of trademark disputes, particularly in infringement matters. However, unlike the arbitrability of patent disputes,[743] most of the jurisdictions have *not* expressly clarified their position (be it positive or negative) about the arbitrability of trademark matters. In fact, most jurisdictions have only indirectly expressed their position, or a position has been inferred by commentators from the generality of applicable laws.[744]

i. Trademark Infringement Disputes

442. Other than China (whose position is difficult to determine), other jurisdictions have all adopted a favorable approach to the arbitrability of trademark infringement disputes.

---

independently of the UPC system through separate mediation, arbitration or ADR"): https://uk.practicallaw.thomsonreuters.com/8-623-0425?transitionType=Default&contextData=(sc.Default)&firstPage=true (last visited 24 February 2021).

740. Erik Schäfer, "Arbitration of Intellectual Property Related Disputes in Germany" in Karl-Heinz Böckstiegel et al, eds, *Arbitration in Germany: The Model Law in Practice*, 2nd ed (Kluwer Law International, 2015) 907 at para. 21.

741. *See* Jacques de Werra, "New Developments of IP Arbitration and Mediation in Europe: The Patent Mediation and Arbitration Center Instituted by the Agreement on a Unified Patent Court" (2014) Revista Brasileira de Arbitragem 17 at 22, 23.

742. *Ibid.*, at 24, 25.

743. *See* above, para. 408.

744. This means that in those jurisdictions, neither their legislative Acts nor their case law has any provision that (even indirectly) discusses the arbitrability of patent disputes. However, commentators have inferred the prevalent approach in those jurisdictions from the relevant legal sources.

443. In China, the Trademark Law, Article 60, states that such disputes can be settled through "consultation" or the parties "*may* bring a lawsuit to the People's Court or request the relevant administrative department for industry and commerce to address the dispute" (emphasis added). The Trademark Law has similar provisions (both in terms of validity and infringement) to the Patent Law. Therefore, the analysis of the arbitrability of patent disputes can be applied to trademark disputes. For the arbitrability of patent disputes, the authors concluded that, while infringement claims appear to be arbitrable in theory, this is not necessarily the case in practice, because as soon as a defense of invalidity is raised, the matter has to be removed from the arbitral proceeding and referred to administrative authorities.[745]

444. However, the Supreme People's Court of China, in *Hong Kong Heung Chun Cereal & Oil Food Co Ltd v. Anhui Cereal & Oil Food Import & Export Co Ltd* (2003), held that the unenforceability of a Hong Kong award concerning a trademark infringement dispute was due to the incapacity of a contracting party, without taking issue with the fact that the arbitral tribunal had decided a trademark infringement matter.[746] Similarly, in *Janful Ltd v. Nanjing Skytech* (2010), the Supreme People's Court partially enforced a foreign-related award between the shareholding companies of a joint venture, without taking issue with the fact that one of the matters addressed by the arbitral tribunal was the transfer of a trademark from one of the shareholding companies to the joint venture.[747]

445. France is positioned at the opposite end of the spectrum. Article L716-6 of the Intellectual Property Code has clearly provided for the arbitrability of disputes in relation to trademarks.

446. In the US, the Trademark Act (also known as the Lanham Act) contains no provision on arbitration. However, US courts have held that infringement disputes arising under the Trademark Act are arbitrable. For example, this was the finding reached by the Court of Appeals for the Seventh Circuit in *Gingiss Int'l, Inc v. Bormet* (1995)[748] and the District Court for the Southern District of New York in *Gidatex, SrL v. Campaniello Imports, Ltd* (1998).[749]

447. Likewise, in Canada, the Trademarks Act has no provision on the arbitrability of trademark disputes, but Canadian courts have long supported the arbitration of trademark infringement matters. In *Bausch & Lomb Inc v. Allergan Inc* (1985), the Trial Division of the Federal Court of Canada stayed the court proceeding in relation to trademark infringement pursuant to an arbitration provision in the parties'

745. Discussed above, para. 410.
746. *Hong Kong Heung Chun Cereal & Oil Food Co Ltd (Hong Kong SAR) v. Anhui Cereal & Oil Food Import & Export Co Ltd (China PR)*, Supreme People's Court, 12 November 2003.
747. *Janful Ltd v. Nanjing Skytech*, Supreme People's Court of the People's Republic of China, [2010] 民四他字第21号 (SPC) & [2010] 苏知民仲审字第 0001号 (Jiangsu HPC), 27 May 2010.
748. *Gingiss Int'l, Inc v. Bormet*, 58 F3d 328 (7th Cir 1995) at 331–332.
749. *Gidatex, SrL v. Campaniello Imports, Ltd*, 13 F Supp 2d 420 (SD NY 1998) at n 2.

manufacturing and supply agreement.[750] Further, in *IMG Canada Ltd v. Melitta Canada Inc* (2001), the Ontario Superior Court of Justice stayed the court proceeding in relation to, inter alia, trademark infringement in favor of arbitration on the basis of the arbitration provision in the parties' sponsorship agreement.[751] In *Dunhill Personnel System Inc v. Dunhill Temps Edmonton Ltd* (1993), the Alberta Court of King's Bench enforced a New York award that was in relation to trademark infringement, and that was rendered pursuant to the arbitration provision in the parties' franchise agreement.[752]

448. In England and Wales, the relevant legislation is the Trade Marks Act 1994 which does not include any provision relating to arbitration. Further, to date, there has been no specific case law addressing the question of the arbitrability of these disputes. However, as noted earlier, commentators consider that, in English law, disputes relating to "the exercise of a contractual registrable intellectual property right—for example, as to royalties due under a licence agreement" are arbitrable.[753]

449. In Germany, the Act on the Protection of Trade Marks and Other Symbols includes no provision on the arbitrability of trademark disputes. And, as with England and Wales, no specific case law on this issue has been reported.[754] However, commentators believe that disputes as to the infringement of IP rights (including trademarks) are arbitrable because they involve economic interests within the meaning of section 1030(1) of the Code of Civil Procedure.[755]

450. In Switzerland, the Trade Mark Protection Act has no provisions on the arbitrability of trademark disputes. However, as mentioned earlier, Swiss law has taken a very liberal approach to the arbitrability of IP disputes. Pursuant to a 1975 decision of the Swiss Federal Institute of Intellectual Property,[756] arbitral tribunals may decide disputes as to the validity of patents, and this reasoning appears to be applicable to trademarks.[757] Although Swiss case law has not expressly discussed the arbitrability

750. *Bausch & Lomb Inc v. Allergan Inc* (1985), 7 CIPR 35 (FCTD) at paras. 1-9, 16, 35, 1985 CarswellNat 591.
751. *IMG Canada Ltd v. Melitta Canada Inc*, [2001] OJ No 2331 (Ont Sup Ct) at paras. 4–6, 8, 12, 13, 18, 20, 2001 CarswellOnt 208.
752. *Dunhill Personnel System Inc v. Dunhill Temps Edmonton Ltd* (1993), 144 AR 272 (Alta QB) at paras. 1, 6, 13 Alta LR (3d) 241.
753. Julian D M Lew & Oliver Marsden, "Arbitrability" in Julian D M Lew et al, eds, *Arbitration in England, with Chapters on Scotland and Ireland* (Kluwer Law International, 2013) at paras. 19.47, 19.48; Michael J Mustill & Stewart C Boyd, *Commercial Arbitration* (2001 Companion to the 2nd edn, Butterworths, 2001) at 73.
754. Erik Schäfer, "Arbitration of Intellectual Property Related Disputes in Germany" in Karl-Heinz Böckstiegel et al, eds, *Arbitration in Germany: The Model Law in Practice*, 2nd ed (Kluwer Law International, 2015) 907 at paras. 18, 29.
755. Rolf Trittmann & Inka Hanefeld, "Commentary on the German Arbitration Law (10th Book of the German Code of Civil Procedure) § 1030" in Karl-Heinz Böckstiegel et al, eds, *Arbitration in Germany: The Model Law in Practice*, 2nd ed (Kluwer Law International, 2015) 94 at para. 13.
756. As quoted in Jacques de Werra, "New Developments of IP Arbitration and Mediation in Europe: The Patent Mediation and Arbitration Center Instituted by the Agreement on a Unified Patent Court" (2014) Revista Brasileira de Arbitragem 17 at 20, n 12.
757. Revue Suisse de la Propriété Industrielle et du Droit d'Auteur (1976) at 36–38 (as cited in Robert Briner, "The Arbitrability of Intellectual Property Disputes with Particular Emphasis on the

of trademark disputes, there are decisions in which the Supreme Federal Court has discussed measures taken by arbitral tribunals deciding trademark disputes in Switzerland, without taking any issue with the arbitrability of these disputes.[758]

451. In Hong Kong, since 2017, the legislative framework has provided a clear and liberal approach to the arbitration of IP disputes, including trademark matters.[759] In 2017, section 103D was added to the Arbitration Ordinance (Cap 609), expressly allowing IP disputes to be submitted to arbitration. Section 103B of the Ordinance defines IP rights to cover a wide range of matters, including trademarks, and section 103C defines "disputes" to cover infringement disputes, among others. The Hong Kong International Arbitration Centre (HKIAC) offers arbitration services for IP disputes.[760]

452. In Singapore, the 2019 amendments to the International Arbitration Act 1994 and the Arbitration Act 2001 expressly provide for the arbitration of IP disputes.[761] Under section 26B(1) of the International Arbitration Act and section 52B(1) of the Arbitration Act, IP disputes are arbitrable. Sections 26A(1) and 52A(1) of the Acts, respectively, define the term "intellectual property" to include a wide range of matters, including trademarks. And sections 26A(4) and 52A(3) of the Acts, respectively, define the term "dispute" to cover infringement matters, among other things.

Situation in Switzerland" [presentation delivered at the Worldwide Forum on the Arbitration of Intellectual Property Disputes, 3–4 March 1994], WIPO Publication No 728(E) at para. 2.2.2), online: http://www.wipo.int/amc/en/events/conferences/1994/briner.html (last visited 10 March 2021). *See* Marc Blessing "Arbitrability of Intellectual Property Disputes" (1996) 12:2 Arb Int'l 191, n 15 DOI: 10.1093/arbitration/12.2.191; Paolo Michele Patocchi, "National Report for Switzerland (2018-2020)" in Jan Paulsson & Lise Bosman, eds, *ICCA International Handbook on Commercial Arbitration* (Kluwer Law International, 2020) 1 at 31; Swiss Federal Institute of Intellectual Property, Newsletter, "Entry into force of the Swiss Code of Civil Procedure (CPC) und arbitral decisions" (6 January 2011), online: (6 January 2011), online: https://www.ige.ch/fileadmin/user_upload/andere/Juristische_Infos/nl_archiv/2011/e/newsletter_jurinfo_1-2011_e.pdf (last visited 10 March 2021).

758. Federal Supreme Court, *BGE 136 III 583, 2 November 2010* (For English translation of the case, *see* Elisabeth Leimbacher and Georgvon Segesser, BGer, 4A_438/2013, Federal Supreme Court of Switzerland, 1st Civil Law Chamber, 4A_438/2013, Case Date 27 February 2014, *A contribution by the ITA Board of Reporters* (Kluwer Law International)); Federal Supreme Court, *Case No 4A_4442009, 11 February 2010* reported in Georg von Segesser & Andrea Meier, *X Ltd v. Y AG*, Swiss Federal Supreme Court, 4A_444/2009, 11 February 2010, *A contribution by the ITA Board of Reporters* (Kluwer Law International).

759. Prior to 2017, Hong Kong law's position on the matter was not very clear. There was no provision in the Trade Marks Ordinance (Cap 559) that would allow or prohibit the arbitration of trademark disputes. Commentators such as Neil Kaplan and Robert Morgan were of the opinion that, in Hong Kong law, IP disputes were only arbitrable where third-party rights were not involved, for example in disputes over royalty rates. *See* Neil Kaplan & Robert Morgan, "National Report for Hong Kong (2013) [Archived]" in Jan Paulsson & Lise Bosman, eds, *ICCA International Handbook on Commercial Arbitration* (Kluwer Law International, 2013) at 24, 25.

760. HKIAC website, News, "HKIAC Introduces a Panel of Arbitrators for Intellectual Property Disputes" (14 March 2016), online: http://www.hkiac.org/news/panel-arbitrators-intellectual-property-disputes (last visited 10 March 2023).

761. Prior to 2019, the relevant legislative Acts in Singapore did not contain any provisions that would expressly allow or prohibit the arbitration of IP disputes. The Trade Marks Act 1998 did not (and still does not) contain any provision on arbitration. However, the legislative history of the Arbitration Act 2001 shows that the drafters of the Act only regarded validity disputes as not suitable for arbitration. Review of Arbitration Act Committee, *Review of Arbitration Laws*, LRRD No 3/2001.

ii. Trademark Validity Disputes

453. The discussion in this Subsection shows that the nine jurisdictions that were studied are divided into two camps in relation to the arbitrability of trademark validity disputes: (a) the arbitrability camp, which includes the majority of the jurisdictions (seven, to be exact) that regard such disputes to be arbitrable[762] and (b) the non-arbitrability camp which includes the other two jurisdictions where trademark validity disputes are non-arbitrable.[763] Further, in the arbitrability camp, only arbitrators in Switzerland may decide the matter in rem.

454. The above summary is similar to the summary presented for patent validity disputes.[764] The only difference is that for patents, the question of the arbitrability of Unitary Patents is not yet settled, whereas for EU trademarks, the answer depends on the EU Member State in which the challenge is filed.

(a) The Arbitrability Camp

455. This camp includes the US, Canada, England and Wales, Switzerland, France, and Hong Kong.

456. In the US, the Trademark Act (also known as the Lanham Act) has no provision on arbitration. However, in a notice issued in 2015, the Trademark Trial and Appeal Board[765] urged parties "to consider alternative dispute resolution as a means of settling the issues raised in any opposition [which is a proceeding to oppose a mark after publication in the Official Gazette] or cancellation proceeding [which is a proceeding to seek cancellation of an existing registration]."[766]

457. In Canada, the Trademarks Act has no provision on the arbitrability of trademarks disputes. The Federal Courts Act provides the Federal Court with *exclusive* jurisdiction over disputes as to the registration, impeachment, or annulment of a

762. Including the US, Canada, England and Wales, Switzerland, France, Hong Kong, and Singapore. It will be explained that the arbitrability position is uncertain in France.
763. Germany and China (Mainland).
764. *See* above, para. 421.
765. The Trademark Trial and Appeal Board is "a neutral body that functions like a court for trademark matters at the US Patent and Trademark Office (USPTO). The Board's administrative trademark judges are authorized to determine a party's right to register a trademark with the federal government. The Board is not authorized to determine whether you have the right to use a trademark, and does not issue injunctions halting use. The Board only determines whether an applicant or registrant has the right to register a mark or to retain a registration under challenge. Additionally, the Board is not authorized to determine questions of trademark infringement or unfair competition or to award money damages or attorney's fees. For anything other than determining the right of federal registration, you must file a case in federal or state court. While the Board is authorized to handle five different types of cases, there are three main categories of proceedings that applicants and registrants should know about: appeals, oppositions, and cancellations." USPTO website, tab "Trademarks"; hyperlink "Trademark Trial and Appeal Board," section "New to TTAB?" online: https://www.uspto.gov/trademarks/trademark-trial-and-appeal-board/about-ttab (last visited 16 June 2022).
766. Trademark Trial and Appeal Board, *Notice Concerning Alternative Dispute Resolution (ADR)* (December 2015), online: https://www.uspto.gov/sites/default/files/documents/USPTO_WEB_POSTING_ON_ADR_%282%29.docx (last visited 16 June 2022).

trademark. Further, section 56 of the Trademarks Act vests the Federal Court with jurisdiction to hear appeals from decisions of the Registrar of Trademarks, whose specialized tribunal (called the Trademarks Opposition Board (TMOB)) decides opposition proceedings[767] and section 45 proceedings.[768]

458. There is not yet a leading Canadian case addressing the arbitrability of trademark validity disputes. However, the Supreme Court of Canada's decision in *Desputeaux v. Éditions Chouette (1987) Inc* (2003) is clear on the general rule that the intention behind statutory provisions providing for a court's jurisdiction over a subject matter is not to exclude arbitration of that matter but is rather to identify which court has jurisdiction over it.[769] As such, the logic of Barry Leon and Jana Stettner's commentary on the arbitrability of patent validity disputes[770] seems to be equally applicable to the arbitrability of trademark validity disputes.

459. In England and Wales, the relevant legislation is the Trade Marks Act 1994 which does not include any provision relating to arbitration. Further, to date, there has been no case law addressing the question of the arbitrability of these disputes. However, again, commentators consider that, in English law, disputes "concerning the existence or validity of a registrable intellectual property right" are arbitrable, but tribunals' declarations in such awards have no impact on third parties.[771] A contrary view has also been expressed.[772]

460. In Switzerland, the Trade Mark Protection Act has no provisions on the arbitrability of trademark disputes. However, as mentioned earlier, Swiss law has taken a liberal approach to the arbitrability of IP disputes, including disputes pertaining to trademark validity. Pursuant to a 1975 decision of the Swiss Federal Institute of Intellectual Property, arbitral tribunals may decide disputes as to the validity of patents, and this rationale seems to be equally applicable to trademarks.[773] The decision reads: "a final and enforceable award rendered by an arbitral tribunal seating

767. *See* Trademarks Act, s. 38.
768. Canadian Intellectual Property Office website, hyperlink "Trademarks," section "Trademarks Opposition Board," hyperlink "Homepage," online: https://ised-isde.canada.ca/site/canadian-intellectual-property-office/en/trademarks/trademarks-opposition-board (last visited 16 June 2022).
769. *Desputeaux v. Éditions Chouette (1987) Inc*, 2003 SCC 17 at paras. 40, 42, 49, 56–58, 61–62, [2003] 1 SCR 178 (holding that disputes as to the ownership of copyrights are arbitrable between the disputing parties).
770. Discussed above, para. 425.
771. Julian D M Lew & Oliver Marsden, "Arbitrability" in Julian D M Lew et al, eds, *Arbitration in England, with Chapters on Scotland and Ireland* (Kluwer Law International, 2013) at paras. 19.47, 19.48; Michael J Mustill & Stewart C Boyd, *Commercial Arbitration* (2001 Companion to the 2nd ed, Butterworths, 2001) at 73.
772. H G Beal et al, eds, *Chitty on Contracts*, vol II (Sweet & Maxwell, 2012) at para. 32.020.
773. Revue Suisse de la Propriété Industrielle et du Droit d'Auteur (1976) at 36–38 (as cited in Robert Briner, "The Arbitrability of Intellectual Property Disputes with Particular Emphasis on the Situation in Switzerland" [Presentation delivered at the Worldwide Forum on the Arbitration of Intellectual Property Disputes, 3–4 March 1994], WIPO Publication No 728(E) at para. 2.2.2), online: http://www.wipo.int/amc/en/events/conferences/1994/briner.html (last visited 10 March 2021). *See* Marc Blessing "Arbitrability of Intellectual Property Disputes" (1996) 12:2 Arb Int'l 191, n 15 DOI: 10.1093/arbitration/12.2.191; Paolo Michele Patocchi, "National

in Switzerland finding the invalidity of a Swiss patent shall constitute a valid basis for cancelling the patent from the Swiss patent registry."[774] The Swiss Federal Institute of Intellectual Property "registers the awards rendered as the basis for entries in the register, provided that the award is accompanied by a certificate of enforceability" that is issued by the competent Swiss court in accordance with Article 193 of the PILA and Article 356 of the Civil Procedure Code.[775]

461. In France, it is not settled whether trademark validity disputes are arbitrable. Article L716-6 of the Intellectual Property Code provides for the arbitrability of disputes in relation to trademarks, but it is not clear whether it includes validity disputes. However, it is likely that such disputes are arbitrable if they are raised in the course of arbitral proceedings in relation to contractual disputes about trademarks, and if the tribunals' decision would be inter partes only. This is based on an analogy to French patent law, as is explained below.

462. Under Article L615-17 of the Intellectual Property Code, French courts have "exclusive jurisdiction to declare that a French patent ceases to produce its effects, in whole or in part." However, in *Liv Hidravlika DOO v. SA Diebolt* (2008), the Paris Court of Appeal held that a patent validity dispute is arbitrable if it is raised in the course of an arbitral proceeding that relates to contractual disputes about the patent, but the tribunal's decision as to patent validity would be limited to the parties.[776] Therefore, trademark validity disputes could be arbitrable in France on the basis of the same reasoning applied by the Paris Court of Appeal in the *Liv Hidravlika DOO* case.

463. In Hong Kong, since 2017, the legislative framework has provided a clear and liberal approach to the arbitration of IP disputes, including patent matters.[777] As already mentioned, in 2017, section 103D was added to the Arbitration Ordinance (Cap

---

Report for Switzerland (2018–2020)" in Jan Paulsson & Lise Bosman, eds, *ICCA International Handbook on Commercial Arbitration* (Kluwer Law International, 2020) 1 at 31.

774. As quoted in Jacques de Werra, "New Developments of IP Arbitration and Mediation in Europe: The Patent Mediation and Arbitration Center Instituted by the Agreement on a Unified Patent Court" (2014) Revista Brasileira de Arbitragem 17 at 20, n 12.

775. Robert Briner, "The Arbitrability of Intellectual Property Disputes with Particular Emphasis on the Situation in Switzerland" [Presentation delivered at the Worldwide Forum on the Arbitration of Intellectual Property Disputes, 3–4 March 1994], WIPO Publication No 728(E) at para. 2.2.2), online: http://www.wipo.int/amc/en/events/conferences/1994/briner.html (last visited 10 March 2021); Swiss Federal Institute of Intellectual Property, Newsletter, "Entry into force of the Swiss Code of Civil Procedure (CPC) und arbitral decisions" (6 January 2011), online: (6 January 2011), online: https://www.ige.ch/fileadmin/user_upload/andere/Juristische_Infos/nl_archiv/2011/e/newsletter_jurinfo_1-2011_e.pdf (last visited 10 March 2021).

776. *Liv Hidravlika DOO v. SA Diebolt*, Paris Court of Appeal, 28 February 2008, reported in (2008) 2008:4 Rev Arb 712 at 714.

777. Prior to 2017, Hong Kong law's position on the matter was not very clear. There was no provision in the Trade Marks Ordinance (Cap 559) that would allow or prohibit the arbitration of trademark disputes. Commentators such as Neil Kaplan and Robert Morgan were of the opinion that validity disputes were generally not arbitrable in Hong Kong law, because they would affect third-party rights and because legislative Acts provided for courts' jurisdiction over these matters. Neil Kaplan & Robert Morgan, "National Report for Hong Kong (2013) [Archived]" in Jan Paulsson & Lise Bosman, eds, *ICCA International Handbook on Commercial Arbitration* (Kluwer Law International, 2013) at 24, 25.

609), expressly allowing IP disputes to be submitted to arbitration. Section 103B of the Ordinance defines IP rights to cover a wide range of matters, including trademarks, and section 103C defines "disputes" to cover any disputes over validity, ownership, or any other aspect of an IP right. Also, arbitration services for IP disputes are offered by the Hong Kong International Arbitration Centre (HKIAC).[778]

464. In Singapore, the 2019 amendments to the International Arbitration Act 1994 and the Arbitration Act 2001 expressly provide for the arbitration of IP disputes.[779] As discussed previously, under section 26B(1) of the International Arbitration Act and section 52B(1) of the Arbitration Act, IP disputes are arbitrable. Sections 26A(1) and 52A(1) of the Acts, respectively, define the term "intellectual property" to include a wide range of matters, including trademarks. And sections 26A(4) and 52A(3) of the Acts, respectively, define the term "dispute" to cover validity and ownership disputes, among other things. The effect of such awards, under sections 26C(3) and 52C(3), does not extend to third-party rights—whether arising from a contract or by the operation of law.

(b) The Non-Arbitrability Camp

465. This camp includes Germany and China (Mainland).[780] In Germany, the Act on the Protection of Trade Marks and Other Symbols does not include any provision on the arbitrability of trademark disputes. There are authorities with exclusive jurisdiction to decide disputes as to trademarks and symbols: under section 54(1) of the Act, the Patent Office must decide any application for cancellation based on absolute grounds and, in accordance with section 140(1), the Regional Courts have exclusive jurisdiction over any dispute as to symbols that arise under the Act. Further, according to commentators, no specific case law on this issue has been reported.[781] Commentators

778. HKIAC website, News, "HKIAC Introduces a Panel of Arbitrators for Intellectual Property Disputes" (14 March 2016), online: http://www.hkiac.org/news/panel-arbitrators-intellectual-property-disputes (last visited 10 March 2023).
779. Prior to 2019, the relevant legislative Acts in Singapore did not contain any provisions that would expressly allow or prohibit the arbitration of IP disputes. The Trade Marks Act 1998 did not (and still does not) contain any provision on arbitration. However, the legislative history of the Arbitration Act 2001 shows that the drafters of the Act regarded trademark validity disputes as matters involving "public policy" and hence not suitable for arbitration (Review of Arbitration Act Committee, *Review of Arbitration Laws*, LRRD No 3/2001). This view was shared by many commentators (until the 2019 legislative changes), who did not distinguish between international and domestic disputes, but opposing views exist in the scholarship. *See* David Joseph & David Foxton, *Singapore International Arbitration: Law & Practice* (LexisNexis, 2014) at para. 5.3; Michael Hwang et al, "National Report for Singapore (2015) [Archived]" in Jan Paulsson & Lise Bosman, eds, *ICCA International Handbook on Commercial Arbitration* (Kluwer Law International, 2015) at 10 (citing *Halsbury's Laws of Singapore*, vol 1(2) (LexisNexis, 2003)); Lawrence Boo, "Arbitrability of Intellectual Property Disputes" (Presentation), International Association for the Protection of Intellectual Property (AIPPI), Forum 07/12, Forum Session 12 at 2.
780. Prior to 2019, Singapore also fit into this Camp. However, due to the changes to its relevant laws in 2019, Singapore now fits into the Arbitrability Camp. *See* above, para. 464.
781. Erik Schäfer, "Arbitration of Intellectual Property Related Disputes in Germany" in Karl-Heinz Böckstiegel et al, eds, *Arbitration in Germany: The Model Law in Practice*, 2nd ed (Kluwer Law International, 2015) 907 at paras. 18, 29.

disagree as to whether disputes concerning the validity of registered IP rights are arbitrable.[782]

466. As seen earlier, according to the explanatory section of the Bill of the Arbitration Law Reform Act (in relation to the 1998 reform in the Code of Civil Procedure) in the case of matters where the Code of Civil Procedure vests exclusive jurisdiction in a court, the exclusivity of the court's jurisdiction should not be considered a decisive factor against the arbitrability of the matter *unless* the court is a special court for specific disputes pertaining to the revocation or nullity of the rights granted through an administrative act of the government, such as in the case of patents.[783] Therefore, given that there are special courts for trademark validity disputes, it is likely that such disputes are non-arbitrable under German law. However, the issue is not settled, as some commentators argue in favor of the arbitrability of validity disputes, at least when the award affects only the parties and not any third party.[784]

467. However, the above discussion (as to the inarbitrability of validity disputes) is likely applicable only to those cases in which a German IP right is involved. If an arbitration proceeding in Germany concerns an IP right granted by another country, then the rule is probably different. This issue has been discussed theoretically, with some commentators arguing that there is no compelling reason why German courts should set aside or refuse to enforce an award as to the validity of an IP right registered in another country solely on the grounds that the validity issue may not be arbitrable under German law.[785]

468. In China (Mainland), given that administrative disputes are inarbitrable,[786] disputes pertaining to the validity of trademarks are believed to be non-arbitrable because they involve administrative authorities.[787] Under articles 44 and 45 of the Trademark Law of the People's Republic of China, trademark validity disputes should be referred to the Trademark Review and Adjudication Board. The Board's decisions are not final, and a party dissatisfied with a decision may file a suit in the People's Court. Jingzhou Tao is of the opinion that the arbitrability of trademarks is "more complicated than that of copyrights and there is no generally accepted attitude toward their arbitrability, since those rights are granted through registration with the State."[788]

782. *Ibid.*, at para. 18.
783. *Bill of the Arbitration Law Reform Act*, BT-Drs 13/5274 at 35, online (in original language): http://dipbt.bundestag.de/doc/btd/13/052/1305274.pdf (last visited 14 February 2021).
784. Erik Schäfer, "Arbitration of Intellectual Property Related Disputes in Germany" in Karl-Heinz Böckstiegel et al, eds, *Arbitration in Germany: The Model Law in Practice*, 2nd ed (Kluwer Law International, 2015) 907 at paras. 18, 22–30.
785. *Ibid.*, at paras. 31–34.
786. Article 3 of the Arbitration Law of People's Republic of China expressly excludes the arbitrability of administrative disputes.
787. Lu Song, "National Report for China (2020 through 2022)" in Lise Bosman, ed, *ICCA International Handbook on Commercial Arbitration* (Kluwer Law International, 2022) at Chapter II.3.a; Jingzhou Tao, "Arbitration Law of the PRC" in Loukas A Mistelis, ed, *Concise International Arbitration*, 2nd ed (Kluwer Law International, 2015) 911 at 914.
788. Jingzhou Tao, *Arbitration Law and Practice in China*, 3rd ed (Kluwer Law International, 2012) at para. 171.

(c) EU Trademarks

469. The Regulation (EU) 2017/1001 on the European Union Trade Mark names specific authorities and courts that have exclusive jurisdiction over validity disputes. Under Articles 59, 60, and 124 of the Regulation, any application relating to the invalidity of an EU trademark must be submitted to the European Union Intellectual Property Office (EUIPO),[789] and any counterclaims for revocation or for a declaration of invalidity of the EU trademark must be submitted to the EU Trade Mark Courts. Under the same Regulation, Article 123 states: "The Member States shall designate in their territories as limited a number as possible of national courts and tribunals of first and second instance, hereinafter referred to as EU trademark courts, which shall perform the functions assigned to them by this Regulation." For example, France has designated the courts of Paris,[790] and Germany has designated the Regional Courts (as the court of first instance) and the Higher Regional Courts (as the court of second instance) for EU Trade Mark Courts.[791]

470. Despite the fact that (according to the provisions set out above) specific courts and authorities have exclusive jurisdiction to decide the invalidity of EU trademarks, the end result may vary from one jurisdiction to another within the EU. For instance, in France, it is likely that such disputes are considered to be arbitrable if they are raised in the course of arbitral proceedings in relation to contractual disputes about EU trademarks and Community designs, and if the tribunals' decision would be inter partes only. This is based on an analogy to French patent law.[792] However, in Germany, unlike France, disputes as to the validity of EU trademarks seem to be non-arbitrable. The explanatory section of the German Bill of the Arbitration Law Reform Act (in relation to the 1998 reform of German arbitration law) relevantly provides that the exclusivity of a court's jurisdiction may not be construed as enforcing the non-arbitrability of a matter *unless* the court is a special court for specific disputes pertaining to the revocation or nullity of the rights granted through administrative act of the government.[793] Given that the EU Trade Mark Courts in Germany could be viewed as special courts designated for validity disputes, it seems unlikely that these courts would stay proceedings in favor of arbitration.

471. Furthermore, given that EU trademarks are EU rights, some commentators have compared them with the other EU IP right: Unitary Patents. Since Article 35(2) of the Agreement on the Unified Patent Court may be viewed as ruling out the arbitrability of validity disputes for Unitary Patents, it has been argued that "there is a risk that in

789. The EUIPO was known as OHIM (Office for Harmonization in the Internal Market) until 23 March 2016. EUIPO website, tab "About EUIP," sub-tab "Who We Are," sub-sub-tab "The Office," online: https://euipo.europa.eu/ohimportal/en/the-office (last visited 24 February 2021).
790. *See* Judicial Organization Code, Art. R211-7.
791. *See* Act on the Protection of Trade Marks and Other Symbols, s. 125e.
792. *See* above, para. 428.
793. Bill of the Arbitration Law Reform Act, BT-Drs 13/5274 at 35, online (in original language): http://dipbt.bundestag.de/doc/btd/13/052/1305274.pdf (last visited 14 February 2021).

regard to community [IP rights] a restrictive approach will be adopted" by the EU Trade Mark Courts and the Community Design Courts.[794]

472. Regarding the status of EU trademarks in the UK after Brexit, it should be noted that those rights are no longer valid in the UK—as EU trademarks—since the date that the UK officially left the EU. Rather, EU trademarks were immediately and automatically replaced by equivalent UK rights.[795] The UK entirely revoked the Regulation (EU) 2017/1001 on the European Union Trade Mark[796] and, thus, those rights are now governed primarily by the Trade Marks Act 1994.

G. LABOUR/EMPLOYMENT LAW

473. The discussion in this section includes two Subsections: the first subsection covers the jurisdictions distinguishing between labour and employment disputes. The majority of jurisdictions that were studied fit into this group, including the US, Canada, France, Germany, Switzerland, and (to a certain extent) England and Wales. In these jurisdictions, the term "labour law" is associated with concepts such as unionized workforce and collective-bargaining agreements[797] while the term "employment law" is associated mainly with individual employment relationships. The second subsection covers the jurisdictions not necessarily distinguishing between labour and employment disputes, which include China (Mainland), Hong Kong, and Singapore. In these jurisdictions, the line between the two terms is not as clear as it is in the first group.

1. Jurisdictions Distinguishing Between Labour and Employment Disputes

474. The jurisdictions that fit into this group are North American and European. This subsection includes two Segments: (i) Labour Disputes and (ii) Employment Disputes. The discussion demonstrates that nearly all jurisdictions in this group consider labour disputes to be arbitrable, while they remain divided over the arbitrability of employment disputes. North American jurisdictions have generally adopted a positive approach to the arbitrability of employment disputes, whereas European jurisdictions (except Switzerland, in domestic matters) are generally reluctant to submit employment disputes to arbitration.

---

794. Erik Schäfer, "Arbitration of Intellectual Property Related Disputes in Germany" in Karl-Heinz Böckstiegel et al, eds, *Arbitration in Germany: The Model Law in Practice*, 2nd ed (Kluwer Law International, 2015) 907 at para. 24.
795. For further information, *see* the official guideline issued by the UK Intellectual Property Office and Government Digital Service, titled *Guidance: Changes to EU and International Designs and Trade Mark Protection*, online: https://www.gov.uk/guidance/changes-to-eu-and-international-designs-and-trade-mark-protection (last visited 28 October 2022).
796. The Trade Marks (Amendment etc.) (EU Exit) Regulations 2019, Schedule 5, para. 6.
797. In English law, the term "trade dispute" has been used as well. *See* Trade Union and Labour Relations (Consolidation) Act 1992, ss. 218, 244.

i. Labour Disputes

475. The discussion in this Subsection shows that the US and the European jurisdictions consider labour disputes to be arbitrable, and that in Canada, although the arbitration of such disputes is a common practice, such arbitration is statutory rather than consensual.

476. In continental Europe, the approach to arbitration of labour disputes is clear:

- France and Germany have a provision in their labour-related legislative Acts which allows collective-bargaining agreements to include an arbitration provision.[798]
- In Switzerland, the Supreme Federal Court, in *BGE 107 Ia 152, 14 October 1981*, held that neither Swiss federal law nor cantonal laws prohibits the parties to a collective-bargaining agreement from including an arbitration clause in their agreement.

477. In England and Wales, under section 212 of the Trade Union and Labour Relations (Consolidation) Act 1992, the Advisory, Conciliation, and Arbitration Service (ACAS) may refer parties' labour dispute (known as trade dispute) to arbitration if all the parties agree to the referral, but Part I of the Arbitration Act 1996 is not applicable to such arbitrations. Article 212A of the Act also allows the ACAS to develop an arbitration scheme. The ACAS assists with the arbitration of both collective and individual disputes[799] through two arbitration schemes: the ACAS Arbitration Scheme for the Resolution of Unfair Dismissal Disputes[800] and the ACAS Arbitration Scheme for the Resolution of Flexible Working Disputes.[801]

478. In the US and Canada, the arbitration of labour disputes has developed into a major field over decades and, as such, the literature on the topic is substantial. The discussion set out below sheds light on the most important aspects of this literature.

The United States

479. Since the US Supreme Court's decisions in the *Steelworkers* trilogy in 1960,[802] US courts have strongly supported the arbitration of labour disputes (known as grievance

798. For France, *see* Labour Code, Arts. L2524-1, L2524-2, and L2524-5. For Germany, *see* Labour Court Act, s. 101(1).
799. ACAS website, tab "Dispute Resolution," sub-tab "Arbitration," online: https://www.acas.org.uk/arbitration (last visited 28 October 2022).
800. Online: https://www.acas.org.uk/sites/default/files/2021-03/acas-arbitration-scheme-for-resolution-of-unfair-dismissal-disputes-england-and-wales.pdf (last visited 12 October 2022).
801. Online: https://www.acas.org.uk/sites/default/files/2021-03/acas-arbitration-scheme-flexible-working-disputes-england-and-wales.pdf (last visited 12 October 2022).
802. *United Steelworkers v. American Mfg Co*, 363 US 564 (1960); *United Steelworkers v. Warrior & Gulf Navigation Co*, 363 US 574 (1960); *United Steelworkers v. Enterprise Wheel & Car Corp*, 363 US 593 (1960).

arbitration) by enforcing arbitration clauses in collective-bargaining agreements. The AAA also offers specific arbitration rules for labour disputes.[803]

480. Given the large number of relevant federal statutes, the arbitrability of a labour dispute should be examined under the statute under which the dispute has arisen. For example:

- Some federal laws, such as the Labor Management Relations Act (§ 171) and the Norris-LaGuardia Act (§ 108), expressly allow for the arbitration of labour disputes.
- Regarding the National Labor Relations Act (NLRA), the Supreme Court, as well as the Courts of Appeals for the Second, Fifth, and Eight Circuits have held that employers may enforce arbitration agreements against employees who are covered by the NLRA.[804]
- In relation to claims under the Fair Labor Standards Act (FLSA), the Courts of Appeals for the Second, Fourth, Fifth, Eight, Ninth, and Eleventh Circuits have held that such disputes are also arbitrable.[805] The Third Circuit has not questioned the arbitrability of FLSA claims but requires the arbitration agreement to *expressly* provide for arbitration of statutory claims or, at least, not limit itself to arbitration of contractual disputes (for example, it should not say "any disputes arising under this agreement").[806]

481. An important category of disputes in US labour/employment law concerns anti-discrimination or civil rights disputes. While the arbitrability of anti-discrimination disputes is discussed in more detail in the section on employment disputes,[807] here it is sufficient to mention that the Supreme Court has adopted a favorable approach to the arbitrability of statutory anti-discrimination claims in labour disputes, but *only when* they are clearly and unmistakably mentioned in the arbitration provision of the collective agreement. For instance, in *14 Penn Plaza LLC v. Pyett* (2009), the Supreme Court held that the provision in a collective-bargaining agreement that clearly and unmistakably required union members to arbitrate claims arising under the Age Discrimination in Employment Act was enforceable and that it falls within the authority of unions to negotiate such arbitration agreements as a part of

803. AAA Labor Arbitration Rules (Including Expedited Labor Arbitration Rules) (2013, amended 2019), online: https://adr.org/sites/default/files/Labor_Arbitration_Rules_Including_Expedited_Labor_Arbitration_Rules.pdf (last visited 16 June 2022).
804. *Epic Systems Corp v. Lewis*, 138 S Ct 1612 (2018); *Sutherland v. Ernst & Young LLP*, 726 F3d 290 at 297 n 8 (2d Cir 2013) at 297 n 8; *DR Horton, Inc v. NLRB*, 737 F3d 344 (5th Cir 2013) at 357, 361; *Owen v. Bristol Care, Inc*, 702 F3d 1050 (8th Cir 2013) at 1053–1054.
805. *Kuehner v. Dickinson & Co*, 84 F3d 316 (9th Cir 1996) at 319–20; *Adkins v. Labor Ready, Inc*, 303 F3d 496 (4th Cir 2002) at 506; *Carter v. Countrywide Credit Indus, Inc*, 362 F3d 294 (5th Cir 2004) at 297; *Caley v. Gulfstream Aerospace Corp*, 428 F3d 1359 (11th Cir 2005); *Owen v. Bristol Care, Inc*, 702 F3d 1050 (8th Cir 2013); *Sutherland v. Ernst & Young LLP*, 726 F3d 290 (2d Cir 2013) at 299.
806. *Moon v. Breathless Inc*, 868 F3d 209 (3d Cir 2017).
807. *See* below, paras. 504–506.

collective-bargaining agreements.[808] The Court also noted that "[n]othing in the law suggests a distinction between the status of arbitration agreements signed by an individual employee and those agreed to by a union representative. This Court has required only that an agreement to arbitrate statutory antidiscrimination claims be explicitly stated in the collective-bargaining agreement."[809]

482. Another issue that should be noted is that there is a difference between the *arbitrability* of labour/employment disputes and the possibility of *waiving an employee's right to join/launch a class action or class arbitration*. The National Labor Relations Board (NLRB),[810] in *DR Horton, Inc* (2012), held that an arbitration agreement waiving the right to join/commence class actions and class arbitrations in any forum for employees covered by the NLRA violated §§ 7 and 8 of the Act and thus was unenforceable under § 2 of the FAA for illegality.[811] The NLRB's interpretation of the interplay between the FAA and the NLRA caused a split between the US Courts of Appeals. The Courts of Appeals for the Second, Fifth, and Eight Circuits favored a more pro-arbitration approach and rejected the NLRB's interpretation,[812] whereas the Courts of Appeals for the Sixth, Seventh, and Ninth Circuits sided with the NLRB and accorded judicial deference to its interpretation.[813] As a result of the split, the Supreme Court granted certiorari and, in *Epic Systems Corp v. Lewis* (2018), ruled that the pro-arbitration approach should prevail.[814]

Canada

483. The arbitration of labour disputes is comprehensively addressed by Canadian labour legislation, at both the federal level and the provincial level.[815] Under the relevant federal and provincial Codes/Acts, all collective agreements must provide for

808. *14 Penn Plaza LLC v. Pyett*, 556 US 247 (2009).
809. *Ibid.*, at 258.
810. The NLRB is "an independent federal agency vested with the power to safeguard employees' rights to organize and to determine whether to have unions as their bargaining representative. The agency also acts to prevent and remedy unfair labour practices committed by private sector employers and unions." NLRB website, tab "About NLRB," Section "What We Do," online: https://www.nlrb.gov/about-nlrb (last visited 16 June 2022).
811. *DR Horton*, 357 NLRB 2277 (2012) at 2278, 2283–2288.
812. *Sutherland v. Ernst & Young LLP*, 726 F3d 290 at 297 n 8 (2d Cir 2013) at 297 n 8; *DR Horton, Inc v. NLRB*, 737 F3d 344 (5th Cir 2013) at 357, 361; *Owen v. Bristol Care, Inc*, 702 F3d 1050 (8th Cir 2013) at 1053–1054.
813. *NLRB v. Alternative Entm't, Inc*, 858 F3d 393 (6th Cir 2017); *Lewis v. Epic Systems Corp*, 823 F3d 1147 (7th Cir 2016) at 1152–54, 1157, cert granted, 137 S Ct 809 (2017); *Morris v. Ernst & Young, LLP*, 834 F3d 975 (9th Cir 2016) at 980–981, 985–986, cert granted, 137 S Ct 809 (2017).
814. *Epic Systems Corp v. Lewis*, 138 S Ct 1612 (2018).
815. For federal laws, *see* Canada Labour Code, RSC 1985, c L-2. For Alberta, *see* Labour Relations Code, RSA 2000, c L-1; Employment Standards Code, RSA 2000, c E-9; Public Service Employee Relations Act, RSA 2000, c P-43. For British Columbia, *see* Labour Relations Code, RSBC 1996, c 244; Employment Standard Act, RSBC 1996, c 113; Public Service Labour Relations Act, RSBC 1996, c 388. For Ontario, *see* Labour Relations Act, RSO 1995, c 1, Schedule A; Employment Standards Act, RSO 2000, c 41. For Québec, *see* Labour Code, CQLR c C-27; Act Representing Labour Standards, CQLR c N-1.1; Civil Code of Québec, CQLR c C-1991.

a means of a final and binding out-of-court dispute settlement mechanism such as arbitration.[816]

484. In Canada, labour arbitration is usually called "grievance arbitration," which is regarded as statutory arbitration and thus is not considered to be consensual.[817] The Supreme Court of Canada in *Port Arthur Shipbuilding Co v. Arthurs* (1969) held that grievance arbitration is statutory arbitration because, under the relevant statutes, the parties to a collective agreement are left with no option but to arbitrate their disputes.[818] Therefore, according to the Court, the awards rendered by such tribunals are subject to judicial review by certiorari as a matter of administrative law.[819] Thirteen years later, in *Roberval Express Ltée v. Transport Drivers* (1982), the Supreme Court came to the same conclusion as it did in *Port Arthur*—that grievance arbitration is statutory arbitration—but questioned its earlier reasoning.[820] Thus, in *Roberval Express*, the Supreme Court held that, if grievance arbitration is statutory arbitration, it is due to the nature of the duties and powers conferred on grievance tribunals by relevant statutes.[821]

485. In terms of the subject matters that may be submitted to grievance arbitration, the Supreme Court of Canada held, in *Weber v. Ontario Hydro* (1995), that grievance arbitrators have exclusive jurisdiction over nearly any dispute if the dispute "in its essential character, arises from the interpretation, application, administration or violation of the collective agreement," even if the dispute goes beyond the traditional subject matter of labour law.[822] In *Weber*, the Supreme Court also held that claims arising under the Canadian Charter of Rights and Freedoms can be submitted to grievance arbitrators if the relevant federal or provincial labour legislation gives them subject matter jurisdiction, as well as the power to grant the remedies sought.[823]

486. However, in the case of *Québec (Commission des droits de la personne et des droits de la jeunesse) v. Québec (Attorney General)* (2004), the Supreme Court of Canada clarified that its decision in *Weber* "does not stand for the proposition that labour arbitrators always have exclusive jurisdiction in employer-union disputes" and held that "depending on the legislation and the nature of the dispute, other tribunals

---

816. *See, e.g.*, Canada Labour Code, RSC 1985, c L-2, s. 57; Alberta's Labour Relations Code, RSA 2000, c L-1, s. 135; British Columbia's Labour Relations Code, RSBC 1996, c 244, s. 84; Ontario's Labour Relations Act, RSO 1995, c 1, Schedule A, s. 48; Québec's Labour Code, CQLR c C-27, Art. 100.
817. The difference between the two types of arbitration is that "consensual arbitration was found to be beyond the scope of judicial review particularly those grounded in certiorari, while statutory arbitration was generally regarded to be subject to the review process." Ronald M Snyder, *Collective Agreement Arbitration in Canada*, 4th ed (LexisNexis, 2009) at paras. 4.3, 4.4.
818. *Port Arthur Shipbuilding Co v. Arthurs*, [1969] SCR 85 at 6–8, 10, 70 DLR (2d) 693.
819. *Ibid.*
820. *Roberval Express Ltée v. Transport Drivers, Warehousemen and General Workers Union, Local 106*, [1982] 2 SCR 888 at 7, 11–14, 144 DLR (3d) 67.
821. *Ibid.*
822. *Weber v. Ontario Hydro*, [1995] 2 SCR 929 at paras. 33–40, 47–53, 56–58, 60–66, 125 DLR (4th) 583.
823. *Ibid.*

may possess overlapping jurisdiction, concurrent jurisdiction, or themselves be endowed with exclusive jurisdiction."[824] As such, the Court held that grievance arbitrators did not have exclusive jurisdiction in a dispute arising under the Québec Charter of Human Rights and Freedoms about an alleged discriminatory clause in the collective-bargaining agreement.[825]

487. In general, a review of decisions by the Supreme Court of Canada[826] and provincial courts[827] indicates that Canadian courts have defined a broad scope of matters that could be submitted to arbitration in labour disputes.

ii. Employment Disputes

488. The jurisdictions (within the group that distinguishes between labour and employment disputes) are divided over the arbitrability of employment disputes. North American jurisdictions have generally adopted a positive approach to the arbitrability of employment disputes whereas European jurisdictions (expect Switzerland, in domestic matters) are reluctant to submit such disputes to arbitration.

European Approach

England and Wales

489. In England and Wales, section 203(1)(b) of the Employment Rights Act 1996 does not allow (save certain exceptions) a party to contract out of the right to gain access to the Employment Tribunal. Likewise, section 144 of the Equality Act 2010 sets limitations on arbitration agreements for discrimination disputes. In *Clyde & Co LLP v. Bates van Winkelhof* (2011), the King's Bench refused to stay an Employment Tribunal proceeding in favor of arbitration for whistleblowing claims brought under the Employment Rights Act 1996, as well as claims of sex and pregnancy discrimination brought under the Equality Act 2010.[828]

Germany

490. In Germany, only disputes arising in limited employment circumstances and in a limited number of occupations are arbitrable. Under section 101(2) of the Labour Court Act, employment disputes of actors, film makers, and artists may be submitted to arbitration provided that: (i) the employment relationship is within the scope of a

824. *Québec (Commission des droits de la personne et des droits de la jeunesse) v. Québec (Attorney General)*, 2004 SCC 39 at paras. 11, 15 [2004] 2 SCR 185.
825. *Ibid.*
826. *See, e.g.*, *Bisaillon v. Concordia University*, 2006 SCC 19 at paras. 1, 2, 5–7, 13, 17, 22, [2006] 1 SCR 666; *Bisaillon v. Concordia University*, 2006 SCC 19 at paras. 1–2, 5–7, 13, 17, 22, [2006] 1 SCR 666.
827. *See, e.g.*, *British Columbia Teachers' Federation v. Port Alberni School District No 70*, 2011 BCCA 148 at paras. 1–3, 9–13, 21–23, 17 BCLR (5th) 179; *Ouellette v. Société de récupération, d'exploitation et de développement forestiers du Québec (Rexfor)*, [1997] JQ No 2753 (Qc CA) at paras. 2–5, 16–18, 1997 CarswellQue 784.
828. *Clyde & Co LLP v. Bates van Winkelhof* [2011] EWHC 668 at paras. 3–5, 37–44, 2011 WL 806822 (QB).

collective agreement that has expressly provided for arbitration of disputes, or (ii) if the employment relationship is not subject to such collective agreement, the parties have incorporated its terms into their contract.[829] Other employment disputes are generally believed to be non-arbitrable.[830] However, disputes arising out of freelance work contracts are arbitrable.[831]

Switzerland

491. In Switzerland, the arbitrability of individual employment disputes depends on whether the applicable law is the PILA or Part III of the Civil Procedure Code. Where the PILA applies (i.e., when one of the parties at the time of conclusion of the arbitration agreement has their domicile or residency in another country), the Federal Supreme Court has noted that the employment dispute will be arbitrable, because such disputes generally involve economic interests and meet the criterion in Article 177(1) of the PILA.[832] Further, in *Case No 4A_388/2012, 18 March 2013*, the Federal Supreme Court held that monetary claims that arise out of employment contracts are arbitrable in Switzerland, even if such claims are not arbitrable under the governing foreign law. However, according to the Court, if the foreign law is the governing law of the contract as per the parties' choice, the prohibition in the foreign law with respect to arbitrability would render the arbitration agreement invalid.

492. Where the Civil Procedure Code applies, the Swiss Federal Supreme Court has held that an employer and an employee may not agree in their contract of employment to submit future disputes to arbitration.[833] The Court's reasoning is that, under Article 354 of the Civil Procedure Code, parties may enter into an arbitration agreement only with respect to the rights that they may freely waive and, according to articles 361 and 362 of the Code of Obligations, an employee may not waive their claims arising out of mandatory or semi-mandatory provisions within the time limits imposed by Article 341 of the same Code.[834] Therefore, where an employee may not waive their employment claims, the claims would not be arbitrable.[835] However, if the employee and employer reach an arbitration agreement where the employee has already filed a case before the

829. *See also* Patrick M Baron & Stefan Liniger, "A Second Look at Arbitrability: Approaches to Arbitration in the United States, Switzerland and Germany" (2003) 19:1 Arb Int'l 27 at 41 DOI: 10.1093/arbitration/19.1.27.
830. Rolf Trittmann & Inka Hanefeld, "Commentary on the German Arbitration Law (10th Book of the German Code of Civil Procedure) § 1030" in Karl-Heinz Böckstiegel et al, eds, *Arbitration in Germany: The Model Law in Practice*, 2nd ed (Kluwer Law International, 2015) 94 at para. 20.
831. *OLG München, 27.02.2020—34 Sch 15/17* (enforcing an arbitral award relating to a dispute arising out of a freelance contract, and rejecting the inarbitrability objection that the parties' relationship was not a freelance relationship but rather an employment relationship). Regardless of whether or not the inarbitrability objection would have been upheld, the decision shows that disputes arising out of a freelance work relationship are arbitrable, as neither the parties nor the court took any issue with the arbitrability of such disputes.
832. *BGE 136 III 467, 28 June 2010.*
833. *Ibid.*
834. *Ibid.*
835. *Ibid. See also* Philippe Bärtsch & Angelina M Petti, "Chapter 3: The Arbitration Agreement" in Elliott Geisinger & Nathalie Voser, ed, *International Arbitration in Switzerland: A Handbook for Practitioners* (Kluwer Law International, 2013) 25 at 39, 40.

Employment Tribunal, the dispute may be submitted to arbitration, as per the Federal Supreme Court's decision in *Case No 4P.69/1989, 23 June 1989.*

493. In a more recent decision, the Federal Supreme Court again confirmed the inarbitrability of domestic employment disputes.[836] The Court reasoned that the criterion for the arbitrability of such disputes has not changed since the entry into force of the Code of Civil Procedure in 2011 and, thus, the Court's 1967 decision regarding the inarbitrability of those disputes under the Concordat remains valid.[837] In obiter, the Court made an important note: that in a purely domestic employment relationship, the parties may *not* circumvent the arbitrability criterion by opting out of the application of the Code of Civil Procedure in favor of the PILA and its arbitrability criterion.[838]

France

494. In France, under Articles L1411-1 and L1411-4 of the Labour Code, the Labour Court has exclusive jurisdiction over disputes arising out of individual employment contracts and any agreement providing otherwise is deemed "unwritten." The only exception to that general rule under the Labour Code is the arbitration of disputes that are raised by journalists with more than fifteen years of experience, where the dispute is with their employer in relation to the compensation due to them. In such a case, under Article L7112-4, there will be a mandatory arbitration that takes the form of an arbitration commission composed of arbitrators appointed jointly by the professional organizations of relevant employers and employees.

495. Another French legislative text that has a provision relevant to the arbitration of employment disputes is the Civil Code. According to Article 2061, which was amended in 2016, "[t]he arbitration clause must have been accepted by the party against whom it is enforced, unless that party has succeeded in the rights and obligations of the party who initially accepted it. Where one of the parties has not entered into the contract in the framework of his *professional activity*, the clause may not be enforced against him" (emphasis added).[839] Under the previous version of Article 2061, "[u]nless provided otherwise in specific legislative provisions, an arbitration clause is valid in contracts which are concluded by reason of a *professional activity*" (emphasis added). Both versions of Article 2061 have the term "professional activity" in common; yet, in the pre-amendment version, it was a *validity* requirement for arbitration agreements, whereas in the current version it is an *enforceability* requirement.[840]

496. Philippe Fouchard considered that "professional activity" refers to an activity that is performed in connection with the exercise of a profession, has a habitual nature, and where its purpose is to provide resources to the professional, but that there is no need

836. *BGE 144 III 235, 18 April 2018.*
837. *Ibid.*
838. For a discussion on the opting out mechanism, *see* above, note 89.
839. Article 2061 was amended by Law No 2016-1547 of 18 November 2016.
840. Laurence Kiffer, "National Report for France (2020)" in Jan Paulsson & Lise Bosman, eds, *ICCA International Handbook on Commercial Arbitration* (Kluwer Law International, 2020) at Chapter II.3.a.

for the contract to be commercial or to be concluded as part of the professional's specialty.[841] In other words, so long as the contract is for the purpose of one's business, the subject matter would be arbitrable.[842]

497. Prior to the 2016 amendment, commentators considered that an arbitration agreement between an employer and an employee in an employment contract should have been a clear example of entering into an agreement "by reason of professional activity," but they believed that employment disputes *could not* fall within the scope of Article 2061 because the Labour Code provides for the exclusive jurisdiction of the Labour Court and, therefore, employment disputes should be regarded as non-arbitrable.[843]

498. The Grenoble Court of Appeal in *Société CFTE v. J Dechavanne* (1994) held that the employment provision in an international agreement for the sale of corporate shares is considered to be an international employment contract and that "the arbitration agreement inserted in an international individual employment contract is valid."[844] The Grenoble Court of Appeal in part relied on the French Government's 1989 withdrawal of its commercial reservation to the New York Convention,[845] which, according to the Court, allowed for the arbitration of disputes arising out of international employment contracts.[846]

499. However, the Court of Cassation, in a line of cases (first international and then domestic), has ruled against the arbitration of employment disputes: not because the subject matter is inarbitrable, but because the arbitration clause is *unenforceable against the employee*. In 2001, the Court of Cassation (Social Chamber) in *Société Kis France v. Lopez-Alberdi*, held that the arbitration clause in an international contract of employment is unenforceable against an employee—who has lodged an application in a competent court under the applicable rules—for any dispute relating to the contract.[847] In this regard, the Court held that the governing law of the contract would be of little importance.[848] In the years following this ruling, the Court of Cassation made

841. Philippe Fouchard, "La laborieuse réforme de la clause compromissoire par la loi du 15 mai 2001" (2001) 3 Rev Arb 397 at paras. 18, 19.
842. *Ibid.*
843. *Ibid.*, at para. 29; Beatrice Castellane, "Arbitration in Employment Relationship in France" (2009) 26:2 J Int'l Arb 293 at 294 DOI: 10.54648/joia2009015; Estelle Courtois-Champenois, "L'Arbitrage des litiges en droit du travail: à la redécouverte d'une institution française en disgrâce" (2003) 2 Rev Arb 349 at paras. 3, 19; Éric Loquin, JurisClasseur Procédure Civile, Fasc 1024 (May 2016) at nos. 107, 108.
844. *Société CFTE v. J Dechavanne*, Grenoble Court of Appeal, 13 September 1993, reported in (1994) 1994:2 Rev Arb 337.
845. *Decree No 90-170 of 16 February 1990*, online: https://www.legifrance.gouv.fr/jo_pdf.do?id=JORFTEXT000000714806 (last visited 10 May 2022).
846. *Société CFTE v. J Dechavanne*, Grenoble Court of Appeal, 13 September 1993, reported in (1994) 1994:2 Rev Arb 337.
847. *Société Kis France v. Lopez-Alberdi*, Court of Cassation (Social Chamber), 9 October 2001, Decision No 99-43.288, reported in (2002) 2002:2 Rev Arb 347.
848. *Ibid.*

similar rulings in other international matters, including *Société Taiphoon limited v. Bobinet* (2005)[849] and *Société Sportive IL Gabbiano v. [not indicated]* (2008).[850]

500. The Court of Cassation later adopted the same approach to domestic employment disputes. In *Société Deloitte conseil v. M E Serant* (2011), the Court of Cassation (Social Chamber) held that the disputes arising out of a corporate charter, which was signed by the two employees and contained provisions in relation to their employment contracts—such as remuneration and notice of termination—may not be submitted to arbitration on the basis of the arbitration clause in the charter. The Court reasoned that, in such circumstances, the charter constitutes an amendment to employment contracts and, as such, the arbitration clause may not, under Article L1411-4 of the Labour Code, be enforced against the employees.[851]

501. The 2016 amendments to Article 2061 (that deems relevant arbitration agreements unenforceable) seem to be in line with the Court of Cassation's decisions on the arbitration of employment disputes.[852] It should be noted that:

- Given that the limitation on arbitration of employment disputes is due to the exclusive jurisdiction of the Labour Court, any matter over which the Labour Court does not have exclusive jurisdiction may be submitted to arbitration.[853] In *Macron (ép Cougoulat) et SARL International Display Design v. Société des Cartonnages de Pamfou* (2002), the Paris Court of Appeal held that a dispute arising out of a non-competition clause in a protocol signed in relation to the parties' employment contract may be submitted to arbitration on the basis of the arbitration clause in the protocol. In that case, the dispute concerned the non-competition clause and not the employment contract.[854]
- The restriction against the arbitration of employment disputes is not applicable when the arbitration agreement is signed after the termination/expiration of the employment contract, because the employee is no longer considered to be in a weaker position with respect to their employer and would as a result be free to waive the rights.[855] In *Société H v. Charles de T* (1984), the Court of Cassation (Social Chamber) upheld the Paris Court of Appeal's decision holding that the parties' arbitration agreement—concluded after the

849. *Société Taiphoon limited v. Bobinet*, Court of Cassation (Social Chamber), 28 June 2005, Decision No 03-45.042, reported in (2005) 2005:3 Rev Arb 799.
850. *Société Sportive IL Gabbiano v. [not indicated]*, Court of Cassation (Social Chamber), 12 March 2008, Decision No 01-44.654.
851. *Société Deloitte conseil v. M E Serant*, Court of Cassation (Social Chamber), 30 November 2011, Decision Nos. 11-12.905 & 11-12.906.
852. *See* Thomas Clay, "La réforme des articles du Code civil sur l'arbitrage en France" (2017) 35:1 ASA Bulletin 40 at 48 DOI: 10.54648/asab2017004.
853. Éric Loquin, JurisClasseur Procédure Civile, Fasc 1024 (May 2016) at no 107.
854. *Macron (ép Cougoulat) et SARL International Display Design v. Société des Cartonnages de Pamfou*, Paris Court of Appeal, 12 September 2002, reported in (2003) 2003:1 Rev Arb 173.
855. Éric Loquin, JurisClasseur Procédure Civile, Fasc 1024 (May 2016) at no 109.

termination of the employment contract—was valid, as the former employee was then free to waive his rights.[856] Non-arbitrability, here, is not permanent.

North American Approach

The United States

502. US courts have generally supported the arbitration of employment disputes. Further, the AAA offers specific arbitration rules for employment disputes.[857] Given the large number of federal statutes on employer-employee relations, the arbitrability of an employment dispute should be examined under the relevant statute under which the dispute has arisen.

503. For example, anti-retaliation claims under the False Claims Act (i.e., employee's claim as to employer's retaliatory measures in violation of whistleblower provisions of the False Claims Act) have been held to be arbitrable.[858] Regarding plan participants' claims arising under the Employee Retirement Income Security Act of 1974 (ERISA), the Courts of Appeals for the Second, Third, Fifth, Sixth, Seventh, Eighth, Ninth, and Tenth Circuits have held that such disputes are arbitrable.[859] However, more recently, the Second and Sixth Circuits[860] as well as some District Courts have—without questioning the arbitrability of such claims—refused to enforce arbitration agreements against plan participants, relying on contract law grounds instead.[861] However, other District Courts have disagreed with this new trend.[862]

504. An important category of disputes in US employment law concerns anti-discrimination or civil rights disputes. Title VII of the Civil Rights Act of 1964 was initially silent on whether the right to a judicial forum could be waived.[863] Later, the

856. *Société H v. Charles de T*, Court of Cassation (Social Chamber), 5 November 1984, reported in (1986) 1986:1 Rev Arb 47.
857. AAA Employment Arbitration Rules and Mediation Procedures (2009, revised 2017), online: https://www.adr.org/sites/default/files/EmploymentRules_Web.pdf (last visited 16 June 2022).
858. *US ex rel Mikes v. Straus*, 897 F Supp 805 (SD NY 1995) at 806, 808; *James v. Conceptus, Inc*, 851 F Supp 2d 1020 (SD Tex 2012) at 1024, 1028, 1039–40.
859. *Bird v. Shearson Lehman/American Exp, Inc*, 926 F2d 116 (2d Cir 1991); *Murphy v. Canadian Imperial Bank of Commerce*, 709 F Supp 2d 242 (2d Cir 2010) at 247; *Pritzker v. Merrill Lynch, Pierce, Fenner & Smith, Inc*, 7 F3d 1110 (3d Cir 1993); *Kramer v. Smith Barney*, 80 F3d 1080 (5th Cir 1996) at 1084; *Simon v. Pfizer Inc*, 398 F3d 765 (6th Cir 2005) at 773; *Smith v. Board of Directors of Triad Manufacturing, Inc*, 13 F4th 613 (7th Cir 2021); *Arnulfo P Sulit, Inc v. Dean Witter Reynolds, Inc*, 847 F2d 475 (8th Cir 1988); *Dorman v. Charles Schwab Corporation*, 934 F3d 1107 (9th Cir 2019); *Williams v. Imhoff*, 203 F3d 758 (10th Cir 2000) at 767.
860. *Cooper v. Ruane Cunniff & Goldfarb Inc*, 990 F3d 173 (2nd Cir 2021) at 180, 183, 185; *Hawkins v. Cintas Corporation*, 2022 WL 1236954 (6th Cir 2022) at 1, 9.
861. *Hensiek v. Board of Directors of Casino Queen Holding Company, Inc*, 514 F Supp 3d 1045 (SD Ill 2021) at 1052–53, appeal dismissed, 2021 WL 6775328 (7th Cir 2022); *Henry v. Wilmington Trust, NA*, 2021 WL 4133622 (D Del 2021) at 1, 5, 6; *Hawkins v. Cintas Corporations*, 2021 WL 274341 (SD Ohio 2021).
862. *Coleman v. Brozen*, 2020 WL 2200220 (ED Tex 2020) at 3; *Holmes v. Baptist Health South Florida, Inc*, 2022 WL 180638 (SD Fla 2022).
863. *Civil Rights Act of 1964*, Pub L 88-352, 78 Stat 241, online: http://www.gpo.gov/fdsys/pkg/STATUTE-78/pdf/STATUTE-78-Pg241.pdf (last visited 15 June 2022).

Civil Rights Act of 1991 "encouraged" alternative means of dispute resolution—including arbitration—for resolving disputes brought under Title VII and various other provisions of federal law. However, the same Act provides that individuals may demand *a trial by jury* when seeking compensatory or punitive damages (42 USC § 1981a.(c)), which makes it unclear whether disputes brought under Title VII are arbitrable. In the process of enactment of the Civil Rights Act of 1991, the Congressional Committee on the Judiciary emphasized in its report that:

> [T]he use of alternative dispute resolution mechanisms is intended to supplement, not supplant, the remedies provided by Title VII. Thus, for example, the Committee believes that any agreement to submit disputed issues to arbitration, whether in the context of a collective bargaining agreement or in an employment contract, does not preclude the affected person from seeking relief under the enforcement provisions of Title VII. This view is consistent with the Supreme Court's interpretation of Title VII in *Alexander v. Gardner-Denver Co.*, 415 U.S. 36 (1974). The Committee does not intend for the inclusion of this section to be used to preclude rights and remedies that would otherwise be available.[864]

505. However, it has been argued that the report by the Committee on the Judiciary "did not establish the intent of the full Congress, as no report on behalf of all of Congress was prepared" and that "[t]hese reports merely offered a hint at Congress' intentions behind the ADR provision in the Act—intentions that still are not clear and have been the basis for much litigation."[865]

506. The Supreme Court, in cases such as *Gilmer v. Interstate/Johnson Lane Corp* (1991) and *Wright v. Universal Maritime Service Corp* (1998), held that anti-discrimination claims arising under the Age Discrimination Employment Act and the Americans with Disabilities Act may be submitted to arbitration, but only when statutory anti-discrimination claims are clearly and unmistakably mentioned in the arbitration agreement.[866]

507. Another category of employment disputes concerns anti-retaliation claims by whistleblowers. The Democrat-controlled 111th US Congress enacted a number of whistleblower protection statutes for certain classes of employees, which prohibit, inter alia, *pre-dispute* arbitration agreements. For example:

- The American Recovery and Reinvestment Act of 2009 § 1553(d) in relation to whistleblower protection for employees of any non-federal employer receiving covered funds.
- The Dodd-Frank Wall Street Reform and Consumer Protection Act (Dodd-Frank Act):
  - § 922(c)(2) in relation to employees of publicly traded companies;

864. H R REP 102-40, pt 2 at 41 (1991), reprinted in 1991 USCCAN 694 at 735.
865. Matthew Gierse, "All Bound up With no Place to Go: A Lack of Individual Alternatives to Binding Arbitration Provisions for Statutory Claims" 2010 J Disp Resol 189 at 192.
866. *Gilmer v. Interstate/Johnson Lane Corp*, 500 US 20 (1991) at 28, 29; *Wright v. Universal Maritime Service Corp*, 525 US 70 (1998) at 79–80.

- § 1057(d)(2) concerning employees of any person that engages in offering or providing a consumer financial product or service; and
- § 748 concerning commodity whistleblower incentives and protection.[867]

508. Federal case law has generally been supportive of the arbitrability of whistleblower claims under the False Claims Act and § 4712 of Title 41 of the US Code (in relation to federal procurement matters).[868] In *James v. Conceptus* (2012), the District Court for the Southern District of Texas held that the amendments introduced by the Dodd-Frank Act (invalidating pre-dispute arbitration agreements for whistleblower claims under certain federal statutes) may not be extended by implication to whistleblower claims under the False Claims Act.[869] More recently, in *Robertson v. Intratek Computer* (2020), the US Court of Appeals for the Fifth Circuit held that the former employee's claims against his former employer arising under 41 USC § 4712 (protecting whistleblowers in federal procurement matters) are arbitrable.[870]

509. Another category of claims in US employment law concerns employees' claims of sexual misconduct in their work environment. In 2022, Congress enacted the Ending Forced Arbitration of Sexual Assault and Sexual Harassment Act,[871] adding a new chapter (Chapter 4) to Title 9 of the US Code—the Title that contains the FAA.[872] Chapter 4 makes a new exception (with respect to sexual misconduct claims) to the FAA rule on the enforceability of arbitration agreements. According to § 402, pre-dispute arbitration agreements and pre-dispute waivers of class claims in sexual harassment and sexual assault claims are no longer enforceable against employees.

867. The Dodd-Frank Act was enacted during the presidency of Mr. Obama as a response to the financial crisis in 2008-2009. After Mr. Trump took office in 2017, he issued a memorandum and signed an executive order, setting out his core policies and directing his administration to review the compliance of the laws and regulations with such policies, which was construed as the first steps to scale back the Dodd-Frank Act. Furthermore, the then Republican-controlled House of Representatives in Congress passed the Financial CHOICE Act of 2017, but it was not passed by the Senate. Had the Financial CHOICE Act been passed, it would have amended and repealed certain portions of the Dodd-Frank Act. Nevertheless, in 2018, Congress enacted the Economic Growth, Regulatory Relief and Consumer Protection Act which, by increasing the applicability threshold of the Dodd-Frank Act, exempted smaller banks from the application of that Act. Financial CHOICE Act of 2017, HR10, 115th Cong (2017), online: https://www.congress.gov/115/bills/hr10/BILLS-115hr10rfs.pdf (last visited 16 June 2022); Economic Growth, Regulatory Relief and Consumer Protection Act, Pub L 115–174 (2018) § 401(a), online: https://www.govinfo.gov/content/pkg/PLAW-115publ174/pdf/PLAW-115publ174.pdf (last visited 16 June 2022).

868. *See, e.g.*, *US ex rel Mikes v. Straus*, 897 F Supp 805 (SD NY 1995) at 806, 808; *James v. Conceptus, Inc*, 851 F Supp 2d 1020 (SD Tex 2012) at 1024, 1028, 1039–1040.

869. *James v. Conceptus, Inc*, 851 F Supp 2d 1020 (SD Tex 2012) at 1024, 1028, 1039–1040.

870. *Robertson v. Intratek Computer, Incorporated*, 976 F3d 575 (5th Cir 2020).

871. Ending Forced Arbitration of Sexual Assault and Sexual Harassment Act, Pub L 117–90 (2022), online: https://www.congress.gov/117/plaws/publ90/PLAW-117publ90.pdf (last visited 16 June 2022).

872. Title 9 of the US Code has four chapters: (i) the FAA, (ii) the Convention Act (incorporating the New York Convention into US law), (iii) the chapter incorporating the Inter-American Convention on International Commercial Arbitration into US law, and (iv) the newly added chapter imposing restrictions on the arbitration of sexual misconduct claims.

This means that employees (if they are in the claimant position) can unilaterally ignore the arbitration agreement in sexual misconduct claims and file those claims in courts (individually or in the form of a class/collection action).[873]

510. It should be noted that the 2022 Act does not ban the arbitration of sexual misconduct claims. The restriction targets only *pre-dispute* arbitration agreements and waivers of class claims, *and* only with respect to enforcing those agreements against *employees*. Thus, post-dispute arbitration agreements remain valid and, with respect to pre-dispute agreements, it will be up to the employee to choose to go to court or arbitration. This is important because some employees may still prefer a private arbitration to a public court proceeding.

511. A statutory exception to the arbitrability of employment disputes is found in § 1 of the FAA, which excludes any "contracts of employment of seamen, railroad employees, or any other class of workers engaged in foreign or interstate commerce" from the coverage of the FAA. The US Supreme Court, in *New Prime Inc v. Oliveira* (2019), held that § 1 is not limited to contracts that establish an employer-employee relationship but also encompasses contracts with independent contractors.[874] The same Court, in *Circuit City Stores, Inc v. Adams* (2001), construed the exception in § 1 as confined to contracts of employment of *transportation* workers only.[875]

512. It should be noted that for a transportation worker to fall under the § 1 exception, they do not have to actually *transport* goods interstate or internationally. In *Southwest Airlines v. Saxon* (2022), the US Supreme Court held that airline workers who load/unload cargo on/from airplanes that then travel in interstate commerce are considered transportation workers covered by the FAA § 1 because they are "*directly involved in* transporting goods across state or international borders."[876] Yet, the Court rejected the argument that § 1 "exempts virtually *all* employees of major transportation providers."[877] Likewise, the Court of Appeals for the Ninth Circuit in *Capriole v. Uber* (2021) held that Uber drivers do not fall under § 1 because they are not "engaged in foreign or interstate commerce."[878]

513. For transportation workers to qualify under the § 1 exemption, the element of timing is important as well. In *Hamrick v. Partsfleet, LLC* (2021), the Court of Appeals for the Eleventh Circuit held that the worker must be involved in the transportation of goods across state lines, i.e., it is not sufficient that the goods were only previously transported interstate.[879]

514. In addition, the Courts of Appeals for the Fifth, Ninth, and Eleventh Circuits have held that the exception in § 1 is *not* applicable to *international* employment disputes,

873. For discussion on the possibility of waiving the right to join/launch a class action or class arbitration, *see* above, para. 482.
874. *New Prime Inc v. Oliveira*, 139 S Ct 532 (2019) at 536, 537, 539.
875. *Circuit City Stores, Inc v. Adams*, 532 US 105 (2001) at 109, 114.
876. *Southwest Airlines Co v. Saxon*, 2022 WL 1914099 (2022) at 5 (emphasis added).
877. *Ibid.*, at 7.
878. *Capriole v. Uber Technologies, Inc*, 7 F4th 854 (9th Cir 2021) at 863–864.
879. *Hamrick v. Partsfleet, LLC*, 1 F4th 1337 (11th Cir 2021) at 1346, 1351.

because an exception in the FAA (which is Chapter 1 of Title 9 of the US Code) does not extend to the Convention Act (which is Chapter 2 of Title 9, incorporating the New York Convention into US law).[880]

515. The last topic to be addressed here is how the preemptive effect of the FAA on contrary state laws plays in the context of employment disputes.[881] Despite the preemptive effect of the FAA, some state courts (or even Circuit courts) have not necessarily applied the rule to the letter. A notable example is the line of cases that has developed in relation to California's Private Attorneys General Act (PAGA). The PAGA allows aggrieved employees to file lawsuits to recover civil penalties on behalf of themselves and other employees (whether current or former) for violations of California's Labor Code.[882]

516. The relevant PAGA cases started with *Iskanian v. CLS Transportation Los Angeles* (2014), where the Supreme Court of California found a waiver of PAGA representative claims to be contrary to public policy, which then rendered unenforceable the pre-dispute arbitration agreement between the employee and employer that provided for such a waiver.[883] This was then followed by the decisions of the Court of Appeals for the Ninth Circuit[884] and the California Court of Appeal,[885] which agreed with the *Iskanian* rule. However, the US Supreme Court in *Viking River Cruises v. Moriana* (2022) abrogated *Iskanian* in part: the part of *Iskanian* that prohibited the division of PAGA claims into individual and representative claims is preempted by the FAA and hence abrogated, while the part that prohibits total waiver of PAGA claims is not preempted by the FAA and thus remains valid.[886]

Canada

517. Canadian courts have generally supported the arbitrability of disputes relating to individual employment contracts. For instance, in Alberta, the Court of King's Bench in *Borowski v. Heinrich Fiedler Perforiertechnik GmbH* (1994) enforced the arbitration clause of an employment contract between an employee and his two foreign employers in a dispute as to whether the notice provision of the employment contract for

880. *Francisco v. Stolt Achievement MT*, 293 F3d 270 (5th Cir 2002) at 273–274, cert denied, 537 US 1030 (2002); *Rogers v. Royal Caribbean Cruise Line*, 547 F3d 1148 (9th Cir 2008) at 1149, 1154, 1159, cert denied, 557 US 920 (2009); *Bautista v. Star Cruises*, 396 F3d 1289 (11th Cir 2005) at 1295–1297.
881. For discussion on the preemptive effect of the FAA, *see* above, para. 88.
882. California Labor Code § 2699(a), online: https://leginfo.legislature.ca.gov/faces/codes_displayText.xhtml?lawCode=LAB&division=2.&title=&part=13.&chapter=&article (last visited 17 June 2022).
883. *Iskanian v. CLS Transportation Los Angeles, LLC*, 327 P3d 129 (Cal 2014) at 133, 148, 149, 151, cert denied, 574 US 1121 (2015).
884. *Sakkab v. Luxottica Retail North America, Inc*, 803 F3d 425 (9th Cir 2015) at 427, 432, 434; *Chamber of Commerce of United States v. Bonta*, 13 F4th 766 (9th Cir 2021) at 775–776, 780.
885. *Perez v. U-Haul Co of California*, 207 Cal Rptr 3d 605 (Cal Ct App 2016) at 614–615; *Moriana v. Viking River Cruises, Inc*, 2020 WL 5584508 (Cal Ct App 2020), cert granted, 142 S Ct 734 (Mem) (2021).
886. *Viking River Cruises, Inc v. Moriana*, 142 S Ct 1906 (2022).

termination was amended.[887] The Court found that the dispute was arbitrable, despite finding that the employment relationship between the parties would not qualify as "commercial" within the meaning of the UNICTRAL Model Law and, as such, the International Commercial Arbitration Act of Alberta would not apply to the dispute.[888] Instead, the Court applied the Arbitration Act of Alberta and enforced the arbitration clause.[889]

518. In British Columbia (BC), the Court of Appeal in *Clayworth v. Octaform Systems* (2020) enforced the arbitration provision in the employment contract with respect to an employer's claims as to a former employee's use of confidential information and trade secrets as well as alleged solicitation of clientele in violation of the terms of the employment contract.[890] The BC trial court (BC Supreme Court) has since strongly supported the arbitration of employment disputes, for example, in *A-Teck Appraisals v. Constandinou* (2020),[891] *Wilson v. Infracon Construction* (2020),[892] and *Kwon v. Vanwest College* (2021).[893]

519. In Ontario, the Superior Court of Justice in *Kocur v. FirstService Corporation* (2017) enforced the arbitration clause and stayed the proceeding initiated by an employee for termination without cause.[894] The same Court, in *Leon v. Dealnet Capital Corp* (2021), enforced the arbitration clause in the parties' employment contract and stayed the proceeding that was brought by an employee who was a senior executive in the defendant company.[895]

520. In Québec, the Court of Appeal in *Ouellette v. Société de récupération, d'exploitation et de développement forestiers du Québec (Rexfor)* (1997) held that a dispute between an employee and employer about payment of severance should be referred to arbitration, applying the arbitration clause in the employment contract.[896] The fact that the severance payments under the contract came from public funds did not render the matter non-arbitrable because of the "public order" ground in Article 2639 of the Civil Code of Québec.[897]

521. However, in Québec and Ontario, international employment disputes may *not* be submitted to arbitration. The relevant case in Ontario is the Court of Appeal's decision in *Patel v. Kanbay International Inc* (2008).[898] In that case, the plaintiff was the former president of the respondent companies. He sued for wrongful dismissal and negligent

887. *Borowski v. Heinrich Fiedler Perforiertechnik GmbH* (1994), 158 AR 213 (Alta QB) at paras. 20, 23, 25, 27–31, 42–45, 22 Alta LR (3d) 366.
888. *Ibid.*
889. *Ibid.*
890. *Clayworth v. Octaform Systems Inc*, 2020 BCCA 117 at paras. 1–6, 58.
891. *A-Teck Appraisals Ltd v. Constandinou*, 2020 BCSC 135 at paras. 1–10, 34–43, 3 BLR (6th) 304.
892. *Wilson v. Infracon Construction Inc*, 2020 BCSC 2074 at paras. 1–4, 11–17, 26, 32.
893. *Kwon v. Vanwest College Ltd*, 2021 BCSC 545 at paras. 3, 5, 30–31, 45, 49.
894. *Kocur v. FirstService Corporation*, 2017 ONSC 6114 at paras. 1–3, 22.
895. *Leon v. Dealnet Capital Corp*, 2021 ONSC 3636 at paras. 1–9, 37–39, 41, 42, 60.
896. *Ouellette v. Société de récupération, d'exploitation et de développement forestiers du Québec (Rexfor)*, [1997] JQ No 2753 (Qc CA) at paras. 2–5, 16–18, 1997 CarswellQue 784.
897. *Ibid.*
898. *Patel v. Kanbay International Inc*, 2008 ONCA 867 at paras. 2, 8–14, 93 OR (3d) 588.

misrepresentation about the value of shares that the plaintiff received upon accepting the offer of employment.[899] The Court of Appeal upheld the lower court's decision to refuse to stay the court proceeding in favor of arbitration on the basis of the arbitration clause in the shareholders' agreement.[900] The Court of Appeal's reasoning was that such disputes are not "commercial" within the meaning of the UNICTRAL Model Law and Ontario's International Commercial Arbitration Act.[901]

522. Article 3149 of the Québec Civil Code prohibits any waiver of court jurisdiction in employment and consumer disputes. Article 3149 is in the part of the Civil Code that covers the international jurisdiction of Québec courts. The Supreme Court of Canada, in *Dell Computer Corp v. Union des Consommateurs* (2007)—deciding a consumer dispute—held that the restriction in Article 3149 applies only when there is a "foreign element" involved.[902] The Supreme Court defined the "foreign element" in this context as "a point of contact that is legally relevant to a foreign country which means that the contact must be sufficient to play a role in determining whether a court has jurisdiction" such as when there is a "fact, event or transaction that is so closely connected with a foreign system of law as to necessitate recourse to that system."[903] According to the Supreme Court, the mere fact that an arbitration proceeding is governed by the rules of a foreign institution would not qualify it as a "foreign element."[904]

523. Although Article 3149 is in the part of the Civil Code that covers the international jurisdiction of Québec courts, the terms "international" in that part of the Code (and the term "foreign" used by the Supreme Court in *Dell*) do *not* mean "outside Canada," but rather "outside Québec." The case supporting this point is *Chung v. Merchant Law Group* (2020).[905] In that case, the Superior Court of Québec first found that the relationship between a law firm (located in the province of Saskatchewan) and an associate lawyer who worked in Québec was an "employment" relationship.[906] The Court then held that the law firm may not rely on the contract's forum selection clause in favor of Saskatchewan courts because Article 3149 of Québec Civil Code prohibits waiver of Québec courts' jurisdiction in international employment disputes.[907] Thus, *Chung* shows that for Article 3149 to apply, it would be sufficient that the subject matter of dispute has elements outside Québec.

---

899. *Ibid.*
900. *Ibid.*
901. *Ibid.*
902. *Dell Computer Corp v. Union des Consommateurs*, 2007 SCC 34 at para. 3, 284 DLR (4th) 577.
903. *Ibid.*, at paras. 25–28 (internal citations omitted).
904. *Ibid.*, at para. 52.
905. *Chung v. Merchant Law Group*, 2020 QCCS 398. Although *Chung* concerns forum selection clause and not arbitration, it is relevant to arbitration because the provisions on which the court relied (Arts. 3148 and 3149 of the Québec Civil Code) provide the same rule for both forum selection and arbitration clauses. As such, any interpretation that applies to forum selection clauses is applicable to arbitration clauses too.
906. *Ibid.*, at paras. 1–6, 10, 13, 84.
907. *Ibid.*, at para. 85.

524. Canadian courts, as explained in the above paragraphs, have been supportive of the arbitration of employment disputes; however, a key decision by the Supreme Court of Canada in 2020 (namely, *Uber Technologies v. Heller*) has set some limitations on the enforceability of arbitration agreements in employment contract.[908] The main question before the Court was whether the arbitration clause in the services agreement between Uber and a driver was valid. The Court made two important rulings.

525. First, the Supreme Court added an exception to the competence-competence rule. It ruled that courts can (despite the competence-competence rule) decide the objection to the validity of an arbitration agreement if referring the parties to arbitration would be "tantamount to denying relief for the claim" (i.e., the objection would likely never be decided).[909] Examples include the following: initiating arbitration would be too costly for the weaker party; it would be difficult for the weaker party to reach the physical location of the arbitration in another jurisdiction; or the foreign choice of law clause would prevent the potential arbitrator from giving effect to the weaker party's substantive local rights.[910] The Court found that the first two were present in *Uber*: access to arbitration was too costly for the driver because the arbitration clause in Uber's services agreement required an up-front payment of administrative fees that were almost equal to the driver's annual income, and also because the driver was required to travel to Amsterdam at his own expense.[911] Accordingly, the Supreme Court held that courts (instead of arbitrators) could decide the driver's objection to the validity of the arbitration agreement.[912]

526. Second, the Supreme Court held that the arbitration agreement between Uber and the driver was invalid because the two requirements of *unconscionability* were met: (i) there was an inequality of bargaining power between the parties, and (ii) such an inequality resulted in an "improvident bargain."[913] The Court defined an improvident bargain as a bargain (here, the arbitration agreement) that "unduly advantages the stronger party or unduly disadvantages the more vulnerable."[914] Nevertheless, the Court noted that the mere fact that a contract is a standard contract or a contract of adhesion does *not* render it unconscionable as long as such contracts "clearly and effectively communicate the meaning of clauses with unusual or onerous effects."[915]

527. *Uber* originated in Ontario, but its effect is not limited to Ontario laws. The decision affects the other two common law provinces (Alberta and BC) as well as Québec. This is so because not only is Ontario's Arbitration Act similar to those of BC and Alberta but also because the Supreme Court expressly relied on its previous

908. *Uber Technologies Inc v. Heller*, 2020 SCC 16.
909. *Ibid.*, at paras. 31, 32, 35, 38, 39, 46.
910. *Ibid.*, at para. 39.
911. *Ibid.*, at para. 47.
912. *Ibid.*, at para. 48.
913. *Ibid.*, at paras. 52, 53, 62, 63.
914. *Ibid.*, at para. 74.
915. *Ibid.*, at paras. 87, 88.

decisions in *Dell*[916] and *Seidel*[917] (which concerned Québec and BC laws respectively). According to the Supreme Court in *Uber*, "the parties agree that the framework from *Dell* and *Seidel* applies to Ontario's Arbitration Act. We agree, based on the similarities between the arbitration regimes in Ontario, British Columbia and Quebec."[918] However, the Court's developments on unconscionability, a common law doctrine, would not apply in Québec.

528. Reacting to the Supreme Court's decision in *Uber*, the Superior Court of Québec in *AGIL OBNL Company v. Bell Canada* (2021), refused to apply *Uber* on the ground that the ruling on the invalidity of the arbitration agreement in *Uber* was based on the notion of fairness in common law, whereas a discussion on the invalidity of an arbitration agreement in Québec is governed by the Québec Code of Civil Procedure and civil law principles.[919]

2. Jurisdictions Not Necessarily Distinguishing Between Labour and Employment Disputes

529. This group includes China (Mainland), Hong Kong, and Singapore. From a terminology perspective, in these jurisdictions, the distinction between labour law and employment law is blurred, in that the term "labour" is not used exclusively in relation to a unionized workforce, nor is the term "employment" used solely in relation to individual employment relationships. Furthermore, in these jurisdictions, disputes that relate to collective-bargaining agreements are often called "trade disputes."[920]

530. The discussion in the following paragraphs shows that, in China and Singapore, employment/labour disputes are considered to be inarbitrable. In Hong Kong, while employment/labour disputes are generally considered arbitrable, there are important legislative and judicial restrictions applied to the arbitration of such disputes.

China

531. Relevant acts, such as the Labour Law of the People's Republic of China (Article 81), the Labour Contract Law of the People's Republic of China (Article 26), and the Law of the People's Republic of China on Mediation and Arbitration of Labour Disputes (Article 17) allow for disputes arising under these laws to be settled by arbitration through the Labour Dispute Arbitration Commissions. It should be noted that although the term "labour" is often used in the English translation of relevant Chinese laws, those laws cover both collective labour matters and individual employment relationships.[921] Labour matters are also regulated by the Trade Union Law of the

916. *Dell Computer Corp v. Union des Consommateurs*, 2007 SCC 34.
917. *Seidel v. Telus Communications Inc*, 2011 SCC 15.
918. *Uber*, at para. 35.
919. *AGIL OBNL Company v. Bell Canada*, 2021 QCCS 365 at paras. 89, 91, 97.
920. *See, e.g.*, China's Trade Union Law of the People's Republic of China and Hong Kong's Trade Unions Ordinance (Cap 332).
921. *See* Labour Law, Art. 2; Labour Contract Law, Art. 2. *See also* Samuel Yang, Liu Zhenghe & Moxue Wang (AnJie Law Firm), "Employment & labour law in China" *Lexology* (24 August

People's Republic of China and the Provisions on Collective Contracts, both of which provide for the arbitration of disputes arising in relation to the performance of collective-bargaining agreements.[922]

532. However, on balance, labour/employment disputes should be categorized as non-arbitrable because, first, the Labour Dispute Arbitration Commissions are not conventional arbitral tribunals that are established by parties to a dispute, but rather they are the administrative arm of the government designated to settle labour disputes. Therefore, labour/employment disputes fall within the scope of Article 3 of the Arbitration Law, which provides for the non-arbitrability of matters that are "administrative disputes falling within the jurisdiction of the relevant administrative organs."[923] Second, labour arbitration, in China, is not based on the parties' arbitration agreements, nor is the award considered to be final.[924] Under Article 84 of the Labour Law, if one of the parties is not satisfied with the arbitration award, they can initiate court proceedings. Likewise, under Article 21 of the Trade Union Law, if the union is not satisfied with the arbitral award, it may take the matter to People's Courts. Chinese case law, too, confirms the conclusion that labour/employment disputes are not arbitrable.[925]

Singapore

533. The Employment Act 1968, as Singapore's primary employment law,[926] makes reference to terms such as "award" and "arbitration" (sections 47, 50, 76(4)), but those references only concern awards issued by the Industrial Arbitration Court under the Industrial Relations Act 1960.[927]

534. Sections 31 and 32 of the Industrial Relations Act provide for labour/employment disputes to be settled through arbitration, but the arbitration is heard by a specific court, namely the Industrial Arbitration Court, which has its own specific rules and

2018), online: https://www.lexology.com/library/detail.aspx?g=bcb63ee3-6f53-4f08-b566-9f270ff564eb (last visited 9 February 2023).

922. Trade Union Law of the People's Republic of China, Art. 21; Provisions on Collective Contracts, Art. 55.

923. *See* WunschARB, "Lianhua Hotel v Puyang Government (2009), Puyang IPC, [2009] 濮中法民二初字第11号 (Puyang IPC), 10 April 2009" Chinese Court Decision Summaries on Arbitration (WunschARB Sàrl & Kluwer Law International) at sec "commentary".

924. Lu Song, "National Report for China (2020 through 2022)" in Lise Bosman, ed, *ICCA International Handbook on Commercial Arbitration* (Kluwer Law International, 2022) at n 1.

925. *See, e.g., Lianhua Hotel v. Puyang Government* (2009), Intermediate People's Court of Puyang, [2009] 濮中法民二初字第11号 (Puyang IPC), 10 April 2009 (holding that the disputes between a landlord and a tenant arising out of a clause in their lease agreement—which provided for the employment rearrangement fees to be paid to the landlord's employees who were laid off in anticipation of the lease agreement, and for the adjustments to the salaries of those employees whom the leaseholder reemployed—are not labour disputes and, as such, the disputes are arbitrable).

926. Ministry of Manpower website, tab "About the Employment Act," online: http://www.mom.gov.sg/employment-practices/employment-act (last visited 11 March 2023).

927. The Industrial Relations Act was enacted to "provide a framework for preventing and settling industrial disputes through collective bargaining, conciliation and arbitration by the Industrial Arbitration Court." Ministry of Manpower website, tab "Legislation," hyperlink "Employment Practices" online: http://www.mom.gov.sg/legislation/employment-practices (last visited 11 April 2023).

procedure. It should be noted that the scope of application of the Industrial Relations Act is not limited to a unionized workforce and matters of an industrial nature. Section 2 of the Act defines the terms "employee" and "industrial matters" broadly.

535. In addition, section 9 of the Employment of Foreign Manpower Act 1990 relevantly provides that disputes as to decisions by the Controller of Work Passes to suspend or revoke the work pass of a foreign employee may not be submitted to arbitration, and the matter is not referable to the Industrial Arbitration Court.

536. In 2016, the Employment Claims Act was enacted to establish the Employment Claims Tribunal (section 8) and gave it jurisdiction over salary-related claims—both statutory and contractual claims—as well as wrongful dismissal disputes (section 12). Decision of the Employment Claims Tribunal are appealable under section 2. Also, under section 28, any contractual provision that would prevent a person from submitting their claim to the Employment Claims Tribunal or from appealing its decisions is void.

537. Under section 11(2) of the International Arbitration Act, a mere reference to a court's jurisdiction does not automatically render the matter non-arbitrable. However, in the context of the legislative framework for labour/employment disputes, commentators generally consider such disputes (and specifically labour disputes) to be non-arbitrable.[928]

538. Nevertheless, according to the website of the Law Society of Singapore, "[b]esides general commercial disputes, the LSAS [the Law Society Arbitration Scheme][929] can be used to arbitrate disputes in the areas of *employment*, tenancy, renovation works, media, entertainment and travel amongst others."[930] This suggests that some employment-related disputes may be arbitrable.

Hong Kong

539. Section 20(2) of the Arbitration Ordinance (Cap 609) allows the arbitration of disputes that are within the jurisdiction of the Labour Tribunal, which includes monetary disputes—but not tortious matters—between employees and employers.[931] Nevertheless, under section 20(2), for a Hong Kong court to enforce an arbitration agreement in this field, two conditions should be met:

---

928. *See, e.g.*, Michael Hwang, Lawrence Boo & Eugene Thong, "National Report for Singapore (2018–2022)" in Lise Bosman, eds, *ICCA International Handbook on Commercial Arbitration* (Kluwer Law International, 2022) at n 25 and the accompanying text; David Joseph & David Foxton, *Singapore International Arbitration: Law & Practice* (LexisNexis, 2014) at para. 5.3.

929. "The Law Society of Singapore administers the Law Society Arbitration Scheme ('LSAS'). The scheme's primary purpose is to help parties come to a resolution." Law Society of Singapore ADR website, tab "Arbitration," online: https://adr.lawsociety.org.sg/law-society-arbitration-scheme/ (last visited 11 April 2023).

930. *Ibid.* (emphasis added).

931. The Labour Tribunal was established by s. 3 of the Labour Tribunal Ordinance (Cap 25) and is a court of record for settling monetary disputes (but not tortious matters) between employees and employers. Section 7 of the Labour Tribunal Ordinance together with its Schedule set out the matters over which the Labour Tribunal has jurisdiction. Online: https://www.elegislation.gov.hk/hk/cap25 (last visited 10 March 2023); Judiciary of Hong Kong website, tab "Court

- (a) that "there is no sufficient reason why the parties should not be referred to arbitration in accordance with the arbitration agreement"; and
- (b) that "the party requesting arbitration was ready and willing at the time the action was brought to do all things necessary for the proper conduct of the arbitration and remains so."

540. Most of the relevant legislative texts, such as the Employment Ordinance (Cap 57), the Trade Unions Ordinance (Cap 332), the Employees' Compensation Ordinance (Cap 282), and the Minimum Wage Ordinance (Cap 608), have no provisions in relation to arbitration. The Hong Kong Court of Final Appeal, in *Paquito Lima Buton v. Rainbow Joy Shipping Limited Inc* (2008), held that statutory claims for work-related injuries under the Employees' Compensation Ordinance (Cap 282) (ECO) may not be submitted to arbitration.[932] The Court reasoned that the wording of the ECO indicates the exclusivity of the District Court's jurisdiction over the matter by stating that any matters "shall" be decided by the District Court and that the ECO identifies the exceptions to jurisdiction without mentioning arbitration as falling within the exceptions.[933]

541. In the *Paquito* case, the Court of Final Appeal reversed the Court of Appeal's decision. The Court of Appeal had ruled in favor of the arbitrability of ECO claims on the grounds that: (a) the exclusivity of District Court's jurisdiction should be seen as excluding other courts and not arbitral tribunals, and (b) the nature of ECO claims (being a statutory claim to compensation) should not bar the claim from being decided in arbitration.[934]

542. Nearly one year after the *Paquito* decision, the Court of First Instance followed the Court of Final Appeal's lead in adopting an unfavorable approach to arbitration in employment disputes. In *Aggressive Construction Co Ltd v. Data-form Engineering Ltd* (2009), a dispute arose between a contractor and a subcontractor as to the wages paid to employees of the subcontractor in order to discharge the statutory obligation under the Employment Ordinance.[935] The Court of First Instance held that, where there are both statutory and contractual bases for a claim ("contractual" here refers to the underlying contract containing the arbitration clause) but the plaintiff has relied only on the statutory basis, the claim "falls outside of the scope of the arbitration agreement."[936]

Services and Facilities," sub-tab "Guide to Court Services," hyperlink "Labour Tribunal," online: https://www.judiciary.hk/en/court_services_facilities/labour.html (last visited 10 March 2023).

932. *Paquito Lima Buton v. Rainbow Joy Shipping Limited Inc*, [2008] HKCFA 30, FACV 26/2007 (28 April 2008) at paras. 3, 4, 7, 48, 50–55.

933. *Ibid.*

934. [2007] HKCA 73, CACV 243/2006 (15 February 2007) at paras. 31–37.

935. *Aggressive Construction Co Ltd v. Data-form Engineering Ltd*, [2009] HKCFI 854, HCA 2143/2008 (4 August 2009) at paras. 1–7, 22–28.

936. *Ibid.*

543. Unlike other relevant legislative texts noted above,[937] the Labour Relations Ordinance (Cap 55) includes a number of provisions on arbitration. Sections 11 and 12 of the Ordinance provide for the possibility of submitting "trade disputes" to arbitration. However, according to section 21, such arbitration is not governed by the Arbitration Ordinance, but rather by specific rules set out in sections 12 to 20 of the Labour Relations Ordinance.

544. The Labour Relations Ordinance "does not apply to employees in the service of the Government of the Hong Kong Special Administrative Region who are governed by appropriate service regulations and procedures."[938] In 1995, following a pay dispute between the Hong Kong Government and the civil servant workforce, when the unions had sought to arbitrate the matter but the Government refused, the Hong Kong Confederation of Trade Unions (HKCTU) reported the matter in the form of an "observation" to the International Labour Organization (ILO)'s Committee of Experts on the Application of Conventions and Recommendations.[939] The Hong Kong Government responded that it did not consider disputes to be arbitrable where they concerned "a matter which [was] trivial, of settled public policy, or affect[ed] the security of Hong Kong."[940]

H. SECURITIES LAW

545. Nearly all jurisdictions that were studied for this book consider securities disputes to be arbitrable.[941] Nevertheless, some of the jurisdictions apply limitations such as a monetary cap (on the claim or the compensation)[942] or limitations on the capacity of a person who may enter into *pre-dispute* arbitration agreements.[943] Further, in a number of jurisdictions, despite the arbitrability of securities disputes, the relevant regulations are more centered on non-binding dispute resolution mechanisms, rather than on arbitration.[944]

546. As such, this section contains four Subsections. The first three subsections address the jurisdictions that regard securities disputes as arbitrable, even though they

937. *See* above, para. 540.
938. Hong Kong Labour Department, *A Guide to the Labour Relations Ordinance* (January 2013), website of Hong Kong Labour Department, online: https://www.labour.gov.hk/eng/public/wcp/GuideLRO.pdf (last visited 10 March 2023).
939. Observation (CEACR)—adopted 1995, published 82nd ILC session (1995). International Labour Organization website, online: http://www.ilo.org/dyn/normlex/en/f?p=1000:13100:0::NO:13100:P13100_COMMENT_ID,P11110_COUNTRY_ID,P11110_COUNTRY_NAME,P11110_COMMENT_YEAR:2141891,103578,China%20-%20Hong%20Kong%20Special%20Administrative%20Region,1995 (last visited 10 March 2023).
940. *Ibid.*
941. The exception is the Canadian province of Alberta.
942. For instance, in Canada, the Canadian Investment Regulatory Organization (CIRO) has an arbitration program for securities disputes, but has a cap of CAD 500,000 in compensation.
943. For instance, in Germany, if one of the parties is neither a merchant nor a public law entity, parties may agree to arbitrate their dispute only after it arises. *See* German Securities Trading Act, s. 37(h).
944. For example, England and Wales, France, and Germany.

have adopted different approaches in this regard: (1) jurisdictions that impose no significant limitation on the arbitration of securities disputes; (2) jurisdictions that impose a monetary cap on the claim or the receivable compensation; and (3) jurisdictions that prefer non-binding dispute settlement mechanisms to arbitration. The last subsection discusses (4) jurisdiction(s) where securities disputes are non-arbitrable.

1. Jurisdictions That Impose No Significant Limitation on the Arbitration of Securities Disputes

547. This group includes the United States, Québec, Switzerland, and China.

The United States

548. The US Supreme Court, in *Scherk v. Alberto Culver Co* (1974), held that international disputes arising under the Securities Exchange Act of 1934 are arbitrable. Later, in *Shearson/American Express, Inc v. McMahon* (1987), the Court held that disputes (whether international or domestic) arising under the Securities Exchange Act of 1934 may be submitted to arbitration.[945] Further, in *Rodriguez de Quijas v. Shearson/American Express, Inc* (1989), the Court held that disputes arising under the Securities Act of 1933 are also arbitrable.[946]

549. The website of the Securities and Exchange Commission (SEC) states that: "Most account agreements between broker-dealers and their customers have arbitration clauses. ... If no agreement to arbitrate exists, a broker-dealer may not compel its customer to arbitrate. However, the FINRA Code of Arbitration Procedure allows a customer to compel a broker-dealer or person associated with a broker-dealer to arbitrate a dispute at the customer's request."[947] "FINRA" refers to the Financial Industrial Regulatory Authority,[948] which has two sets of arbitration rules:

- the Customer Code, which governs arbitrations between investors and industry parties;[949] and
- the Industry Code, which only governs arbitrations between or among industry parties.[950]

945. *Scherk v. Alberto Culver Co*, 417 US 506 (1974) at 513. For a recent decision enforcing an arbitration agreement with respect to claims arising under the Securities Exchange Act of 1934, *see Donelson v. Ameriprise Financial Services, Inc*, 999 F3d 1080 (8th Cir 2021).
946. *Rodriguez de Quijas v. Shearson/American Express, Inc*, 490 US 477 (1989) at 478–484.
947. SEC website, tab "Introduction to Investing," sub-tab "Glossary," term "Arbitration and Mediation," online: http://www.sec.gov/answers/arbproc.htm (last visited 17 June 2022).
948. FINRA is "authorized by Congress to protect America's investors by making sure the broker-dealer industry operates fairly and honestly." FINRA website, tab "About FINRA," online: http://www.finra.org/AboutFINRA/ (last visited 17 June 2022).
949. Online: https://www.finra.org/rules-guidance/rulebooks/finra-rules/12000 (last visited 17 June 2022).
950. Online: https://www.finra.org/arbitration-mediation/rules-case-resources/13000 (last visited 17 June 2022).

550. It should be noted that the Dodd-Frank Wall Street Reform and Consumer Protection Act § 921(a) added a section to the Securities Exchange Act of 1934, thereby allowing the SEC to prohibit or impose limitations on the use of arbitration in securities disputes (§ 78o.(o)).[951]

Québec

551. In Canada, there is currently no federal legislative Act on securities, and each province (including Québec) has its own Securities Act and securities regulator.[952] In *Carboni v. Financière Banque Nationale* (2004), the Québec Superior Court held that disputes arising under the Securities Act of Québec are arbitrable.[953] Section 11.1 of the Québec Consumer Protection Act prohibits pre-dispute arbitration agreements as against consumers, but section 6 provides that the Act does not apply to securities disputes. This means that the limitations on arbitration within the Act likewise do not apply to securities disputes.

552. The Securities Act of Québec contains no provision on arbitration. Nevertheless, section 168.1.1 of the Act obliges all dealers and advisers to have a policy for processing complaints, and they must process the complaints in a fair manner. Also, according to section 168.1.4, if the complainant is dissatisfied with the result, they may request the complaint to be examined by the Autorité des Marchés Financiers, which may act as "conciliator or mediator or designate a person to act as such."

553. It should be noted that the province of Québec is *not* one of the participating jurisdictions in the Cooperative Capital Markets Regulatory System (CCMRS), which is a system between the Canadian federal government and the governments of some provinces.[954] As such, Québec will not enact the relevant uniform provincial legislation, namely the Capital Markets Act.[955]

951. For discussion on the fate of the Dodd-Frank Act after Mr. Trump took office, *see* above, note 867.
952. The efforts at the federal level to enact a federal law on securities failed when, in 2011, the Supreme Court opined that the proposed federal Securities Act was unconstitutional because the Act, as drafted, was not within the federal Parliament's power over the regulation of trade and commerce. *Reference Re Securities Act*, 2011 SCC 66. For discussion on securities law at the federal level, *see* below, para. 562 et sec.
953. *Carboni v. Financière Banque nationale*, [2004] RJQ 1945 (Qc Sup Ct) at paras. 1–4, 55–62, [2004] JQ No 7254.
954. The participating provinces and territories include Ontario, British Columbia, Saskatchewan, New Brunswick, Prince Edward Island, Newfoundland and Labrador, and Yukan. Neither Québec nor Alberta participates in the CCMRS. For discussion on the CCMRS, *see* below, para. 564.
955. The Capital Markets Act is a uniform provincial/territorial legislation to be adopted by each of the participating jurisdictions in the CCMRS. The Québec Court of Appeal (responding to the questions from the government of Québec in relation to the constitutionality of the proposed uniform provincial law and the proposed federal Act under the CCMRS) ruled that the proposed laws, as drafted, were unconstitutional. *Québec (Procureure générale) c Canada (Procureure générale)*, 2017 QCCA 756, 2017 CarswellQue 4199. However, its decision was overturned by the Supreme Court of Canada in 2018, which ruled that the proposed cooperative system is constitutional but that the provinces have the right not to join the system. *Reference re Pan-Canadian Securities Regulation*, 2018 SCC 48 at paras. 129, 131.

Switzerland

554. Securities disputes are arbitrable under Swiss law. The Federal Act on Financial Services, while providing for the settlement of disputes through an ombudsman (Article 74), states that mediation services can be requested if the dispute has not been dealt with by, inter alia, an arbitral tribunal. Moreover, Article 177(1) of the PILA provides that disputes involving economic interests are arbitrable, which is the case with securities disputes.[956] Other relevant securities laws and ordinances include no provisions on the arbitration of securities disputes.[957]

555. It should be noted that former rules of the SIX Swiss Exchange[958] provided that any disputes with SIX would have to be settled "solely and finally by their Zurich-based arbitration court" and that the proceedings would not be governed by Chapter 12 of the PILA.[959] However, that provision has been repealed, and there is no equivalent provision in the new rules.[960]

China (Mainland)

556. There is no provision relating to arbitration in the Law of the People's Republic of China on Securities, but Articles 94 and 166(7) allow for the mediation of securities disputes through the Investor Protection Bureau and the Securities Association of China (known as SAC—a self-regulatory organization of the securities industry). Similarly, the Securities Investment Funds Law does not have a provision addressing the arbitrability of securities disputes. However, under Article 52, a "fund contract for a publicly offered fund" should include a dispute resolution provision. In 2013, SAC signed an agreement with the Beijing Arbitration Commission to use arbitration in securities disputes.

557. The China International Economic and Trade Arbitration Commission (CIETAC) has a specific set of arbitration rules, called the Financial Disputes Arbitration Rules

956. *See* Harold Frey, Patrick Schleier & Patrick Schärli, "Switzerland" in Antony Ryan & Philippe Z Selendy, eds, *Getting the Deal Through: Securities Litigation 2016* (Law Business Research Ltd, 2016) 73 at 77 (question 33); Pierre Yves Tschanz, "The Chamber of Commerce and Industry of Geneva's Arbitration Rules and their Expedited Procedure" (1993) 10:4 J Int'l Arb 51 at 56.
957. *See, e.g.*, Federal Act on Financial Institutions (FinIA); Ordinance on Financial Services (FINSO); Federal Act on Financial Market Infrastructures and Market Conduct in Securities and Derivatives Trading (FinMIA); Federal Act on Collective Investment Schemes (CISA).
958. According to the SIX's website, "SIX operates the infrastructure for the Swiss financial center, thus ensuring the flow of information and money between financial market players. SIX offers exchange services, financial information and banking services with the aim of increasing efficiency, quality and innovative capacity along the entire Swiss banking value chain. ... SIX connects financial market participants in Switzerland and throughout the world. The company is owned by around 120 national and international financial institutions that are active in the Swiss financial center. They are the main users of our services and our most important customers." SIX website, online: https://www.six-group.com/en/company.html (last visited 10 March 2021).
959. SIX Swiss Exchange Ltd Rule Book (2016), clause 24(2).
960. *See* SIX Swiss Exchange Ltd Trading Rules (2020), clause 16.2.8.

that apply to disputes arising out of financial transactions, including securities trading.[961] Article 2 of the Rules reads:

> The term "financial transactions" shall refer to transactions arising between financial institutions *inter se*, or arising between financial institutions and other natural or legal persons in the currency, capital, foreign exchange, gold and insurance markets that relate to financing in both domestic and foreign currencies, and the assignment and sale of financial instruments and documents denominated in both domestic and foreign currencies, including but not limited to: loans, deposit certificates, guarantees, letters of credit, negotiable instruments, fund transactions and fund trusts, bonds, collection and remittance of foreign currencies, factoring, reimbursement agreements between banks, and securities and futures.

558. There is also a Supreme People's Court decision (*ED & F Man Co v. China National Sugar* (2003)) where the Court opined that disputes arising out of futures contracts have a commercial contractual nature and, as such, are arbitrable.[962] Xiuming Tao has also noted that "financial investment disputes have increasingly become a major part of the disputes administered by China's major arbitration institutions."[963]

559. In 2018, the Chinese Supreme People's Court, together with the China Securities Regulatory Commission, issued an Opinion providing for the diversification of dispute resolution mechanisms for securities/futures disputes, including the establishment of institutions for the mediation of such disputes.[964] An example is the Shenzhen Securities and Futures Dispute Resolution Centre, which combines mediation and arbitration for securities and futures disputes.[965] In the same year, the Shanghai Financial Court was established as a specialized court to hear civil and administrative financial disputes,[966] including the judicial review of arbitral awards and deciding applications for recognition and enforcement of foreign awards on financial disputes.[967]

560. In 2021, the China Securities Regulatory Commission and the Ministry of Justice issued an Opinion on conducting a pilot program in Beijing, Shanghai, and Shenzhen,

961. Online: http://www.cietac.org/index.php?m = Page&a = index&id = 108&l = en (last visited 9 February 2023).
962. *ED & F Man (Hong Kong) Co v. China National Sugar & Wines Group Corp*, Supreme People's Court of the People's Republic of China, [2003] Min Si Ta Zi No 3 ([2003] 民四他字第3号).
963. Xiuming Tao, "Annual Review on Financial Dispute Resolution in China (2016)" in *Commercial Dispute Resolution in China: An Annual Review and Preview (2016)* (Kluwer Law International, 2016) 187 at 188.
964. Notice by the Supreme People's Court and the China Securities Regulatory Commission of Issuing Opinions on Comprehensively Advancing Establishment of Diversified Resolution Mechanism of Securities and Futures Disputes, No 305 (2018).
965. Online: http://www.scia.com.cn/index.php/En/index/serviceinfo2/id/27.html (last visited 9 February 2023).
966. Decision of the Standing Committee of the National People's Congress on Forming the Shanghai Financial Court (2018).
967. Provisions of the Supreme People's Court on the Jurisdiction of the Shanghai Financial Court (2018).

in relation to the arbitration of securities and futures disputes.[968] The Opinion encourages all parties involved to choose arbitration as the dispute resolution mechanism and to designate the arbitration commissions in the pilot program as their arbitration institutions. Article 4 of the Opinion lists the type of disputes that may be submitted to arbitration.

2. Jurisdictions That Impose a Monetary Cap

561. This group consists of jurisdictions that allow the arbitration of securities disputes but impose a monetary cap on the claim or the receivable compensation. The group includes Canada (other than the provinces of Québec and Alberta),[969] Hong Kong, and Singapore.

Canada

562. There is currently no federal legislative Act on securities in Canada.[970] Each province has its own securities Act and securities regulator that are brought together by the Canadian Securities Administrators (CSA).[971] However, there is a regulatory authority at the national level: the Canadian Investment Regulatory Organization (CIRO), which regulates investment dealers and mutual fund dealers.[972] The CIRO was formed in 2023 to take over the functions of the Investment Industry Regulatory Organization of Canada (IIROC) and the Mutual Fund Dealers Association of Canada (MFDA).[973]

563. The IIROC had an arbitration program for securities disputes, which has now been transferred to the CIRO.[974] However, the program has a cap of CAD 500,000 in

968. Opinions of the China Securities Regulatory Commission and the Ministry of Justice on Conducting the Pilot Program of Arbitration in the Securities and Futures Industry in Accordance with the Law (2021).
969. For discussion on the approach in Québec, *see* above, paras. 551–553. For discussion on the approach in Alberta *see* below, paras. 591–592.
970. The efforts at the federal level to enact a law on securities failed when, in 2011, the Supreme Court opined that the proposed federal Securities Act was unconstitutional because the Act, as drafted, was not within the federal Parliament's power over the regulation of trade and commerce. *Reference Re Securities Act*, 2011 SCC 66.
971. The CSA defines itself as "the umbrella organization of Canada's provincial and territorial securities regulators whose objective is to improve, coordinate and harmonize regulation of the Canadian capital markets." CSA website, tab "About," sub-tab "About Us," online: https://www.securities-administrators.ca/about/ (last visited 9 September 2023).
972. CIRO website: https://www.ciro.ca (last visited 9 September 2023).
973. The IIROC was a self-regulatory organization that oversaw investment dealers and trading activity on Canada's debt and equity marketplaces. IIROC website: https://www.iiroc.ca (last visited 9 September 2023). The MFDA was a national self-regulatory organization that oversaw mutual fund dealers in Canada. MFDA website: https://mfda.ca (last visited 9 September 2023).
974. *See* Corporation Investment Dealer and Partially Consolidated Rules (2023), Rule 9502, which replaced the IIROC Rules (2022), rule 9502. Online: https://www.ciro.ca/media/16/download?inline (last visited 9 September 2023).

compensation, which does not include fees, interest, or legal costs.[975] Unlike the IIROC, the MFDA had no arbitration program[976] but recognized the arbitration of securities-related disputes.[977]

564. In 2014, the federal government and the governments of Ontario, British Columbia and two other provinces (Saskatchewan and New Brunswick) signed a memorandum of agreement to formalize the terms of a new system called the Cooperative Capital Markets Regulatory System (CCMRS).[978] Since then, the governments of Prince Edward Island, Newfoundland and Labrador, and Yukon have also agreed to join the CCMRS.[979] The proposed CCMRS includes:

- a regulator (called the Capital Markets Regulatory Authority);
- uniform provincial/territorial legislation to be adopted by each of the participating jurisdictions (titled the Capital Markets Act), where section 17(1) gives the regulator the power to designate a dispute resolution service; and
- complementary federal legislation (titled the Capital Markets Stability Act) to address criminal matters and those relating to systemic risk in the capital markets, with no provision on arbitration.[980]

It seems unlikely that the CCMRS will render already-arbitrable disputes non-arbitrable.

565. In 2018, the Supreme Court of Canada ruled that the proposed CCMRS is constitutional but that the provinces have the right not to join it.[981] Although initially the CCMRS was expected to be implemented in 2018,[982] no specific launch date has been confirmed to date.

566. Currently, the applicable Act in the province of British Columbia (BC) is the BC Securities Act, which contains no provision on arbitration. However, the BC Securities

975. IIROC News Release (14 January 2011), online: https://www.iiroc.ca/news-and-publications/notices-and-guidance/iiroc-announces-changes-arbitration-program (last visited 9 September 2023). As of 2023, the cap on compensation is still CAD 500,000. IIROC website, tab "Arbitration-FAQ", question "How much money can I get back through arbitration?" online: https://www.iiroc.ca/arbitration-faq (last visited 9 September 2023).
976. MFDA website, tab "Investors," online: http://mfda.ca/investors/ (last visited 9 September 2023).
977. *See* MFDA Bulletin No 0123-M (24 January 2005), online: https://mfda.ca/wp-content/uploads/Bulletin0123-M.pdf (last visited 9 September 2023).
978. Memorandum of Agreement Regarding the Cooperative Capital Markets Regulatory System (30 September 2014), online: https://www.canada.ca/en/news/archive/2014/09/memorandum-agreement-regarding-cooperative-capital-markets-regulatory-system.html (last visited 3 December 2021).
979. *See* the latest version of the Memorandum of Agreement Regarding the Cooperative Capital Markets Regulatory System (25 September 2020), online: http://ccmr-ocrmc.ca/wp-content/uploads/MOA_Conformed-2020-09-25.pdf (last visited 9 November 2021).
980. Section 3 of the Memorandum of Agreement Regarding the Cooperative Capital Markets Regulatory System (30 September 2014).
981. *Reference re Pan-Canadian Securities Regulation*, 2018 SCC 48 at paras. 129, 131.
982. Website of the Cooperative Capital Markets Regulatory System, online: http://ccmr-ocrmc.ca/capital-markets-regulatory-authority-initial-board-directors-new-implementation-timelines-announced/ (last visited 3 December 2021).

Commission[983] allows the arbitration of securities disputes if the dispute is with a firm member of the CIRO (replacing the IIROC) and the amount in dispute does not exceed CAD 500,000.[984]

567. Likewise, in the province of Ontario, the current applicable Act is the Ontario Securities Act, which has no provision on arbitration. However, the Ontario Securities Commission[985] allows the arbitration of securities disputes if the dispute is with a firm member of the CIRO (replacing the IIROC) and the amount in dispute does not exceed CAD 500,000.[986]

568. Under section 7(2) of the Consumer Protection Act of Ontario, pre-dispute arbitration agreements in consumer contracts are invalid, but section 2 relevantly provides that the Act does not apply to securities disputes and, thus, the limitations on arbitration set out in the Act likewise do not apply to securities disputes. In *Advanced Explorations Inc v. Storm Capital Corp* (2014), the Ontario Superior Court expressly held that securities disputes are arbitrable.[987] Prior to that, it could be understood from cases such as *Webber v. Seltzer* (2005) and *Forbes v. Siskind, Cromarty, Ivey and Dowler LLP* (2003) that securities disputes were arbitrable.[988]

Hong Kong

569. The Hong Kong Financial Dispute Resolution Centre (FDRC) commenced operations in 2012.[989] The task of the FDRC is to administer the Financial Dispute Resolution Scheme (FDRS). All financial institutions or financial service providers that are authorized by the Hong Kong Monetary Authority or are licensed by/registered with the Securities and Futures Commission (except institutions that only provide

983. The BCSC is a provincial government agency that regulates securities trading and administers the Securities Act of British Columbia. Securities Act, RSBC 1996, c 418, ss. 4(1)-(2), 5(1), 184(1). *See also* BCSC's website, tab "About Us," sub-tab "Who We Are," online: http://www.bcsc.bc.ca/About_Us/Who_We_Are/ (last visited 3 December 2021).
984. BCSC InvestRight website (the website that the BCSC has launched to inform investors of their rights), tab "Avoid Fraud," sub-tab "Report Fraud or Misconduct," sections "Find the Right Regulator" and "Binding Arbitration" online: https://www.investright.org/avoid-fraud/where-to-get-help/report-fraud-or-misconduct/ (last visited 9 September 2023).
985. The OSC is a provincial regulatory body that administers the Securities Act of Ontario. Securities Act, RSO 1990, c S5, ss. 3.2(2), 143(1). *See also* OSC's website, tab "About Us," sub-tab "Role of the OSC," online: http://www.osc.gov.on.ca/en/about-us/role-osc (last visited 3 December 2021).
986. OSC website (section "GetSmarterAboutMoney), topic "What is the Arbitration Program?" online: https://www.getsmarteraboutmoney.ca/protect-your-money/investor-protection/making-a-complaint/making-complaint-getting-money-back/ (last visited 9 September 2023).
987. *Advanced Explorations Inc v. Storm Capital Corp*, 2014 ONSC 3918 at paras. 1, 29–31, 57–61, 64–67, 30 BLR (5th) 79.
988. *Webber v. Seltzer* (2005), [2005] OJ No 453 (Ont Sup Ct) at paras. 1, 3, 5, 17, 2005 CarswellOnt 465; *Forbes v. Siskind, Cromarty, Ivey and Dowler LLP* (2003), [2003] OJ No 4533 (Ont Sup Ct) at paras. 1, 2, 60, 61, 2003 CarswellOnt 4455.
989. Government of Hong Kong website, Press Releases (19 June 2012), online: http://www.info.gov.hk/gia/general/201206/19/P201206190504.htm (last visited 10 March 2023).

credit rating services) are required to join the scheme as a member.[990] Under the scheme, if there is a monetary dispute (up to HKD 1,000,000) between a member institution and any customer or receiver of financial services, the dispute is generally resolved through the "Mediation First, Arbitration Next" process, in which the arbitral award will be final and binding.[991]

570. Under section 118(1)(b) of the Securities and Futures Ordinance (Cap 571), for a financial institution involved in leveraged foreign exchange trading to obtain a license from the Securities and Futures Commission, the institution is "obliged, if the client so requires, to have the dispute settled by arbitration." An arbitration panel was established by the Securities and Futures (Leveraged Foreign Exchanged Trading) (Arbitration) Rules (Cap 571F), which also outlined the rules governing such arbitrations.

571. It should also be noted that the Hong Kong International Arbitration Centre (HKIAC) has specific arbitration rules for securities disputes.[992]

Singapore

572. Under section 28A(1) of the Monetary Authority of Singapore Act 1970, the Monetary Authority has the power to approve a dispute resolution scheme "for the resolution of disputes arising from or relating to the provision of financial services by financial institutions." The Monetary Authority passed a regulation in 2007 (last revised in 2021), which approves the dispute resolution scheme operated by Singapore's Financial Industry Disputes Resolution Centre Ltd (FIDReC) and names nine financial institutions that should be members of the scheme. The FIDReC provides a dispute resolution scheme for disputes between financial institutions and consumers,[993] but its jurisdiction is limited to claims up to SGD 100,000.[994] The FIDReC decisions are final and binding, but only on the financial institutions and not on the consumers.[995]

573. Also, the Singapore Exchange Limited (SGX) has a set of rules (called the Rulebooks) that govern activities in relation to securities and derivatives,[996] as follows:

---

990. FDRC website, tab "Resolving Disputes," sub-tab "Financial Dispute Resolution Scheme (FDRS)," online: http://www.fdrc.org.hk/en/html/aboutus/aboutus_fdrs.php (last visited 10 March 2023).
991. Financial Dispute Resolution Centre (FDRC) Terms of Reference (2018), para. 2 (definitions of "Arbitral Award" and "Maximum Claimable Amount") together with paras. 12 and 18.4, online: https://www.fdrc.org.hk/en/doc/FDRC_ToR_Full_2018_en.pdf (last visited 10 March 2023).
992. HKIAC Securities Arbitration Rules (1993), online: http://www.hkiac.org/images/stories/arbitration/Securities%20Arbitration%20Rules.pdf (last visited 10 March 2023).
993. FIDReC website, tab "About Us," headline "Our Mission," online: https://www.fidrec.com.sg/about/ (last visited 11 April 2023).
994. FIDReC website, tab "About Us," headline "FIDReC's Jurisdiction," online: https://www.fidrec.com.sg/about/ (last visited 11 April 2023).
995. FIDReC website, tab "Processes," headline "Key Features of the two Schemes," online: https://www.fidrec.com.sg/process/ (last visited 11 April 2023).
996. SGX website, Chart of Rulebooks, online: http://rulebook.sgx.com/# (last visited 11 April 2023).

- In terms of derivatives, in 2005, the SGX appointed the Singapore International Arbitration Centre (SIAC) to administer disputes between SGX members and market participants in relation to derivatives and futures trading.[997] In 2006, the provisions of Chapter 6 of the SGX Futures Trading Rules were amended, providing for SIAC arbitration of these disputes. In the same year, a new chapter (Chapter 5) was added to the Singapore Exchange Derivatives Clearing Limited (SGX-DC) Clearing Rules that provides for SIAC arbitration.
- Regarding securities, the SGX Securities Trading Rules (SGX-ST Rules), the Central Depository (Pte) Limited Clearing Rules (CDP Clearing Rules),[998] the CDP Depository Rules, and the CDP Settlement Rules contain no provision on arbitration.

574. It should be noted that, according to section 2(1) of the Consumer Protection (Fair Trading) Act 2003, the Act applies to the consumers of, among other things, "financial products" and "financial services."[999] The Act does not contain any provision on arbitration, but sections 7(10)(b), 7(11), and 35(3) provide for the possibility of having "dispute resolution schemes" in consumer disputes and for the "settlement of disputes." In addition, section 322(2)(f)(i) of the Securities and Futures Act (Cap 289) indicates that parties may conclude a settlement in or out of court.

3. Jurisdictions That Prefer Non-Binding Dispute Settlement Mechanisms to Arbitration

575. This group includes jurisdictions that consider securities disputes to be arbitrable, but they favor non-binding dispute settlement mechanisms for such disputes, rather than arbitration. The group includes France, England and Wales, and Germany.

997. SGX—Derivatives Circular For All Members, Circular No DT/ AM 69 of 2005 (30 June 2005), online: https://rulebook.sgx.com/rulebook/circular-no-dtam-69-2005 (last visited 11 April 2023).
998. "The Central Depository Pte Limited (CDP) is a wholly owned subsidiary of the Singapore Exchange Ltd (SGX), providing integrated clearing, settlement and depository facilities for customers in the Singapore securities market, including both equities and fixed income instruments." DBS website, online: https://www.dbs.com.sg/personal/investments/stp-cdp-forms.page (last visited 11 April 2023).
999. The financial products and services regulated under the following nine Acts are all within the scope of coverage of the Consumer Protection (Fair Trading) Act: the Banking Act, the Finance Companies Act, the Financial Advisers Act, the Insurance Act, the Monetary Authority of Singapore Act (s. 28), the Money-changing and Remittance Businesses Act, the Securities and Futures Act, the Commodity Trading Act, and the Moneylenders Act (w.e.f. 1 April 2010). Ministry of Trade and Industry website, tab "Resources," sub-tab "Legislation," hyperlink "Consumer Protection (Fair Trading) Act," hyperlink "FAQs on the Consumer Protection (Fair Trading) Act and Consumer Protection (Fair Trading) (Amendment) Act 2008," online: https://www.mti.gov.sg/Resources/Legislation/Consumer-Protection-Fair-Trading-Act (last visited 11 April 2023).

France

576. Under Articles L212-1, L212-3, and L241-1 of the Consumer Code, any clause in a contract "between professionals and consumers" that causes a significant imbalance between the rights and obligations of the parties is considered to be "unfair" and hence "unwritten" because the rule is of "public order." Further, under Article R212-2 of the same Code, arbitration clauses are included in the category of those clauses that are *presumed* to be "unfair" unless proved otherwise by the professional.

577. However, French case law, prior to 2020, was supportive of arbitrating securities disputes. For example, in two cases concerning stock portfolios, namely *Pourdieu v. SAS Merril Lynch Pierce Fenner & Smith SAF* (2003) and *Mattei et autres v. SAS Merril Pierce* (2004), the Paris Court of Appeal held that the possible unfairness of the arbitration clause would not render it manifestly invalid and that it is the arbitral tribunal (not the court) who should decide whether the arbitration clause is unfair under consumer laws.[1000] Further, in *Rado v. Société Painvewebber* (2005), the Court of Cassation rejected arguments as to the invalidity of an arbitration clause in the parties' international securities contract and instead referred the parties to the arbitral tribunal to decide the arbitrability question.[1001]

578. However, in 2020, the Court of Cassation made a ruling that has been understood as overturning the *Rado* case and as a major shift from the above approach.[1002] In *PwC Landwell-PricewaterhouseCoopers Tax & Legal Services v. [not indicated]* (2020), the Court of Cassation held that the arbitration clause in a contract between the Spanish arm of an international legal service provider and its French client was "unfair."[1003] The Court rejected the argument whereby arbitrators should first decide the unfairness of an arbitration clause under Article 1448 of the Code of Civil Procedure (on the negative effect of the competence-competence principle).[1004] The Court relied on the Council Directive 93/13/EEC of 5 April 1993 on Unfair Terms in Consumer Contracts

1000. *Pourdieu v. SAS Merril Lynch Pierce Fenner & Smith SAF*, Paris Court of Appeal, 2 April 2003, reported in (2005) 2005:1 Rev Arb 115; *Mattei et autres v. SAS Merril Pierce, Fenner & Smith SAF*, Paris Court of Appeal, 28 April 2004, reported in (2004) 2004:1 Rev Arb 115.

1001. *Rado v. Société Painvewebber*, Court of Cassation (1st Civil Chamber), 30 March 2004, reported in (2005) 2005:1 Rev Arb 115.

1002. *See, e.g.*, Practical Law Arbitration, Quinn Emanuel Urquhart & Sullivan UK LLP, "Final Clap for Consumer Disputes in International Arbitration? (French Cassation Court)," published online at Practical Law a Thomson Reuters Legal Solution (21 October 2020): https://uk.practicallaw.thomsonreuters.com/w-027-9940?transitionType=Default&contextData=(sc.Default)&firstPage=true (last visited 3 February 2021).

1003. *PwC Landwell-PricewaterhouseCoopers Tax & Legal Services v. [not indicated]*, Court of Cassation (1st Civil Chamber), 30 September 2020, Decision No 18-19.241.

1004. Article 1448 of the Code of Civil Procedure reads: "When a dispute relating to an arbitration agreement is brought before a State court, the latter declares itself incompetent unless the arbitral tribunal has not yet been seised and if the arbitration agreement is manifestly null or manifestly inapplicable of being performed." According to Art. 1506 of the same Code, Art. 1448 applies to international arbitration.

(articles 6 and 7)[1005] and a relevant ECJ's decision,[1006] to hold that the relevant rule in the Directive is a public policy rule and that Article 1448 of the Code of Civil Procedure must not make it excessively difficult for consumers to exercise their rights under the Directive.[1007]

579. Thus, *where the consumer is protected by EU consumer law* (whether a domestic dispute case or an international dispute), the rule in the Consumer Code (about the presumed unfairness of arbitration clauses)[1008] provides a significant impediment to the arbitration of consumer disputes, including securities disputes.[1009] It remains to be seen whether French courts apply the new approach to international matters that do not involve EU consumer law.

580. The current legislative framework in France provides more for the mediation of securities disputes than for arbitration. Under Article L316-1 of the Monetary and Financial Code, consumers of financial instruments, equity securities, banks' payment services, services of the issuance and management of electronic money, and account information service providers, are entitled to free-of-charge mediation services where disputes arise with their relevant financial institution. The Directive 2004/39/EC (known as MiFID I), Article 53(1), *encouraged* the Member States to provide for alternative dispute resolution mechanisms that are accessible to financial consumers.[1010] The MiFID I was transposed into French law through a number of laws, ordinances, and decrees,[1011] none of which contained any provision on out-of-court dispute settlement mechanisms for consumers.

581. The MiFID I was then repealed by the Directive 2014/65/EU (known as MiFID II), which requires Member States to *ensure* that out-of-court dispute resolution mechanisms are available to consumers (Article 75).[1012] France transposed the MiFID

1005. It is worth noting that the Directive is the same instrument based on which the rule on the unfairness of arbitration clauses was first introduced into the Consumer Code (then Art. L131-1) in 1995. For the 1995 version of Art. L131-1, *see* online: https://www.legifrance.gouv.fr/codes/id/LEGIARTI000006292180/1995-02-02/ (last visited 1 February 2021).
1006. *OTP Bank Nyrt. and OTP Faktoring Követeléskezelő Zrt v. Teréz Ilyés and Emil Kiss*, ECJ, Case No C-51/17, Judgment, 20 September 2018, at para. 89.
1007. *Ibid.*
1008. Discussed above, para. 576.
1009. *See* Antoine Cottin & Florian Renaux, "2020 in Review: Arbitration-related Developments in France" Kluwer Arbitration Blog (31 January 2021), online: https://arbitrationblog.kluwerarbitration.com/2021/01/31/2020-in-review-arbitration-related-developments-in-france/ (last visited 3 February 2021).
1010. Directive 2004/39/EC of the European Parliament and of the Council of 21 April 2004 on Markets in Financial Instruments (MiFID I) (consolidated version as of 4 January 2011), online: http://eur-lex.europa.eu/legal-content/EN/TXT/?uri=CELEX:02004L0039-20110104 (last visited 31 January 2021).
1011. Online: http://eur-lex.europa.eu/legal-content/EN/NIM/?uri=celex:32004L0039 (last visited 31 January 2021).
1012. Directive 2014/65/EU of the European Parliament and of the Council of 15 May 2014 on Markets in Financial Instruments (MiFID II) (consolidated version as of March 2020), online: https://eur-lex.europa.eu/legal-content/EN/TXT/?uri=CELEX%3A02014L0065-20200326 (last visited 31 January 2021).

II into its law[1013] but again made no provision in relation to out-of-court dispute settlement mechanisms. However, this is likely due to the fact that Article L316-1 of the Monetary and Financial Code already provides for the mediation of securities disputes.[1014] The current Article L316-1 was introduced in 2015 as an amendment by Ordinance No 2015-1033 of 20 August 2015,[1015] which was enacted to implement, among other things, the Directive 2013/11/EU on Alternative Dispute Resolution for Consumer Disputes.[1016] Article L316-1 was then amended in 2017 by the Ordinance No 2017-1252 of 9 August 2017 (Article 7) in order to be applicable to "account information service providers" as well.[1017]

582. Also, according to the Autorité des Marché Financier (AMF)[1018] General Regulation, Article 516-3, "at the request of a market operator, the AMF can put in place an arbitration procedure to resolve disputes arising between the operator and its market members, between market members themselves, or between members and their clients."[1019] The AMF Ombudsman offers mediation services to "any saver, retail investor or professional (company, non-profit association, pension fund, etc.) that has an individual dispute with a financial intermediary or an issuer" over matters such as "financial product marketing, asset management, transmission and reception of stock market orders, account keeping services for a security account, personal equity plan, etc."[1020] However, the AMF does not have jurisdiction over disputes as to "taxation, life insurance or banking (savings passbooks, term deposits, home savings plans, loans)" or "individual investment opportunities or on whether a financial intermediary has made an appropriate choice."[1021]

583. In any case, the fact that these disputes may be submitted to mediation indicates that they are of the type of rights that the parties may freely waive, and hence the arbitrability of these disputes under Article 2059 of the Civil Code. However, the Court

1013. Online: http://eur-lex.europa.eu/legal-content/EN/NIM/?uri = celex:32014L0065 (last visited 31 January 2021).
1014. *See* above, para. 580.
1015. Online: https://www.legifrance.gouv.fr/jorf/id/JORFTEXT000031070940 (last visited 31 January 2021).
1016. Directive 2013/11/EU of the European Parliament and of the Council of 21 May 2013 on Alternative Dispute Resolution for Consumer Disputes. For discussion on the Directive and the relevant Regulation, *see* above, paras. 268–269.
1017. Online: https://www.legifrance.gouv.fr/jorf/id/JORFTEXT000035394629/ (last visited 31 January 2021).
1018. The AMF "regulates the French financial marketplace, its participants and the investment products distributed via the markets." The AMF website, tab "The AMF," sub-tab "Our Missions" online: https://www.amf-france.org/en/amf/our-missions (last visited 31 January 2021).
1019. Online: https://www.amf-france.org/en/eli/fr/aai/amf/rg/20230730/notes (last visited 31 January 2021).
1020. AMF website, tab "The AMF Ombudsman," sub-tab "How Mediation Works," sub-sub-tab "What is the Ombudsman's remit?" online: https://www.amf-france.org/en/amf-ombudsman/how-mediation-works/what-ombudsmans-remit (last visited 31 January 2021).
1021. *Ibid.*

of Cassation's recent decision in the *PwC* case[1022] can impose significant limitations to the arbitration of securities disputes.

England and Wales

584. As early as the 1990s, commentators were of the opinion that English securities law imposed no obstacle to the arbitration of securities disputes.[1023] In this regard, three cases should be discussed. In *Philip Alexander Securities and Futures Ltd v. Bamberger* (1996), the Commercial Court refused to grant a declaration that the judgments by German courts (which had refused to enforce an arbitration agreement in a dispute relating to futures and options) could not be recognized in the UK.[1024] The English Court of Appeal then upheld the Commercial Court's decision, not because disputes relating to futures and options were inarbitrable in English law, but rather because: (i) a proper construction of the arbitration clause indicated that the arbitration clause did not make it mandatory for German customers to arbitrate disputes for less than a specific amount; and (ii) that futures and options were not considered securities under the then applicable law and, as such, they did not fall within the scope of the exception in the then Consumer Arbitration Agreements Act 1988 section 2(b), which excluded securities from the prohibition on consumer arbitration.[1025]

585. The two other cases indicate that English courts have generally assumed that securities disputes (defined broadly) are arbitrable. In *Profilati Italia SRL v. Painewebber Inc* (2001), the King's Bench refused to set aside an arbitral award concerning options and futures, rejecting allegations that the award was improperly procured and would be contrary to public policy.[1026] In *Deutsche Bank AG v. Sebastian Holdings Inc* (2009), the Commercial Court noted that one of the agreements between a foreign bank and its customer in relation to lending and borrowing securities included a valid arbitration clause for technical disputes regarding securities.[1027]

586. Despite the arbitrability of securities disputes under English law, the current regulatory framework provides for non-binding dispute resolution mechanisms. The English financial market is overseen by two regulatory bodies, namely the Prudential Regulation Authority (PRA)[1028] and the Financial Conduct Authority (FCA).[1029] Under the Alternative Dispute Resolution for Consumer Disputes (Competent Authorities and Information) Regulations 2015, regulation 8(2) and Schedule 1, the FCA is "the

1022. Discussed above, para. 578.
1023. *See, e.g.*, Jr John J Kerr, "Arbitrability of Securities Law Claims in Common Law Nations" (1996) 12(2) Arb Int'l 171 DOI: 10.1093/arbitration/12.2.171.
1024. *Philip Alexander Securities and Futures Ltd v. Bamberger* [1996] 5 WLUK 104 (QB), 1996 WL 1093286.
1025. *Philip Alexander Securities and Futures Ltd v. Bamberger* [1996] CLC 1757 (CA) at 1780–1782, 1786–1787, [1997] ILPr 73.
1026. *Profilati Italia SRL v. Painewebber Inc*, 2001 WL 14918 (QB) at paras. 1, 2, 7, 11, 36.
1027. *Deutsche Bank AG v. Sebastian Holdings Inc*, [2009] EWHC 2132 (Comm) at paras. 1–4, 22, 76, [2009] WL 2392326.
1028. Bank of England website, tab "Explore," sub-tab "Prudential regulation," online: https://www.bankofengland.co.uk/prudential-regulation (last visited 28 October 2022).
1029. FCA website, tab "About us," sub-tab "About the FCA," online: https://www.fca.org.uk/about/the-fca (last visited 28 October 2022).

relevant competent authority in relation to alternative dispute resolution services offered by the [Financial Ombudsman Service]." The FCA website explains the typical process to follow for making a complaint about financial products or services:

- The first step is to contact the financial firm that has offered the product or services. The firm must then decide on the complaint and inform the customer of its decision (as to whether the firm resolved the matter or it needs more time to investigate it) within a specific timeline (depending on the type of firm).
- If not satisfied with the result, the customer may then contact the Financial Ombudsman Service (FOS)[1030] within six months of receiving the firm's decision.
- If not satisfied with the FOS' decision, the customer may initiate court proceedings as a last resort if they have not already "used an independent complaints scheme."[1031]

Germany

587. Securities disputes are generally arbitrable in Germany, but there are limitations that apply in terms of subjective arbitrability (i.e., the capacity of a person to arbitrate) when entering into *pre-dispute* arbitration agreements. Under section 101 of the Securities Trading Act, only merchants and public law entities may enter into pre-dispute arbitration agreements where the underlying contract concerns "investment services, ancillary services or financial futures and forward transactions." The Federal Court of Justice in *BGH, 09.03.2010—XI ZR 93/09* applied the then section 37(h) (now section 101) and noted that the restriction concerns subjective arbitrability.

588. As a result of the above, if one of the parties is neither a merchant nor a public law entity, the parties may agree to arbitrate their dispute only after it arises. In *BGH, 08.06.2010—XI ZR 349/08,* the arbitration clause was printed on the reverse side of an account management contract between a US brokerage house and two German investors for securities trading services and futures transactions in the US stock market. The Federal Court of Justice held that an arbitration clause would be invalid where it is established that investors are not "merchants." This is because the then section 37(h) (now section 101) of the Securities Trading Act requires that, for an arbitration agreement in securities disputes to be valid, the parties to the dispute must be merchants.

589. For regular consumers of financial services in Germany, the most readily available out-of-court dispute resolution mechanism is mediation. The Directive 2004/39/EC on Markets in Financial Instruments (MiFID I) encouraged EU Member States (in Article 53(1)) to provide alternative dispute resolution mechanisms that are

---

1030. FOS website, online: http://www.financial-ombudsman.org.uk/default.htm (last visited 28 October 2022).

1031. FCA website, tab "Consumers," sub-tab "How to Complain," online: http://www.fca.org.uk/consumers/complaints-and-compensation/how-to-complain (last visited 28 October 2022).

accessible to financial consumers.[1032] The MiFID I was repealed by the Directive 2014/65/EU on Markets in Financial Instruments (MiFID II), which requires Member States to "ensure" (rather than "encourage") that out-of-court dispute resolution mechanisms are available to consumers (Article 75).[1033] Another important instrument is the Directive 2013/11/EU on Alternative Dispute Resolution for Consumer Disputes which Germany transposed into its law through the Act on Alternative Dispute Resolution in Consumer Matters (VSBG) in 2016. Under section 5(2) of the VSBG, a consumer conciliation body "may not employ a dispute resolution method that imposes a binding solution on the consumer or excludes the consumer's right to access to courts."

590. In Germany, different dispute resolution mechanisms for financial consumers are already in place, but they do not seem to include arbitration. Under section 14(1) of the Act on Injunctive Relief (UKlaG), "without prejudice to consumer's right to access courts," consumers should be able to contact private dispute resolutions entities, the Arbitration Body at the Deutsche Bundesbank, or the Arbitration Board of the German Federal Financial Supervisory Authority (BaFin). However, despite the fact that these boards include the term "arbitration" in their title, they may not issue final and binding decisions.[1034]

4. Jurisdiction(s) Where Securities Disputes Are Non-Arbitrable

591. Of the jurisdictions that were studied, only the Canadian province of Alberta does not regard securities disputes as arbitrable. Alberta (like Québec) is not one of the participating jurisdictions in the Cooperative Capital Markets Regulatory System (CCMRS)[1035] and, as such, it will not enact the relevant uniform provincial legislation, namely the Capital Markets Act.[1036]

592. The Securities Act of Alberta has no provision on arbitration. However, section 22 of the Financial Consumer Act of Alberta requires parties to "attempt to resolve the

1032. The MiFID I was transposed into German law by the Financial Markets Directive Implementation Act (2007), which mirrored the wording of the former s. 33(1)(4) of the Securities Trading Act. Section 33(1)(4)—which was removed from the Act in 2017—obliged investment services enterprises to have in place "procedures for the reasonable and prompt handling of complaints."

1033. Germany transposed the Directive into its law by the Second Financial Market Amendment Act (2017).

1034. Deutsche Bundesbank website, tab "Service," sub-tab "Schlichtungsstelle," section "Schlichtungsverfahren," online (in original language): https://www.bundesbank.de/de/service/schlichtungsstelle/-/schlichtungsverfahren-613580 (last visited 24 February 2021); BaFin website, tab "Consumers," sub-tab "Complaints," sub-tab "Filing a complaint with BaFin," headline "Only court rulings are binding," online: https://www.bafin.de/EN/Verbraucher/BeschwerdenStreitschlichtung/BeiBaFinbeschweren/BeiBaFinbeschweren_node_en.html (last visited 24 February 2021).

1035. A system between the Canadian federal government and the governments of the provinces and territories of Ontario, British Columbia, Saskatchewan, New Brunswick, Prince Edward Island, Newfoundland and Labrador, and Yukan. For discussion on the CCMRS, *see* above, para. 564.

1036. A uniform provincial/territorial legislation to be adopted by each of the participating jurisdictions in the CCMRS.

dispute themselves," which seems to indicate that parties are allowed to submit their securities disputes to arbitration. However, section 26(1) of the same Act offers consumers the option "to start court proceedings instead of arbitration proceedings." If consumers have the option to take their claim to courts—even when there is an arbitration agreement—it seems reasonable to conclude that arbitration agreements regarding securities disputes are unenforceable against consumers. This conclusion is further supported by section 16 of the Consumer Protection Act of Alberta, which prohibits arbitration of consumer disputes unless the arbitration agreement is signed after the dispute arises or (in case of a pre-dispute arbitration agreement) if the agreement "allows the consumer to decide, after a dispute has arisen, whether the consumer will use arbitration or an action in court to resolve the dispute."

EXECUTIVE SUMMARY 3

This summary consists of two Tables: Table 3.1 summarizes the major approaches to arbitrability across all the fields discussed in this chapter except bankruptcy/insolvency law. Table 3.2 covers the approaches to bankruptcy/insolvency law.

Table 3.1 Major Approaches to Arbitrability (All Fields Except Bankruptcy/Insolvency)

Subject Matters (whether disputes in the fields below are arbitrable in the following jurisdictions)[1037]	Jurisdictions									
	Common Law Jurisdictions					Civil Law Jurisdictions				
	Canada (AB, BC, ON)	England & Wales	Hong Kong	Singapore	United States	Canada (Québec)	China (Mainland)	France	Germany	Switzerland
Antitrust/ Competition	Yes	Yes	Yes	No[1038]	Yes	Yes	No	Yes	Yes[1039]	Yes
Consumer	In AB and ON: Yes[1040] In BC: Depends[1041]	Yes[1042]	Yes[1043]	Unsettled	Yes[1044]	Yes[1045]	Yes	Yes[1046]	No[1047]	Yes[1048]

1037. It should be noted that for some fields, there is not a definite "Yes" or "No" answer, either because the legislative texts and case law in that jurisdiction have not provided a clear answer, or because there are conditions to be fulfilled for a matter to be arbitrable or there are considerable restrictions on the arbitrability of that dispute. In the latter case, those conditions or restrictions are briefly set out in a footnote next to the "Yes" or "No."
1038. Unless no regulatory issues are involved.
1039. But it is likely that awards on competition disputes are subject to full merits review.
1040. But pre-dispute arbitration agreements are "unenforceable" in AB and "invalid" in ON.
1041. The answer is "Yes" if the consumer is the one who has suffered damages, and "No" if the consumer is acting as a public interest plaintiff (usually in the form of class action).
1042. But the arbitration clause may be found "unfair," depending on the circumstances.
1043. But, for an arbitration agreement to be enforceable, it should be signed by the consumer after the dispute arises, and if it is a pre-dispute arbitration agreement, only the consumer may invoke the arbitration clause.
1044. But there are many federal statutes protecting consumers' rights, some of which prohibit pre-dispute arbitration agreements.
1045. But pre-dispute arbitration agreements are "prohibited."
1046. But in domestic matters, only the consumer can invoke the arbitration clause; and where the consumer is protected by EU consumer law (whether a domestic or an international matter) the arbitration clause is presumed to be "unfair."
1047. Unless the arbitration agreement is in a separate document and signed by both parties or, alternatively, the entire contract is notarized.
1048. But in domestic matters, consumers may not enter into pre-dispute arbitration agreements.

Subject Matters (whether disputes in the fields below are arbitrable in the following jurisdictions)[1037]	Jurisdictions									
	Common Law Jurisdictions					Civil Law Jurisdictions				
	Canada (AB, BC, ON)	England & Wales	Hong Kong	Singapore	United States	Canada (Québec)	China (Mainland)	France	Germany	Switzerland
Corporate	AB: Yes[1049] BC: Yes[1050] ON: Yes[1051]	Yes[1052]	Yes[1053]	Yes[1054]	Yes	Yes[1055]	Yes[1056]	Yes[1057]	Yes[1058]	Yes

1049. Even for oppression claims.
1050. But there are restrictions as to the remedies a tribunal may award.
1051. Even for oppression claims.
1052. But there are restrictions as to the remedies a tribunal may award.
1053. But there are restrictions as to the remedies a tribunal may award.
1054. But there are restrictions as to the remedies a tribunal may award. The Singapore Court of Appeal has drawn a clear distinction between minority oppression claims arising under s. 216 of the Companies Act and disputes over liquidation of an insolvent company that arise upon insolvency. The former are arbitrable, whereas the latter are not.
1055. Even for oppression claims.
1056. But not when the dispute involves administrative matters.
1057. An arbitral tribunal may even decide on the dissolution and liquidation of a company.
1058. But for the arbitrability of disputes as to the validity of shareholder resolutions in limited liability corporations and partnerships, the Federal Court of Justice has set a number of conditions to be fulfilled. Further, the arbitrability of disputes as to shareholder resolutions in stock corporations remains unsettled.

Subject Matters (whether disputes in the fields below are arbitrable in the following jurisdictions)[1037]	Jurisdictions									
	Common Law Jurisdictions					Civil Law Jurisdictions				
	Canada (AB, BC, ON)	England & Wales	Hong Kong	Singapore	United States	Canada (Québec)	China (Mainland)	France	Germany	Switzerland
Family/Domestic Relations: • Financial matters (F) • Non-financial matters (NF), except divorce	AB: Yes (F & NF) BC: Yes (F & NF)[1059] ON: Yes (F & NF)[1060]	No	No[1061]	No[1062]	Yes (F) Unsettled (NF)	No	No	No	Yes (F), except for child support No (NF)	No, except for (F) in international matters
Intellectual Property:[1063]										
• Copyright	Yes	Yes	Yes	Yes	Yes	Yes	Yes	Yes	Yes	Yes
• Patent infringement • Patent validity (in personam)	Yes Yes	Yes Yes	Yes Yes	Yes Yes	Yes Yes	Yes Yes	Unsettled No	Yes Yes[1064]	Yes No[1065]	Yes Yes

1059. But, generally, only post-dispute arbitration agreements are enforceable, and only FDRPs are allowed to sit as arbitrator.
1060. But, generally, only post-dispute arbitration agreements are enforceable.
1061. Arbitration has not yet effectively opened its way into Hong Kong family law, but mediation is encouraged in family disputes.
1062. Except court-ordered arbitrations in Islamic law-related matters.
1063. For the EU members, this Table does not cover EU IP rights, including Unitary Patents and EU Trademarks.
1064. But only when the issue is raised in the course of an arbitral proceeding in relation to contractual disputes about a patent.
1065. But German courts are likely to enforce an award on the validity of a patent registered in another country, if under the law of that country the matter is arbitrable.

Subject Matters (whether disputes in the fields below are arbitrable in the following jurisdictions)[1037]	Jurisdictions									
	Common Law Jurisdictions					Civil Law Jurisdictions				
	Canada (AB, BC, ON)	England & Wales	Hong Kong	Singapore	United States	Canada (Québec)	China (Mainland)	France	Germany	Switzerland
• Trademark infringement • Trademark validity (in personam)	Yes Yes	Yes Yes	Yes Yes	Yes Yes	Yes	Yes Yes	Unsettled No	Yes Yes[1066]	Yes No[1067]	Yes Yes
Labour	No[1068]	Yes	Yes[1069]	No	Yes	No[1070]	No	Yes	Yes[1071]	Yes
Employment	AB: Yes BC: Yes ON: Yes (but not in international matters)	Depends on the applicable Act			Yes	Yes (but not in international matters)		Yes[1072]	Yes[1073]	Yes (but not in domestic matters)

1066. But opposite view exists too.
1067. But German courts are likely to enforce an award on the validity of a trademark registered in another country under whose law the matter is arbitrable.
1068. Although arbitration of labour disputes is a common practice in Canada, it is considered statutory arbitration and not consensual.
1069. But there are important legislative and case law restrictions on arbitration of labour/employment disputes in Hong Kong.
1070. Although arbitration of labour disputes is a common practice in Canada, it is considered statutory arbitration and not consensual.
1071. But merits review of awards is allowed.
1072. But the arbitration clause may not be enforced against an employee.
1073. But only for a limited number of occupations and in limited employment circumstances.

Subject Matters (whether disputes in the fields below are arbitrable in the following jurisdictions)[1037]	Jurisdictions									
	Common Law Jurisdictions					Civil Law Jurisdictions				
	Canada (AB, BC, ON)	England & Wales	Hong Kong	Singapore	United States	Canada (Québec)	China (Mainland)	France	Germany	Switzerland
Securities	AB: No BC: Yes ON: Yes	Yes	Yes	Yes	Yes	Yes	Yes	Yes[1074]	Yes[1075]	Yes

1074. But the current legislative framework in France provides more for the mediation of securities disputes than arbitration; and where the consumer is protected by EU consumer law (whether a domestic or an international matter) the arbitration clause is presumed to be "unfair."
1075. But only merchants and public law entities may enter into pre-dispute arbitration agreements if the underlying contract concerns investment services, ancillary services, or financial futures and forward transactions. As a result, if one of the parties is neither a merchant nor a public law entity, parties may agree to arbitrate their dispute only after it arises.

Table 3.2 Major Approaches to the Arbitrability of Bankruptcy/Insolvency-Related Disputes

Jurisdiction	**Types of Claim**		**Location of the Bankruptcy/Insolvency Proceeding**		
	Core Claims[1076]	**Non-Core Claims**[1077]	**Local Proceeding (Scenario A)**		**Foreign Proceeding (Scenario B)**
			With No Pending Arbitration	**With a Pending Arbitration**	
Canada	No specific discussion distinguishing the two types of claims.		• If the bankruptcy/insolvency is subject to the BIA: arbitration may not commence (with certain exceptions). • If the bankruptcy/insolvency is subject to the CCAA or WORA: arbitration may commence, but courts have discretion to not allow any arbitration against the debtor.	• If the bankruptcy/insolvency is subject to the BIA: arbitration may not continue (with certain exceptions). • If the proceeding is subject to the CCAA or WORA: no automatic stay of arbitration, but courts have discretion to stay the arbitration.	• Adopted the UNCITRAL Model Law on Cross-Border Insolvency. • Upon the recognition of the foreign proceeding, no arbitration may commence or continue against the debtor.
China (Mainland)	Inarbitrable	The law is not clear.	The law is not clear on this, but it is likely to allow commencing the arbitration proceeding against a debtor; but, only after an administrator takes over the debtor's property.	Automatic stay of the arbitration but may resume once the bankruptcy administrator takes over the debtor's assets. This seems not to apply strictly in "foreign-related" arbitrations.	Has no statutory regime regulating foreign proceedings.

1076. Those are disputes that arise only following the onset of bankruptcy/insolvency and due to the operation of the bankruptcy/insolvency regime (Default Definition 1).
1077. Those are disputes that stem from the debtor's pre-insolvency rights and obligations (Default Definition 2).

Jurisdiction	Types of Claim		Location of the Bankruptcy/Insolvency Proceeding		
	Core Claims[1076]	Non-Core Claims[1077]	Local Proceeding (Scenario A)		Foreign Proceeding (Scenario B)
			With No Pending Arbitration	With a Pending Arbitration	
England & Wales	Inarbitrable[1078]	Arbitrable	• For companies: arbitration may commence, except when arbitration is against a company in administration, or when a winding up order is made, or a provisional liquidator is appointed. • For individuals: it depends on whether the trustee adopts the underlying contract. However, once the bankruptcy order is made, creditors may not commence any arbitration.	• For companies: no automatic stay of arbitration unless the company goes into administration, or when a winding up order is made, or a provisional liquidator is appointed. • For individuals: no automatic stay of arbitration, but courts have discretion to stay the arbitration.	• Adopted the UNCITRAL Model Law on Cross-Border Insolvency. • Upon the recognition of the foreign proceeding, no arbitration may commence or continue against the debtor.

1078. In English law, the definition of core claims includes Default Definition 1, plus the following: disputes arising under provisions of the Insolvency Act 1986 which apply to liquidation, as well as those provisions that apply to liquidators' power to intervene in and set aside transactions with third parties in the context of the insolvency regime. However, more recently, English courts have relaxed the sharp distinction between disputes arising from a company's pre- and post-insolvency rights to the extent that England and Wales are likely to move from their current category (those jurisdictions that differentiate between core and non-core disputes) to the other category (those jurisdictions that do not recognize such difference).

Jurisdiction	Types of Claim		Location of the Bankruptcy/Insolvency Proceeding		
	Core Claims[1076]	Non-Core Claims[1077]	Local Proceeding (Scenario A)		Foreign Proceeding (Scenario B)
			With No Pending Arbitration	With a Pending Arbitration	
France	Inarbitrable	Arbitrable	Arbitration may commence against the debtor, but a bankruptcy judge must first check the legality of the creditor's claim declaration.	Automatic stay of arbitration until the claimant creditor files the declaration of their claim. After resuming the arbitration, the arbitral tribunal may only validate the claims and quantify their amount, without having any jurisdiction to order the debtor to pay.	• Upon the recognition of the foreign proceeding, it is treated like local proceedings. • Applies the Regulation (EU) 2015/848, which provides for automatic recognition of proceedings in other EU Member States, except Denmark.
Germany	Inarbitrable[1079]	Arbitrable (however, an award against a bankrupt can only establish the validity of a claim and its amount.)	Arbitration may commence unless the debtor does not have sufficient funds to cover its share of the arbitration costs.	Arbitration may continue, but three conditions must be met: (i) the claimant creditor must file its claim with the insolvency administrator when the insolvency proceeding is opened; (ii) the insolvent party must be replaced with the insolvency administrator; and (iii) the arbitral tribunal may only establish the validity of the claim and its amount and may not order the insolvency administrator to pay or release any assets.	• Provides for automatic recognition of foreign proceedings.[1080] • Upon the recognition of the foreign proceeding, arbitration is stayed. • Applies the Regulation (EU) 2015/848 which provides for automatic recognition of proceedings in other EU Member States, except Denmark.

1079. In German law, for a dispute to be considered "core," not only does it have to fulfill the conditions under Default Definition 1, but also the dispute must arise as a result of the administrator's application of specific rights granted to them by the German Insolvency Act.
1080. Certain exceptions apply.

Jurisdiction	Types of Claim		Location of the Bankruptcy/Insolvency Proceeding		
	Core Claims[1076]	Non-Core Claims[1077]	Local Proceeding (Scenario A)		Foreign Proceeding (Scenario B)
			With No Pending Arbitration	With a Pending Arbitration	
Hong Kong	No specific discussion distinguishing the two types of claims. However, disputes that are settled through particular courts or tribunals, including bankruptcy, company liquidation and winding up disputes, are inarbitrable.		No specific rule prohibiting the commencement of arbitration against a debtor where the dispute is arbitrable. An exception seems to be when a winding up order is made.	No automatic stay of arbitration, but courts have discretion to stay the arbitration. However, when a winding up order is made, arbitration is stayed.	Has no statutory regime regulating foreign proceedings.
Singapore	Inarbitrable	Arbitrable[1081]	• For individuals: arbitration may commence if either the Official Assignee adopts the underlying contract, or the court enforces the arbitration agreement. • For companies: arbitration may commence unless a winding up order is made, or if the company has applied for a judicial management order or an arrangement order, or if the company is in a simplified debt restructuring.	No automatic stay of arbitration, but courts have discretion to stay the arbitration. However, arbitration is stayed when a winding up order is made or when the company has applied for a judicial management order or an arrangement order.	• Adopted the UNCITRAL Model Law on Cross-Border Insolvency, but only in relation to corporate insolvency. • Upon the recognition of the foreign proceeding, the company is treated as if the insolvency proceeding has been opened in Singapore.

1081. In Singapore, non-core claims have the same definition as Default Definition 2 (*see* above, note 1077), but it does not include claims that affect creditors' rights.

Jurisdiction	Types of Claim		Location of the Bankruptcy/Insolvency Proceeding		
	Core Claims[1076]	Non-Core Claims[1077]	Local Proceeding (Scenario A)		Foreign Proceeding (Scenario B)
			With No Pending Arbitration	With a Pending Arbitration	
Switzerland	Inarbitrable[1082]	Arbitrable	Arbitration may commence against the debtor.	Automatic stay of arbitration but may resume after 10 or 20 days (depending on the type of liquidation).	• Provides for the recognition of a foreign bankruptcy proceeding if: it is enforceable in the country where it was rendered and there is no ground for refusal under Article 27 of the PILA. • Upon the recognition of a foreign proceeding, it is treated like local proceedings.
The United States	Inarbitrable[1083]	Arbitrable	Arbitration may not commence (with certain exceptions).	Automatic stay of arbitration (with certain exceptions and the possibility of lifting the stay).	• Adopted the UNCITRAL Model Law on Cross-Border Insolvency. • Upon the recognition of the foreign proceeding, it is treated like local proceedings.

1082. In Swiss law, core matters are limited to "the initiation of insolvency proceedings; appointment of trustees; verification and acceptance of the creditor's claims and the administration of the reorganisation or liquidation of a company pursuant to the [Federal Act on Debt Enforcement and Bankruptcy]." Robert B Kovacs, "A Transnational Approach to the Arbitrability of Insolvency Proceedings in International Arbitration" (2012) 21 J Bankr L & Prac 5 Art. 3 at para. 7.2.2.1. In addition, arbitrators may not decide on an application to set aside (definitively or provisionally) the debtor's objection to a collection order. *BGE 136 III 583, 2 November 2010.*

1083. In US law, for a non-exhaustive list of matters that are regarded as "core," *see* § 157(b)(2) of the Judiciary and Judicial Procedure Code. Different Circuit courts have adopted different tests in relation to coreness.

www.ingramcontent.com/pod-product-compliance
Lightning Source LLC
LaVergne TN
LVHW020638300926
849161LV00004B/749